PENGUIN BO(
U.G. KRISHNAM

Mahesh Bhatt is one of the most p1
Bombay film industry. He began his ca.__ ___
Aur Bhi Hain (which was initially not released because it was
banned by the Censor Board of India for speaking against the
institution of marriage). He went on to make landmark films
like *Arth, Saaransh, Janam* and *Naam*. His other films include
Daddy, Sadak, Saathi, Sir, Naajayaz, Tamanna (National Award
winner), *Dil Hai Ki Manta Nahin, Hum Hain Raahi Pyaar Ke* and
Aashiqi. The last film he directed was *Zakhm*, the story of a mother
and her illegitimate son against the backdrop of the 1992–93
communal riots in Bombay. It won the Nargis Dutt Award for
the best film on National Integration, in addition to five *Screen*
awards one *Filmfare* award.

Mahesh Bhatt is the Guest Editor of the entertainment
supplement of *Dainik Bhaskar*, the largest selling Hindi
newspaper in the country, and writes regularly for leading
English- and Hindi-language newspapers, including the *Times
of India*, the *Indian Express*, the *Hindustan Times, Dainik Bhaskar*
and *Dainik Jagran*. He also compiled and edited *The Little Book of
Questions*, a collection of the sayings of U.G. Krishnamurti.

U.G. KRISHNAMURTI
A Life

Mahesh Bhatt

PENGUIN BOOKS

PENGUIN BOOKS
Published by the Penguin Group
Penguin Books India Pvt Ltd, 11 Community Centre, Panchsheel Park, New Delhi
110 017, India
Penguin Group (USA) Inc., 375 Hudson Street, New York, New York 10014, USA
Penguin Group (Canada), 90 Eglinton Avenue East, Suite 700, Toronto, Ontario,
M4P 2Y3, Canada (a division of Pearson Penguin Canada Inc.)
Penguin Books Ltd, 80 Strand, London WC2R 0RL, England
Penguin Ireland, 25 St Stephen's Green, Dublin 2, Ireland (a division of Penguin
Books Ltd)
Penguin Group (Australia), 250 Camberwell Road, Camberwell, Victoria 3124,
Australia (a division of Pearson Australia Group Pty Ltd)
Penguin Group (NZ), cnr Airborne and Rosedale Roads, Albany, Auckland 1310,
New Zealand (a division of Pearson New Zealand Ltd)
Penguin Group (South Africa) (Pty) Ltd, 24 Sturdee Avenue, Rosebank, Johannesburg
2196, South Africa

Penguin Books Ltd, Registered Offices: 80 Strand, London WC2R 0RL, England *

First published by Penguin Books India 1992
This revised edition published 2001

Copyright © Mahesh Bhatt 1992, 2001

10 9 8 7 6 5 4

Typeset in Sanskrit Palatino by S.R. Enterprises, New Delhi
Printed at Chaman Offset Printers, New Delhi

To my children
Pooja, Sunny, Shaheen and Aalia

Contents

Acknowledgements

*My grateful thanks to Dr J.S.R.L. Narayana Moorty
and Dr Larry Morris for their heartfelt and untiring
helpfulness in writing this book. If it were
not for them this work would never
have seen the light of day.*

Introduction

'I have no message for mankind.'

–U.G.

'Why a biography of me?' asked U.G. when I first expressed my desire to write the story of his life. 'Tell me, how would you go about writing the biography of a person who says he has no story to be told? If my life story is never told, the world would be none the worse for it. For those who delight in reading biographies, my story would be disappointing indeed. If they are looking for something in *my* life to change their lives for the better, they haven't got a chance. You can fit my life neatly into that rhyme for children, "Solomon Grundy". That, in a nutshell, is yours, mine and everybody's story. There's no more to it than that.'

'What are you, U.G?' asked the eighty-four-year-old Swiss lady, Valentine de Kerven, ten years ago over lunch. She had been with U.G. for over twenty years. Most of us at the table stared blankly at her. Her question is the same question asked by all those who have come in contact with U.G. The friend who was instrumental in introducing U.G. to me was himself in a dilemma for years, trying to figure out 'who' and 'what' U.G. is. His efforts were frustrated at every turn. So one day he decided to put this question to the *I Ching*. He received the following answer: 'He is not a guru, not a priest, not a teacher, nor a savant. He has no interest in enlightening you, and in fact does not intend to do anything. He burns brightly with passion and without purpose. He is as lost without you as you are without him. His light dies if you do not reflect it. Your life is dark without his light.' I might add that U.G.'s passion is certainly not that of an evangelist.

On 9 July 1967 in Saanen, Switzerland, on his forty-ninth birthday, U.G. Krishnamurti died. What brought about this death? What brought him back to life? 'I don't know. I can't say anything about that because the experiencer was finished. There was nobody to experience that death at all,' says U.G. He insists that it was a completely physical and not a psychological death. From that point, his life was not under his control nor was there any entity controlling it. 'What I am left with is a sort of burnt-out case. The flame still burns. Whether these dying embers of life would have any impact on others or on society is not my concern.'

Here perhaps for the first time is a man who talks of enlightenment as a neurobiological state of being. He says that it is utterly free of religious, psychological or mystical implications. This represents a whole new concept, a new and genuinely fresh approach to the experience. U.G. also scoffs at the sacred, the religious and, particularly, at the whole idea of 'enlightenment'. To religious buffs, his shocking statements are largely unacceptable. He sounds to them like a man wise in his own conceit. And yet, what he says has tremendous significance to those who are searching for enlightenment. U.G. does not give lectures or write books. Furthermore, he emphatically says, 'If you are searching for someone who will enlighten you, you have come to the wrong man.'

There are days in our lives which, once lived through, change us forever. In July 1995 I tasted such days. On a dark, rainy morning, I got a call from Europe. Without any forewarning U.G. ordered me to take a break from my hectic shooting schedules in Mumbai and come to stay with him in his beautiful chalet, nestled in the midst of the towering Alps, in Switzerland. The diary I kept during this time has been added to this new edition in a section called 'A Taste of Death'.

Having intimately known U.G. for almost 16 years and having witnessed a rage in him that tears through all the institutions which man has built for centuries, I should have been adequately prepared to shield myself from this man, who I believe to be the most subversive human being that has ever lived. But I wasn't. I didn't know that sharing the same roof with U.G. for a month would feel as if my insides were being bathed in fire. I could not imagine that in that summer, in the dazzling beauty of Gstaad, I would taste death.

My daily conversations with U.G. on transience and endings, held over a cup of coffee, in the deep silence of the pre-dawn light made me see death everywhere. One morning, as I strolled through the fragrance-filled streets of the traffic-free town of Gstaad, I noticed how death slowly spreads over the world. I began to see how it kills an old tree which had survived so many storms, how it penetrates one's dark dreams, how it withers a gorgeous flower outside my window and how it gnaws at individuals and cultures and eventually destroys even civilizations. And it struck me suddenly that, in fact, the only genuine fear I had grappled with all my life was the fear of life ending. Even as a child I would often go to a crematorium near my home on the sea shore, and for hours I would sit there, watching human bodies burn. And when the fire had burned the corpse down to embers and the last flame of the pyre had sputtered and died, I would gaze at the last wisps of smoke rise to the sky, and sceptically wonder whether the person consumed by the flames had escaped into the heavens as the elders believed or had actually turned into ashes and dust! It was there in that cremation ground that the thought that one day even my body would be reduced to ashes took root in my heart. I began to see that I too, like civilizations before me, was only a guest on this earth.

As days dissolved into weeks in the stark beauty of Gstaad, I began to feel death intensifying all around me, like blood surges to the head in moments of great anger. Every conversation with

U.G., no matter how it started, ended in the discussion of death. He set the very core of my being ablaze. Everything I had thought, felt, known, and aspired to was being reduced to ashes by this man and there was precious little I could do to protect myself from him. He was a firestorm raging around me all the time. So, I decided to fortify myself. I began writing this journal. This diary of death.

Some times I wonder, however, whether it might have been better for me to totally surrender to the flames that U.G. was blowing at me, and let them burn me completely, instead of objectifying my feelings in the form of this diary. All my life, I have agonized over man's inability to keep his most intense experiences locked inside his heart. Always I have wondered why do we want to escape the terrible chaos of life by talking about it or writing about it? Maybe because giving it the order and symmetry of words and sentences and paragraphs on pages is the only way of saving a part of ourselves from dying.

Whoever has seriously contemplated the question of death has felt fear. The reason we fear death is because we fear nothingness. And writing is a way of fighting that black nothingness into which death threatens to throw us. Above all it's an attempt to keep the 'I' going. Because as long as there is an 'I', there is no death. And once dead there is no 'I' any longer.

This diary originates from the deepest part of my being. The reason I want people to read about the taste I had of death is that curiously enough it is in these pages that I come alive. I come alive because of the abundant love I have received from U.G. Because only one who loves you deeply will expose you to the kind of fire that U.G. threw at me that summer. And in that dark abyss, where U.G. demolishes all the institutions that hold up the world, my heart begins to beat. In this glow after death I feel frightened but I also discover that it's when we die, we live.

Once while sitting in a coffee shop I asked U.G., 'Is there nothing you want from me?' He replied, 'Only one thing. After

I'm dead and gone there should be no trace of me inside of you and outside of you.' This complete self-smashing jolted my entire being. His will to stand alone and then just die quietly washed me head to toe. Here I was in this moment in time face to face with a phenomenon who not only embraced nothingness but was, in fact, nothingness. I've always without question and with absolute consent done everything U.G. has asked me to do, but I wonder if I'll ever be able to fulfil this impossible 'wish' he has for me. Because I know for certain that the day U.G. fades out from my heart and mind, that'll be the end of all I know and the end of me. And I certainly do not want to end.

The afterglow of a thousand yesterdays spent with U.G. simmers within me. All art is perhaps born out of the overriding compulsion to share with someone, somewhere, somehow, the intense experiences of the heart. Every artist preserves, deep within him, a single source from which, throughout his lifetime, he draws what he is and what he says. And when the source plays out, the work withers and crumbles.

Man is intrinsically a teller of stories. He lives surrounded by his own story and the stories of others. Splicing together the scenes from my memory, I tell you in the pages that follow, my story of this extraordinary man, U.G.

Mumbai, India   *Mahesh Bhatt*
June 2001

PART I

1. The Encounter

*'If you are searching for someone who
will enlighten you, you have come to the
wrong man.'*

–U.G.

27 August 1991. My flight from Bombay to London is on schedule. Leaving home and your near and dear ones even for a while is tough. I wonder how U.G. has turned his back to the entire experience.

As I take off for forty days and forty nights to join U.G. in London and thereafter journey with him to California to write his biography, I am overcome by a feeling of dread. Will I be able to do justice to this self-imposed task of presenting U.G. to the world? I wonder.

The legend of Icarus from Greek mythology leaps out of a page of the magazine of *New Writing*. The legend: Daedalus secretly made two sets of wings—one pair for himself and one for his son Icarus. The wings were cleverly fashioned with feathers set in beeswax. The father showed his son how to use them and warned him not to fly too high as the heat of the sun would melt the wax. Then he led him up to the highest tower and, flapping their wings, they flew off like two birds. Nobody could stop their flight. The young and foolish Icarus could not resist the temptation to rise ever higher into the sky. The whole world seemed to lie at his feet. He flew too close to the sun and the wax began to melt. The feathers came loose, the wings fell apart and Icarus plunged into the sea and drowned.

INVERTED BINOCULAR SYNDROME!

It is said that one cannot stare at death or the sun too long without blinking. Looking into U.G.'s desolate life is no different.

Perhaps the only way to write this biography is to give myself the permission to fail. One cannot be intimidated into living up to anyone's high standards, even one's own.

It is not always possible to wander backward through the blur of years and remember the exact moment when you met someone. When did I first meet U.G.? Where and how? Looking at one's past is like looking at things from the wrong end of a telescope. It makes everything look distant and small. As the aircraft plunged into a sea of clouds, I floated backwards into time, descending into a mist of images....

Those were the days of living dangerously—of reading *Jonathan Livingston-Seagull*, listening to John Lennon and taking LSD. I was meditating that morning when the telephone rang. As I walked to pick up the phone, little did I know that this call would change my entire life.

'U.G. is here... when would you like to meet him?' asked Pratap Karvat. 'Now,' I said. 'Take down my address....' I had met Pratap Karvat, a soft and meek intellectual, by chance at a film shooting. Seeing me dressed in orange robes (I was a Rajneeshi sannyasi then), reading the latest J. Krishnamurti book, *The Awakening of Intelligence*, Pratap approached me, wanting to take a look at that book. He is a voracious reader, a book addict. He spoke about J. Krishnamurti, Rajneesh and the whole spiritual game. Then, just like that, out of nowhere, he mentioned the name of another Krishnamurti called U. G. Krishnamurti who visited India every year but remained anonymous. 'Would you like to meet this U.G.?' he asked. I was curious. 'Why not, the more the merrier. Let us see what he has to say.'

The scent of tobacco, the clamour of the city and the dark, squeaky staircase. How vivid the memory of my first meeting with U.G. is. His face slowly eclipsed everything around me. A volcanic silence blazed through my guts. How can I ever forget what he said that day!

4

I am not a godman. I would rather be called a fraud. The quest for God has become such an obsessive factor in the lives of human beings because of the impossibility of achieving pleasure without pain. That messy thing called the mind has created many destructive things. By far the most destructive of them all is God. God has become the ultimate pleasure. The variations of God—self-realization, *moksha* or liberation, fashionable transformation gimmicks, the first and the last freedom and all the freedoms that come in between—are the ones that are pushing man into a manic-depressive state. Somewhere along the line of evolution, man experienced self-consciousness for the first time in contradistinction to the way consciousness functions in other species. It was there, in that division of consciousness, that God, along with the nuclear doctrine that is threatening the extinction of all that nature has created with such tremendous care, was born.

No power on this earth, no god, no *avatar*, can halt this. Man is doomed. He has no freedom of action. All we can do is to wait for the end of the world— even while we talk of ways to stop a nuclear holocaust. This may sound like Jeremiah or an apocalyptic warning of a prophet of doom.

U.G. was like a raging bull; his fury was stunning. It was strangely attractive.

'Are you not taking hope away from us, Sir?' I questioned. U.G. smiled and said, 'Am I? I am no jaunty optimist. You can live in hope and die in hope.' 'Do you have any special attitude toward sexuality?' I asked. U.G. answered:

God and sex spring from the same source. God is the ultimate pleasure. God has to go first before

5

sex goes. Why should sex go? Let me mention *en passant* that my whole thinking on the subject of sex had been found at the hands of the holy men. Now I maintain that the life of ascetic austerity, denial of sex and all the disciplines associated with the religious life, have had nothing to do with whatever has happened to me. That is not to say that indulgence in sex or a life of promiscuity is the springboard to enlightenment or whatever you want to call it. You have been fed on that rubbish and I am not in any way compelled to disillusion you. You can delude yourself that smoking marijuana or preaching sexual freedom is a sure path to 'selfhood' or 'samadhi'. The fact that you are violating both moral injunctions and legal codes of conduct is a matter between you and your society. Social attitudes may be changing but your actions are still considered to be antisocial. Your guru has given you the licence and cover, so you don't feel guilty or immoral or impure. Similarly, those aspiring starlets who have sex—on what they call in Hollywood the casting couch—with the producer-director to get a part in his film, also feel superior to professional whores. They get away with that because they belong to a glamorous profession. I have no moral position. Are you happy? Who amongst you is happy? You? Your girlfriend? Your wife? Or her boyfriend? Everybody is unhappy. Don't forget that your actions affect everybody. Everybody is miserable.

I felt scorched. Accidentally I had touched a live wire. Walked into a field of mines. His words jolted me out of the spiritual coma I had sunk into. I was desperate. I needed a 'trip' badly. It was LSD which had initiated me into the world of meditation. It had given me and an entire generation of the 'flower children' a taste of the mystical. The desire to relive this chemically-induced experience drew me into by-lanes of the spiritual bazaar.

That evening, as I dimmed the lights of my room and sat down to meditate, the after-image of U.G. loomed there in the darkness. His words resonated in my head. 'Meditation is warfare,' said U.G., as I was leaving his place. For the first time in two years, since my acquaintance with Rajneesh, I panicked and found that I could not meditate. I wandered out into the streets. The street dogs, which at first sight barked, soon knew that I was one of them. I stood by a fire with strangers. The night was cold. Flames rushed up in yellow sheets. Sparks glittered in our eyes. All the men around the fire were drunk. The fire held us and comforted us all. 'Are you Mahesh Bhatt?' asked one of them. 'Yes,' I answered. They smiled. They were happy to have me amidst them. I wondered why. Why was I not happy to be with myself? All the faces around the fire looked haggard. Later, I tried to sleep but I couldn't. Something told me, 'Friend, you're heading for trouble.'

'I feel lost, alone. I am frightened and full of doubt. Help me!' I said when I met Bhagwan Shree Rajneesh in his ashram on a cold winter evening in Pune. He stared at me, gently placed his hand on my head and said, 'Jesus too was seized by such doubt when he was crucified. "Oh God, why hast thou forsaken me?" he screamed, doubting if God was with him. But as soon as he had uttered these words, he saw for himself that God was very much by his side. I am very much with you.' That evening he gave me a gift—his white robe. 'Wear this, Mahesh. Everything will be fine. You are doing well.' His words comforted me. He told me things I wanted to hear. Unfortunately, this feeling of well-being did not last long. I had to go back again and again to the ashram front office, begging for one more *darshan* with the Bhagwan. I was like a drug addict, desperately hunting for his next fix. Rajneesh had become my crutch.

7

It was a paradox. My quest for freedom was transformed into a trap, a prison from which I blurted out concepts of liberty and independence. My encounter with U.G. had left me traumatized. Deep within me a wound festered. You can run but you cannot hide. You can lie to the whole world but you cannot lie to yourself. I knew my days with Rajneesh were numbered. The walls of paradise had begun to crack. My Bhagwan was dying within me and there was nothing I could do.

It was inevitable, I said to myself as I watched the remains of my broken *mala* (given to me by Rajneesh) slowly disappear down the toilet. It felt so strange to be free of the dog-collar which had kept me on a leash for almost three years. I was tired of the life I had been leading. I was tired of the man I was. The years spent in the Rajneesh Ashram had not contributed in any way toward my self-improvement. Progress in that area was perhaps an illusion. 'If books and talks could change people, this world would become a paradise,' says U.G. A chapter in my life was over.

'Bhagwan is very angry with you, Mahesh. I am shooting a movie at Filmistan Studios. Come over right away. I have his message to pass on,' said Vinod Khanna, the film star, a few days after my breakup with Rajneesh. News about my dumping the *mala* down the commode had got back to the ashram. I was ready for the repercussions. 'Why, Mahesh? Why did you do that?' asked Vinod. His concern for me was sincere. 'I have never seen Bhagwan in such a temper. He wants you to come to the ashram and hand the *mala* back to him in person. It's a breach of trust on your part. He says he works so hard on you. If you don't do that, he says he will destroy you, Mahesh.' He looked at me as if my days on this earth were numbered. There was a heavy silence in the make-up room. I had rebelled against 'God'. His wrath was now directed at me.

I was angry. I remembered how Rajneesh had given discourses on unconditional love and had spoken at great length about how detestable it was for man to be possessive. It was disgusting now to see him behave just like any jilted lover, unable to swallow a rejection. He was just a wordsmith peddling half-truths, high-sounding phrases and holy concepts. And that's what people wanted, not the blunt facts. At this time U.G.'s words came to my rescue: 'A guru is one who tells you to throw away all crutches. He would ask you to walk and if you fall, he would say that you will rise and walk.' These words gave me unimaginable courage. 'Who is afraid of Bhagwan Shree Rajneesh? Get up,' I said to myself. 'Get up on your own two feet, no matter how shaky they are, and walk.' Once I did that, there was no looking back.

1977 to 1979. During those years I met U.G. whenever he passed through Bombay. In those days U.G., Lalubhai Shah and I went for a walk almost every morning. 'You should write U.G.'s biography someday,' said Lalubhai Shah to me on a misty morning. (Lalubhai was a prosperous diamond merchant who had given up his flourishing trade to join Vinoba Bhave in the Sarvodaya movement. He had also worked under Mahatma Gandhi during the Quit India movement against the British Raj.) At that time I was a struggling film maker who made advertisement films to make ends meet. My personal life was a big mess, to put it mildly. I was a married man with a lovely daughter, yet I was involved with a famous film star: 'the *Time* magazine cover girl', as she was popularly known in those days—Parveen Babi.

The front office of the Rajneesh Ashram had warned the sannyasis against seeing U.G. After they met U.G., many of Rajneesh's very close devotees had quit the ashram. I remember in those days, Rajneesh gave four talks against U.G., calling him all sorts of names. 'U.G., you have not said a word in response to the repeated attacks Rajneesh has been making on you of late. Why? I have also noticed that you don't say much against any particular guru,' I asked. His reply was unusual:

9

> Gurus play a social role; so do prostitutes.
> Unfortunately in society what the gurus are offering
> is not only socially acceptable but also considered
> the be-all and end-all of our existence. The others
> are not. You choose what suits you best....

Ever since I can remember, I was always frightened of the
dark, and I still am. When I am alone at home or out in a hotel I
just cannot sleep in the dark. Right from the *kalmas* which my
Muslim mother taught me up to the explanations and techniques
given by godmen and psychotherapists, all have failed to free
me from this phobia. When I placed my problem before U.G. he
said:

> All the phobias that the psychiatrists are trying to
> free you from are essential for the survival of the
> living organism. Society wants to free you from
> these fears so that it can use you to fulfill its own
> needs.... If you don't have one fear, you will have
> some other f ear.

> I know a famous film producer from the United
> States who has this phobia about cats. Every time
> he comes to see me his aides first make sure that
> there are no cats around. One day this man, who
> was embarrassed by his phobia, and had seen
> every psychiatrist in the US, mentioned his fear to
> me. He thought there was something wrong with
> him. He was relieved when I told him that there
> was no need for him to try and free himself from
> his phobia. That ended his problem. So, what's
> wrong with your having a fear of the dark...?

His words freed me from the search for the solution to my
phobia. I am still scared of the dark but I am not scared that I am
scared of the dark!

Amongst those that came to see him that day was a gentleman connected with many institutions and president of an organization dedicated to social work. He asked U.G., 'You don't seem to have any love for your fellow-men. Are you indifferent to the poverty and suffering around you? Your teaching has no practical utility for mankind.' U.G.'s reply was blunt:

> You are just a good man blinded by the folly of doing good to others. What is a good man good for? What makes you think that you are living to do good unto others? To live to do good to others is a self-absorbed, self-centred activity of yours. You are not honest enough to admit that. You call it a mission in life to serve humanity. You have been amply rewarded for service to your country. Humanity is just an abstraction. Death will lay its icy hands on you too. You know perfectly well that there is an end for you too. That is why you project permanence on mankind by struggling against all change. The belief in the eternity of your soul and the afterlife springs from the same source.

A parapsychologist intervened. 'Do you have any comment to make on clairvoyance, clairaudience, extrasensory perception and psychic phenomena?' U.G. nodded and explained:

> Man is one of the species on this planet to inherit these things in common with all the other species. Man in his anxiety to maintain his non-existing and illusory identity has been using thought to translate sensory perception. Now the yogis are promising these things back to us and making a business out of it.
>
> Let me give you an example of how effectively it operates in animals. In Switzerland, where we live up in the Alps, hunting of deer is permitted from

11

16 September every year. Would you believe it, on
15 September every year, hordes and hordes of deer
come down from all over into the safety of the
animal sanctuary next door to us. How do you
explain this phenomenon?

'U.G. is the most radical man I have met,' said my writer
friend, Sujit Sen. He was keeping a hawk-like eye on everything
U.G. said and did. He had come to meet U.G. reluctantly,
hesitantly and unwillingly on my insistence. Sujit is an
intellectual, devoid of any religious or spiritual aspirations. He
is a leftist who was once a member of a terrorist group that failed
to achieve its revolutionary goals. Now he is full of bitterness.
His life is drained of any purpose and he is simmering with
anger and frustration. Sujit asked, 'Has life any purpose, U.G.?'
'Why must there be any meaning or purpose to life?' replied
U.G. 'We must latch on to *something* to prevent us from
disappearing. Or else, why should I not commit suicide?' Sujit
persisted. U.G. said:

Do you have the courage to do it? Go right ahead
and do it! Don't forget that if you fail in your
attempt, the law will be after you. You don't have
the courage to live. You don't have the courage to
die. And yet you don't begrudge laying down your
life in the name of freedom or communism or
whatever happens to be your particular fancy. Or
you can give a name and philosophy to that thing
called despair and market it. That may bring you
into the limelight.

Sujit said, 'This is no laughing matter. Jokes aside, let me ask
you a question that is of great importance. The end of civilization
seems to be around the corner. New weapons are threatening
our very existence....' U.G. interrupted him saying, 'Isn't it strange
that you are talking of suicide in one breath and nuclear
holocaust in another?' Sujit answered, 'Paradoxical as it may

seem to you, the fact remains that mankind too seems to have opted for suicide.' This discussion really got U.G. going.

> Your minds pose as much a threat to the future of mankind as the nuclear weapons. The hydrogen bomb has its origin in the jawbone of an ass. The caveman used it to kill his neighbour. Here your civilized man is doing what the caveman did but you do it for the 'good of mankind.' Those who still hold that right is all on their side and that their eternal good will burn away the evil of others are the real enemies of mankind. It doesn't matter how the world will blow itself up—with a bomb that has the markings of the stars and stripes or a hammer and sickle or a crescent or a Jewish star or the Ashok Chakra.

Sujit was speechless. At this point, a politician waylaid U.G. and asked, 'If humanity is to be saved from the chaos of its own making, what role can India play in restoring peace to mankind? Can the heritage of India be of any value to mankind?' U.G.'s answer was: 'India has neither the spiritual power nor the material strength to be of any help to mankind. Sorry.' Every word he said that day had a sense of finality. Yet I knew he did not intend to evoke paranoia within us. I asked, 'Is it possible to avert the catastrophe by somehow changing or improving human nature?' What he said to me was something I had not asked for:

> Man is merely a biological being. There is no spiritual side to his nature. All your virtues, principles, beliefs, ideas and spiritual values imposed on you by your culture are mere affectations. They haven't touched anything in you. Religion exploited for centuries the devoutness, piousness and whole-souled fervour

13

of the religious man. Not in 'Love thy neighbour as thyself' but in the terror that if you try to kill your neighbour you will also be destroyed along with him, lies the future of mankind. How long is anyone's guess.

The wounds of sexual betrayal leave a lasting scar. A famous film star made an overture to the woman I was living with in those days. I was furious. Every cell in my body vibrated with jealousy. I felt like strangling that man and my girlfriend. I fought hard with the upsurge of my wild emotions and realized that it was a losing battle. 'Love is unconditional,' said Rajneesh. The writing was there on the wall. My guru's maxim was not working in my life. That's when I ran up to U.G. and asked him: 'Is it possible for me to be free from jealousy and at the same time have sex, pleasure, companionship and exchange ideas and opinions with my girlfriend?' U.G. said:

> Wanting to kill that man and woman is something natural. That is a healthy reaction. If you felt differently for any reason, religious or otherwise, then something is wrong with you. You are a sick man. What culture has done to you has unfortunately turned you into a hypocrite. When someone makes a pass at your girlfriend or when you suspect unfaithfulness, you are bound to be tortured by jealousy, by hate and by the agony that is going on inside you. If some ugly saint in the market-place says that it is possible, that there is a way out, that you can be free from jealousy and yet have sex and the rest of it, he is taking you for a ride. I am sorry I cannot swallow that pill. If jealousy goes, sex goes too. If you can make it possible without going mad, good luck to you!

14

Every time I went to him, my mental processes were put to rout. I went to U.G. for help and what I got was despair. The hopelessness of my situation was like the story of a man who is lost in a pitch dark jungle. He is in great pain because of a thorn stuck in his foot. He gropes around and finds another thorn to remove the thorn which is causing him agony. Instead of freeing himself of the first thorn, what he finds to his dismay is that he is now stuck with two thorns instead of one. So there I was, stuck with two thorns—jealousy and despair. I had come to a dead end. Perhaps the only way out then from that feeling of utter hopelessness and desperation was to resort to an act of recklessness.

It was two o'clock in the morning when this drunken man, myself, walked to U.G.'s house and rang his bell U.G. opened the door. I still remember what I said: 'I want to kill you. Why on earth did I ever have to meet a man like you? No matter what topic I begin with, it ultimately ends in despair.' U.G. said, 'Why don't you go to sleep, Mahesh. There is a sofa and there is a blanket. If you want to kill me, you will do well to wait till tomorrow when people will be around. Then you can make a ritual of the whole thing.' Minutes later I bade 'Good night' to him and kissing his hand said, 'U.G., I love you.' That was the beginning of my one-way love story with U.G.

As days wore on in his company, I realized that this man's sagacity was not acquired by years of learning and experience. What spilt out of him did not seem to be laboured. There was something indefinable about him. He had a peculiar quietening quality about him that seemed to affect the people that came to see him. The peace he radiated was not obtrusive. It seeped into you. What was its source? How or by what means had U.G. stumbled into this 'state' of being? Had his life been a preparation for this? These questions began to weigh on me. And then one day, he told me the story of his life and his search....

WISE = SAGACITY

15

2. Early Years

'A real guru, if there is one, frees you
from himself.'

–U.G.

Uppaluri Gopala Krishnamurti was born on 9 July 1918 in the small town of Masulipatam in South India and was brought up in the nearby town of Gudivada. Those were the days of the First World War. 'This boy is born to a destiny immeasurably high,' predicted U.G.'s mother just before she died, seven days after she gave birth to him. His maternal grandfather, Tummalapalli Gopala Krishnamurti, a wealthy Brahmin lawyer, took his dying daughter's prediction seriously. He gave up his flourishing law practice to devote himself to his grandson's upbringing and education. The grandparents and their friends were convinced that this child that was born in their family was *yogabhrashta*, one who had come within inches of enlightenment in his past life. U.G.'s father played no role in his life except the 'hereditary role', as U.G. put it. Although they lived in the same town, they never lived under the same roof for any length of time. U.G.'s father remarried soon after his wife's death and left his son to be cared for by his grandparents.

In the year 1873, Helena Petrova Blavatsky, a Russian immigrant to the United States, along with Colonel Olcott, an American lawyer, founded the Theosophical Society. The Theosophical Society was built largely on their reading of Buddhism and Hinduism and on a fusion of assorted occult presuppositions. Its object was to delve into the riddles of creation to discover the dormant power in man. It was open equally to believers and non-believers, as well as to the orthodox and the unorthodox. In those days Theosophy had a strong appeal to those who found little solace in orthodoxy and yet were not content to call themselves atheists. It attracted an articulate group of free thinkers and avowed atheists searching for some order and spiritual support.

Strangely, even though he was a Theosophist, T.G. Krishnamurti was also a very orthodox Brahmin. He was, according to U.G., a 'mixed-up' man. With orthodoxy and tradition on the one side and Theosophy on the other, T.G.Krishnamurti failed to strike an equilibrium. And that was the beginning of U.G.'s problems.

When U.G. was three, instead of playing with toys, he sat crosslegged in meditation, imitating all those holy men who visited his house. His grandfather not only invited every holy man that he could to his house but he also kept learned men on his payroll. He was totally dedicated to creating a profound atmosphere in which to educate his grandson in the right way. Every day, from dawn to dusk, U.G. was made to listen to the *Upanishads, Panchadasai Naishkarmya Siddhi,* the commentaries, and also the commentaries on the commentaries. By the time U.G. reached his seventh year he could repeat from memory most of the passages from these holy books.

In the year 1925, when he was barely seven years old, God became irrelevant to U.G. The incident that led to this break also ended his faith in the efficacy of prayer forever. The incident occurred in December 1925. The Theosophical Society was commemorating its Golden Jubilee celebration at its headquarters in Adyar, Madras. Since they did not have room reservations in Adyar, U.G.'s grandparents were uncertain about participating in this gala event. U.G. was very keen to go. He thought of praying to Hanuman and gifting him with coconuts. But now U.G. had a problem: there was an unsettled account of almost 500 coconuts for all of U.G.'s prayers which Hanuman had already gratified. U.G. was a defaulter. He did not have the money to buy 500 coconuts. Should he steal? Even if he did, what would he do with all the other coconut halves that the temple would return? Where would he keep them? He was cornered.

Then suddenly U.G. learned that his grandparents had decided to attend the celebrations after all. How did this happen? He had not settled his account with Hanuman. How was it possible that his prayer had been granted? It was then that he saw for himself that it was the power and vigour of his own thought which had swayed his grandparents. He had found fulfilment not through the efficacy of prayer but through the strength of his own desire.

On 29 December 1925, the Golden Jubilee function took place in Adyar. It was a regal affair. Scores of people from all over the world participated in the celebration with great fervour. It was there that U.G. saw and heard J. Krishnamurti speak for the first time. As an orator, Krishnamurti did not impress U.G. On the stage the man stammered and struggled for words. Compared to Annie Besant (whose oratory, according to U.G., could make inanimate objects pulsate with life) Krishnamurti was a 'pygmy'.

The next evening, on Elliot Beach in Adyar, as U.G. was wading in the water, collecting shells, he saw Krishnamurti taking a walk with some admirers. For an instant, the two Krishnamurtis' eyes met. Krishnamurti moved away from the crowd. He joined U.G. and began helping him collect shells. I wonder whether U.G. had the slightest inkling then of the part Krishnamurti would play in his life in the years to come.

Around the time when U.G. was twelve, printers would leak test papers to students for a price. To prevent this, the school authorities used stencils and destroyed the master copy immediately after making copies. One day U.G. devised a scheme for defeating the authorities with the help of ten other boys in his class. Between them they collected a hundred rupees. U.G. was able to bribe the attendant who ran the machine into giving them the original stencil. Then just before the examination, U.G. thought to himself, 'Why should we alone be benefited?' So, he and his friends distributed the question sheets to all the students in the class. Naturally, the authorities of the school came to know of this. The poor attendant was dismissed. A re-examination was held and U.G. and all his friends failed. The authorities would have expelled them were it not for the fact that U.G.'s uncle happened to be on the governing committee of the school.

The event that propelled U.G. into his quest for truth was a traumatic one. His grandfather had a personal meditation room in which he used to meditate every day for hours. U.G. was not permitted to enter this room since he had meddled with the photographs of the Masters (of Theosophy). After all, one had to be initiated into the Esoteric Group of the Theosophical Society to even catch a glimpse of these Masters. The Esoteric Society (or E.S. as it came to be called) was strictly for those who had proved their dedication to Theosophy, mostly through work. These select members were deemed ready for exposure to the ancient wisdom which would help them along the path of the Masters. Membership of the E.S. was supposed to be absolutely secret. U.G. was too young to be initiated into that group. Later, when he reached the age of fourteen, he was admitted as one of its privileged members. Only so-called 'spiritually evolved' people were enrolled in this elite group.

T.G. Krishnamurti was meditating one day when his great-granddaughter, a little baby, started to cry for some reason. The child's wailing interrupted the old man's meditation. This infuriated him. He came down and thrashed the child brutally. 'There must be something funny about the whole business of meditation,' said U.G. to himself, as he helplessly witnessed his grandfather savaging his own great-granddaughter: 'Their lives are shallow and empty. They talk marvellously. But there is a neurotic fear in their lives. Whatever they preach does not seem to operate in their lives. Why?' This was the beginning of his search, a search that lasted till his forty-ninth year.

In the year 1932, when U.G. was fourteen, three significant events took place which steered him further away from the world of orthodoxy and tradition. One day, a pontiff of great repute, a Shankaracharya of a well-known *math*, visited U.G.'s house. Not everybody in those days could afford to have guests. The Shankaracharya travelled with a huge entourage of disciples and attendants. The religious ceremony that was performed extended to several days. All this cost a lot of money. The pomp and the colour, the crown and the sceptre of the pontiff fascinated U.G. He wanted to be like him when he grew up. He wanted to leave his house, his grandparents and everything else to become the pontiff's assistant. He wanted to succeed him and inherit all that he had.

The pontiff turned U.G.'s request down saying that he was too young for that kind of life and that leaving his home would make his family extremely unhappy. This did not distract U.G. from his aspirations. 'There must be somebody else somewhere who can fulfil this desire of mine,' he thought to himself. The pontiff, when leaving, gave U.G. a Shiva *mantra*. For the next seven years U.G. recited this *mantra* three thousand times a day, every day, everywhere he went.

The 1932 convention of the Theosophical Society was once again held in Adyar. Scores of people stood in a line to pay their respects to the Society's President, Annie Besant. U.G., holding flowers in his hands, waited along with his grandfather in the line. When his turn came, he noticed that Annie Besant did not recognize his grandfather. She was more absorbed in looking at U.G. As he laid the bunch of flowers he was carrying on to the quilt in her lap, she asked him affectionately, 'You are going to work for the Theosophical Society in Adyar, aren't you?' U.G. did not respond.

Mr. Jinarajadasa, the Vice-President of the Theosophical Society, who had been standing behind Annie Besant, overseeing the occasion, heard what she had said to the boy. He was amazed.

He called U.G.'s grandfather aside and asked him to visit him along with U.G. that evening.

Later in the evening, as the gathering at Adyar dispersed, Mr Jinarajadasa gave an autographed copy of the book entitled *I Promise* to U.G. The book dealt with the process of receiving acceptance by the Masters and with the ways and means of preparing for discipleship.

It was on the death anniversary of his mother that U.G. finally broke away from the practice of all religious rites. Every year on this day U.G. was made to fast. The little boy was permitted to eat only at the end of the day, after feeding a couple of Brahmin priests and washing their feet. U.G. was also made to meditate and recreate in his mind the image of his dead mother whom he had hardly seen.

U.G. was enraged that day when he discovered the Brahmin priests eating heartily in a nearby restaurant. 'They too are supposed to be fasting. Enough is enough. They are all fakes,' he said to himself. Furious, he raced back to his grandfather and, in an act of defiance, broke his sacred thread, the symbol of his religious heritage, and threw it away. He then asked his grandfather for money. He was leaving home to begin his own search. 'You are a minor. You cannot have the money,' said his grandfather. 'I don't want your money. I want my mother's money,' answered U.G. 'If you go on this way, I'll disown you,' said his grandfather, hoping to frighten the little boy. What U.G. said was the last thing the old man expected. 'You don't own me. So how can you disown me?'

Between the ages of fourteen and twenty-one, U.G. undertook all kinds of spiritual exercises. He practised all the austerities. He was determined to find out if there was any such thing as *moksha*, about which all the great teachers of mankind had spoken endlessly. He wanted that *moksha* for himself. He had also resolved to prove to himself and to everybody that there cannot be hypocrisy in the people who have realized themselves. He searched for a person who was an embodiment of this realization.

21

There was in those days a Hindu evangelist, a strict and self-righteous 'spiritual authority' called Sivananda Saraswati with whom U.G. spent seven summers in the Himalayas studying classical Yoga. Those years laid the foundation for his quest.

While practising Yoga and meditation, U.G. had every kind of experience talked about in the sacred books—*samadhi*, super *samadhi*, *nirvikalpa samadhi*. 'Thought can create any experience you want—bliss, beatitude, ecstasy, melting away into nothingness—all those experiences. But this can't be the thing, because I have remained the same person, mechanically doing these things. This is not leading me anywhere,' thought U.G. to himself.

About the same time, sex became an issue for U.G. He wondered why religious people wanted to deny or suppress a natural biological urge. He wanted to find out what happened to that urge he did not do anything with it. He wanted to understand everything about sex. 'Why do I want to indulge in auto-erotism. I don't know anything about sex. Then why is it that I have all kinds of images about sex?' U.G. inquired. *This* became his meditation:

> How am I able to form these sexual images? I have never gone to a movie or seen anything of a sexual nature. How is it that these sexual images exist inside of me and are not put in me from outside? All stimulation apparently comes from outside. But there is another kind of stimulation which comes from within. I can cut out all external stimulation. But how can I eliminate what is inside of me?

U.G. had not experienced sex but he says that even then he seemed to know what the sex experience was. Since his aim in those days was to become an ascetic or a monk, he did not entertain the thought of marriage. He saw for himself that though he thought of gods and goddesses, he had wet dreams. He questioned why he felt guilty about this when he had no control over it. His meditation, his discipline and his study of holy books had not helped him with this issue. Even his staying away from salt, chillies and spices had not worked.

U.G.'s Yoga Master, Sivananda, was startled when U.G. caught him devouring hot pickles behind closed doors. 'How can this man deceive himself and others, pretending to be one thing while doing another. He has denied himself everything in the hope of getting something but he cannot control himself. He is a hypocrite. This kind of life is not for me.' So U.G. gave up his Yoga practice and left Sivananda.

As U.G. moved into adulthood, he became a cynic, rejecting the spiritual bonds of his culture and questioning everything for himself. He displayed a healthy contempt for his religious inheritance, a contempt which was to develop into an acute repugnance towards what he was later to call, 'the hypocrisy of the holy business.' He wanted to 'do things my way.' He relentlessly questioned the authority of others over him. No wonder his grandmother said of him that he had 'the heart of a butcher.'

By twenty-one, U.G. had become a quasi-atheist. He joined the University of Madras and for some years studied Psychology, Philosophy, Mysticism and Modern Sciences.

The human mind had always intrigued U.G. 'Where is this mind? I want to know something about it; here inside of me I don't see anything,' he introspected. 'Why read all this? All this knowledge does not satisfy me.' With the passage of time, the intensity of his search had grown. One day, he asked his professor:

> We are talking about the mind all the time. Do you know for yourself what the mind is? All the stuff I know about the mind is from these books of Freud, Jung, Adler and so on, that I have studied. Apart from these descriptions and definitions that are

23

there in the books, do *you* know anything about the mind?

'These are dangerous questions. If you want to pass your examinations, memorize what there is in the books and repeat it in your examination papers. You will get your degree,' said the professor. U.G. retorted, 'I am not interested in a degree. I am interested in finding out about the mind.' Even now, looking back, U.G. fondly refers to this professor as the 'only honest person' he ran into in those days.

'There is a man at Tiruvannamalai called Ramana Maharshi. Come, let us go and see him. It is said that he is a human embodiment of the Hindu tradition,' said a friend to U.G. one day during the course of a discussion. U.G. by then had arrived at a point where he felt certain that all the teachers of mankind—Buddha, Jesus, Sri Ramakrishna, etc. had deluded themselves and deluded others. The description of that state which these teachers talked about had absolutely no relation to the way he was functioning. He had a revulsion, an 'existentialist nausea' against everything sacred, everything holy:

> I am a brute, I am a monster. I am full of violence. This is a reality. I am full of desire. Desirelessness, non-greed, non-anger, those things have no meaning for me. They are false. They are not only false, they are falsifying me. I am finished with this whole business. I don't want to sit at the feet of any holy man. If you have seen one, you have seen them all.

'Go there just for once. It is said his look changes you. In his presence you feel silent, your questions disappear,' the friend persisted. He gave U.G. a book to read, entitled, *Search in Secret India* by Paul Brunton. U.G. read the chapter relating to Ramana and, in the year 1939, reluctantly, hesitantly, unwillingly went along with his friend to meet the famous sage of Arunachala.

Bhagwan Sri Ramana Maharshi was reading comic strips when U.G.first saw him.At the very first glimpse of him, U.G. thought, 'How can this man help me?' As he sat there for two hours, watching the Bhagwan cut vegetables and play with this, that or the other, he wasn't at all surprised to find that all those fancy assertions to the effect that this man's look changed you and that all questions disappeared in his presence, remained fables.

'Is there,' asked U.G., 'anything like enlightenment?' 'Yes, there is,' replied Ramana. 'Are there any levels to it?' The Master replied, 'No, no levels are possible. It is all one thing—either you are there or you are not there at all.' Finally U.G. asked, 'This thing called enlightenment, can you give it to me?' Sri Ramana did not answer. After a pause U.G. repeated the question, 'I am asking you whether you can give me whatever you have.' Looking U.G. in the eyes, Bhagwan replied, 'I can give it to you but can you take it?'

'What arrogance!' U.G. thought to himself. 'I can give it to you but can you take it? Nobody had said anything like that before.' Everybody that he had met had advised him to do something. For seven years he had been through all kinds of *sadhanas*. He had also gone through a 'masochistic' period of self-denial. 'If there is any individual who can take it, it is me. But what is that state? What is it that he has?' queried U.G. 'He can't be very different from me. He was also born to parents. People say something happened to him. How do I know if there is anything like enlightenment? I must find out. Nobody can give me that state. I am on my own....'

U.G. never visited Sri Ramana again. As he left Tiruvannamalai, his real search began, and with it, his long involvement with the Theosophical Society.

3. Life among the Theosophists

'When you know nothing you say a lot;
when you know something there is
nothing to say.'

—U.G.

28 August 1991, 5:50 a.m. I am in London. The landing was smooth. I get out of the aircraft with my handbag. That is the only luggage I carry. I hurry through the Immigration and Customs and head towards the taxi stand. As I get into a taxi I see a big orange sun climbing up in the sky, ushering in a perfect summer day. It's unusually warm here in London. As I drive into the sleepy city a voice on the radio predicts the end of the Soviet Union. My mind flashes back to what U.G. had said about Mikhail Gorbachev two years ago when the entire world was applauding him as the man of the decade. 'Gorby has opened a can of worms, Mahesh. This is the beginning of the end of the Soviet Union.'

The streets of London are littered with memories of half-lived yesterdays. Nostalgia is pain. I am reminded of Parveen Babi. Her memory doesn't seem to have faded with time. It was with her that I first walked down these streets of London. 'Man is memory. You are nothing but the past,' says U.G. I remember 1979, a year which marked a turning point in my life.

Parveen's first breakdown is an old story. I wonder if anyone can imagine what it is like to live with a person who is going mad. Parveen's madness, the threat from the film industry to get her back in front of the camera at any cost, the psychiatrists throwing up their hands, her mother yielding to the pressure for shock treatment—God, what a mess it was! 'There must be an end to this misery,' I said to myself then. 'For God's sake, help us,' I cried out to U.G., 'We are at the end of our rope.' My mood was such that I was ready to follow him over the wall and even venture to assay the first jump, if he so commanded. U.G. did come to our rescue and he shielded us from all those pressures. Even now, I feel guilty for imposing my problems and Parveen's illness on him. I engulfed him in our private hell. How can I ever forget that every time I sought his help, he stretched out his hand! And he was even blamed for it by the media.

In September 1979, I shanghaied Parveen to Kodaikanal where U.G. was spending a month. Being there with U.G. helped her. Her condition was slowly improving. All her fears that somebody wanted to kill her gradually dissipated. U.G. was like a solitary tree in a wasteland, sheltering us in its shade so we could breathe awhile.... But not for long. Soon Kodai turned out to be something like a page from Dante's *Inferno*.

Parveen locked herself up in her room and would come out only to have her meals. U.G. too was not well because of his cardiospasms. He just couldn't eat or drink anything for thirty-six hours. To make matters worse, Parveen too stopped eating and drinking—perhaps in sympathetic response to U.G.'s condition. The damp, cold, wet weather added to our discomfort.

Suddenly, one night, a gripping pain seized U.G. Looking at his friend Valentine, he said, 'It looks like the time has come for me to go.' To this Valentine remarked, half-jokingly, 'U.G., I don't think it is practical to die in a place like this, at a time like this.' U.G. burst into laughter—that was the only laughter that echoed within the four walls of that cottage in a week. That outburst of laughter freed U.G. from his difficulty, much to everybody's relief.

The last seven days I spent in Kodai were the most harrowing, agonizing, vexing and tormenting I have ever had. I think I was more deeply depressed than anybody there. One evening, when it was almost midnight, U.G. was in the living-room alone, watching the fire glowing in the fireplace. As I joined him, I was in a troubled state of mind over the uncertainty of Parveen's and my future together. U.G. sensed my anxiety, sadness and despondency. He said he saw little chance of complete recovery; that all mental maladies were genetic in origin. 'The psychiatrists know it too. But they won't admit it. It would put them out of business.' U.G. suggested that we leave for Bangalore and seek the help of his friends at the Institute of Mental Health. In Bangalore, Parveen's condition improved.

I had heard intriguing stories about U.G.'s walks with king cobras. I had dismissed these stories as myths but was nevertheless curious. So, one day, at Mr Brahmachari's ashram, I said to U.G., 'I hear that you go for walks with a king cobra. This I would like to see.' U.G. responded saying, 'We will see.' Late that same evening, Parveen and I went for a stroll with U.G. As we were walking along, all of a sudden U.G. said, 'Stop,' and holding us both back said, 'Look and see for yourselves.' There they were—not only the king cobra but the whole family. Parveen and I ran away in terror.

After this incident I asked U.G., 'Were you not frightened?' U.G. replied:

> The cobra would only strike if it sensed fear. A frightened being emits odours. The cobra strikes in order to protect itself. It does not trust human beings. It may kill one human being to protect itself, while humans kill hundreds of cobras for no reason. Naturally when this happens, the field mice have a field day with the crops in the field because there are no cobras left to eat them.

That was some lesson in ecology!

I still remember the day when U.G. spoke to me about distancing myself from Parveen. 'I know it's going to be tough,

Mahesh,' he said hesitantly, 'but make possible what is inevitable....' I knew the end was near. Strange as it may seem, U.G. had in a way prepared both Parveen and me for this separation. It was in Gstaad, Switzerland, on a quiet morning that U.G., seeing Parveen's palm, predicted a break in her career. She was right on top in those days. He also predicted the termination of our relationship. The manner in which he said it seemed frivolous but somewhere within both of us a feeling of impending doom surfaced. For months Parveen woke up in the middle of the night staring at her palm, terrified. She tried to prevent me from meeting U.G. whenever he passed through Bombay, saying, 'He will take you away from me. Don't meet him. Don't you see, he wants us to break up?' U.G. persuaded Parveen to save money for what he called a 'rainy day'. How helpful those savings are to her now!

On 26 October 1979, U.G., seeing me off in a taxi said, 'When you look back, you will see for yourself that this was the happiest day of your life. Go, Mahesh, and carve out a new future for yourself. You cannot help this girl. It's finished.' There is an end and there is an ending to that end. With that, my two-and-a-half-year relationship with Parveen Babi, my dependence on her and our mutual exploitation ended.

My relationship with U.G. had left me shattered and alone. My facades had all collapsed. At that point in my life, I felt like a total failure. My professional identity was that of a 'flop director', talked about only as Parveen Babi's boyfriend. Yet the encounter with this blunt realization gave me an extraordinary drive to become somebody on my own. 'Don't make a virtue of failure. I will never forgive you if you are not a success,' demanded U.G., rubbing salt into my wounds. Thirteen years later, as I drive down the streets of London, I realize that by amputating me from that sordid, dependent relationship and not even offering me a helping hand as a crutch, U.G. gave me the courage to walk by myself. Yes, today I *can* look back and call that the happiest day of my life!

29

The place where U.G. and I lived in London is situated opposite 33 Ovington Square. This is the place from where Mr C. Jinarajadasa, the Head of the Esoteric Section of the Theosophical Society, who later became its President, wrote to U.G. who was then in India.

12 July 1940

Dear Brother,

I can only reply briefly to your letter of appreciation and enquiries.

It is excellent that you should have the ideals which you have of being of service, but you can work out a great part of the problem before you in the light of the many teachings which you find in Theosophy. Regarding the matter of your desiring to find a Teacher, I might here quote the answer which the Master K.H. gave to the late Bro. C.W.L, who asked that question of the Master in 1883:

'To accept any man as a chela does not depend on my personal will. It can only be the result of one's personal merit and exertions in that direction. Force any one of the "Masters" you may happen to choose; do good works in his name and for the love of mankind; be pure and resolute in the path of righteousness (as laid out in our rules); be honest and unselfish; forget yourself but do remember the good of other people—and you will have forced that "Master" to accept you.'

The hymn of Frances Havergel is often used by me to explain to my hearers certain aspects of the great ideal.

When I return to India and I can meet you, I can give you further advice. In the meantime, look within yourself for the guidance which you think

you need. You will find that if you are in a quiet
state of meditation, with a feeling of aspiration,
some suggestion will come in the matter of helping
others. Put it into operation even if the result seems
not noticeable. But remember the teaching of the
Gita that you must have no thought of fruit or
reward, but act righteously because that is a law of
your being, or because it is an offering from your
heart to God.

Yours sincerely,
C. Jinarajadasa

Jinarajadasa returned to India toward the end of 1940. He opened
the facility built by U.G.'s grandfather for the use of the Andhra
Theosophical Federation as its headquarters. He stayed with
U.G.'s family in their home for two days. This was in January
1941.

That summer, U.G. worked in C.W. Leadbeater's personal
library, rearranging his books for almost three months. He had
always wondered how Leadbeater wrote about the past lives of
Krishnamurti, published under the title, *Lives of Alcyone*. When
U.G. looked at the collection of books Leadbeater had in his
personal library, he said to himself, 'He has read all the ancient
histories of practically every civilization in the world. No wonder
he could fit Krishnamurti's past lives into these histories.' This
confirmed his scepticism about Leadbeater's powers of
clairvoyance which he was credited with by the members of the
Theosophical Movement. As a child U.G. had sat in front of
Leadbeater every day, expecting that he would see some spiritual
potential in him. To his disappointment, Leadbeater never
showed any such recognition.

Be that as it may, the opportunity of working in this library
brought U.G. and Jinarajadasa close to each other. Every now
and then Jinarajadasa used to walk into the library, talk to U.G.
about some of the rare books and recommend them to him.

31

U.G.'s early life, according to him, in no way resembled the life story of a saint. U.G. himself says he was never a good student, either in high school or in college. He never passed any examination on the first attempt. Throughout his college years, however, he received letters of support from Dr Arundale, the President of the Theosophical Society. These letters offered encouragement and sympathy.

10 July 1939

Thank you for your letter dated July 8th. I quite realize that examinations are a very great nuisance, and are indeed of extremely little worth. But one has to go through them for the sake of equipment from the standpoint of the outer world.

We were very glad to have you here in the Office and hope to see you again when you are next in Madras.

10 February 1940

I myself certainly have high hopes for you, and I am always glad to see you at Adyar. I do hope you will pass your examinations successfully.

20 May 1940

I am so sorry you have failed in your examination again. Some of us are not really fit for examinations. We can do other and better things, and if you have an income which will suffice, then why should you not follow your own inclinations and study along your own lines. For my own part, I should not think it is necessary for you to have a university career.

23 October 1940

I am very delighted to hear that you have passed the examination. This is very good news. I offer you my very affectionate congratulations.

U.G. offers the following remarks on his college education:

> Although I was a student with the lowest grades, barely passing grades, I was admitted into the Philosophy Honours class at Madras University. These courses were primarily for brilliant students. Though I wasn't brilliant, the professor of Philosophy needed students. There were only four students in the class. So, he admitted me. Because of my lack of interest in studies, he always joked that he had four-and-a-half students in his class. I never attended any mid-term examinations, let alone the final ones. My report card revealed nothing but absenteeism.
>
> One day the Principal sent for me and confronted me with my last report card. I had struck off the 'Parent or Guardian' entry and signed it myself. The Principal said that I should get the signature of my grandfather. If I failed to do so, he would fine me twenty-five rupees. I said that wouldn't hurt anybody and that I could write a cheque immediately for that amount drawn on the Imperial Bank of India (the bank for Government agencies and rich people). The principal asked me, 'Why are you attending this college, then?' I said, 'For want of a better occupation.' He was not impressed. He insisted that I should still produce the report card duly signed by my grandfather. Luckily for me and unfortunately for him, the principal died of a heart attack the next day.

U.G. comments on the value of political sages and experts:

During those years I lived in Adyar most of the time, the headquarters of the Theosophical Society, and worked for Dr Arundale as one of his personal assistants. My job was to read newspapers and periodicals from all over the world and choose articles of permanent interest for him to read at a later date.

It was during that time I discovered the *Time* magazine. (I continued to read it from cover to cover for fifty years and enjoyed its style and coverage of world events.) That was when I discovered that there is no such thing as objectivity and an unprejudiced view of human affairs. Those were the War years. The magazine used to arrive six months behind schedule. But we followed the course of events of the war from day to day through the B.B.C. and the daily newspapers.

Two of the noted journalists and columnists at that time were Walter Lippman and H.V. Kaltenborn. Walter Lippman knew everything and predicted everything but most of the time he was wrong about the course of events of the War. Kaltenborn, a news broadcaster and analyst, was famous for predicting the outcome of the election between Truman and Dewey. He proclaimed with great gusto that Dewey would win by a landslide, even when there were reports that he was lagging behind in the race. Kaltenborn explained the reports away saying that it was only a temporary set-back. The next morning, the headlines announced that Truman had won. From such incidents I have concluded that the viewpoint of an uneducated person in some remote corner of India is just as valid as that of the world-acclaimed pundits.

I can say without hesitation that I have learned precious little from either spiritual or secular teachers.

In 1946 Jinarajadasa was elected President of the Theosophical Society and U.G. the Joint General Secretary of the Indian section. U.G. occupied that position for three years and when that office was eventually abolished, he became a national lecturer for seven years. In this capacity, he spoke at almost every college in India. He then went to England, Ireland, Europe and North America on an extensive lecture tour. He spoke at the annual convention of the Theosophical Society in England, presided over by Mr Jinarajadasa.

It was when he was in England, in May 1953, that he met Jinarajadasa for the last time. It is ironical that the beginning and the end of U.G.'s association with the Theosophical Society took place at 33 Ovington Square, Knightsbridge, London. This is what Jinarajadasa said to U.G.:

> I have heard about your reactions with reference to the Theosophical Society and Krishnaji—how critical you have become of everything and everybody! I should like to know your exact viewpoint and would certainly like to discuss it with you. I suggest that you contribute a series of articles to the *Theosophist*. You can very freely criticize anybody—the President, the General Secretaries and anybody else, in support of your position. Such articles would be welcome in order to maintain absolute freedom on the platform of the Theosophical Society. It is only by such frank and free expression of opinions that organizations can retain their vigour and vitality. If you feel that the Theosophical Society should be closed down,

> say so in the articles. Let the members know it and
> let them begin to think. I feel that I at any rate will
> be greatly benefited.

Yet, in response to this, U.G. told him of his intention to resign from both the Theosophical Society and its Esoteric Section. Jinarajadasa was disappointed. He said that he was leaving soon for the United States and that he would be back in India before the end of the year. He wanted to discuss the matter further with U.G. then. But he died in America in July, the same year.

U.G. continued his lecture tour for the Theosophical Society in Europe. At Oslo, he addressed the One World Movement. At a German Summer School in Rendsberg, he was the guest of honour and gave a series of lectures on 'Man, Nature and Reality'. At the invitation of the General Secretary of the Council of the Theosophical Society in Europe, which was celebrating its Golden Jubilee, he attended meetings and addressed them on Indian ideals of life and thought.

He also gave a public lecture in Brussels. The audience consisted of twenty-eight people—twenty-five of whom were old women in tennis shoes, knitting sweaters. It was then that U.G. said to himself, 'Is this how I am going to serve the cause of Theosophy and the Theosophical Society? All this is second-hand information. Anybody who has brains can gather this information and then throw it out. This is not something real for me. What am I doing? Why am I wasting my time?' Given below is U.G.'s opening address to the German Summer School at Rendsberg in July 1953.

PERSONAL EXPERIENCE IN RELATION TO THEOSOPHY

> The history of Theosophical thought is the history
> of the evolution of modern thought. As of all others,
> the survey of Theosophical thought in successive
> periods of the Society's history is the general
> evolution and progress of human thought. The
> leaders of the Society have a place not only in the

Theosophical Movement but also in the history of world thought itself, in the whole intellectual advance that has been registered these seventy-seven years. Every leader has contributed to this onward and forward movement some small fresh fragment to the Temple of Theosophical Wisdom. Progress always appears in different lights to different people. The Society is not simply a working institution; it is a spiritual organization. It is different from the ordinary human societies or clubs that men form for ordinary purposes of human association; but it is still a Society composed of people of various nationalities, and therefore, not something that you can talk about in the abstract. It is like any other organization made up of members. Sometimes in the life of any spiritual movement, we seem to be just jogging along; nothing very much appears to be happening and we do not seem to be getting anywhere in particular; it is only when we pause to look back and to take our bearings that we realize what a long way we have, in fact, come from where we started and what tremendous advances we are really making. There is bound to be loss as well as gain but the leaders have, during these seventy-seven years, made significant contributions in and through the Theosophical Society, to the religious life of the community as a whole. Each of them had something new to say and that is why we revere them, but each of them in a different fashion proclaimed a different facet of Theosophy and they carried the Society forward with them because they journeyed with their faces towards the light. They have left their mark upon its outlook and activities and have also helped to set the general tone.

37

Let us look at the different stages of growth and the gradual objectivization of the ideals of Theosophy. Let me very briefly survey the background of the Theosophical Movement and the conditions of the world before its advent.

The world was then divided into two camps, that of rigid materialism and that of a narrow and bigoted form of religion. It was an age of conquering science when religion was on the defence. The increase of 'valid knowledge' called Science was having a disturbing effect on the religious traditions. Religion had become bankrupt, for it had no real life in it. The mechanistic theory of man and the Universe grew in clarity and prestige. The philosophy that emanated was a materialistic philosophy which sought in matter the solution of all mysteries. Into this maelstrom of opposing and conflicting forces was heralded the Theosophical Society. Thus what was wanted, the Theosophical Society supplied. So the work of H.P. Blavatsky is of great consequence, as she supplied a philosophy of life which was broad enough to include both spirit and matter. The great Theosophical treatise, *The Secret Doctrine,* by Madame Blavatsky, brought together all sorts of facts in the domain of mysticism, religion, philosophy and science to prove that quite apart from science and religion, dogma and worship, there is one step beyond mind touching spirit, which may be called the transcendental aspect of Theosophy. She tried to establish the Law of Reincarnation, the Theory of Karma, the power of mind over matter and she stressed the practice which, in fact, is Occultism. It appealed to the intellectuals of that time and so she was able to gather around her great personages like Edison,

Sir William Crookes, Alfred Russell Wallace, W.t.Stead and Sir Oliver Lodge, though they dropped out of our ranks later. Thus the early efforts of H.P.B. proved the supremacy of spirit over mind.

But when Dr Annie Besant came to the scene, she tried to contact that spirit and to make that Transcendental into Immanent. And her method of achieving this was the service of mankind. What is the motive for service? Each one of us has to try and delve as deeply as possible within himself to see what really is the propelling force or hidden motive behind his activities. This is how a modern psychologist, E.M.Delfield, warns us when he says:

'The philanthropist is relatively safe when he acknowledges safely to himself the elements of satisfaction in his work. The person who says, "I give freely and look for no return; I wear myself out for the sake of others; I accept honours and responsibility unwillingly; the money I receive for my work is nothing to me; I do not want gratitude," is being hoodwinked by his unconscious. People do not consider it decorous to realize that they are doing more interesting work and getting better pay than ever before, an outlet for their energies and many are the better for it.' Why the urge for service at all? ... Dr Besant taught us that life is only for service. She stressed the central truth as distinct from dogmatic and institutional forms. This appealed to the moderm mind, which was becoming increasingly rationalistic in temper and outlook. She made the evolving Universe intelligible to millions of people and from the heights of her idealism, she set in motion thought currents which spiritualized them more than any other single influence. -

Leadbeater helped us to see the other worlds to which we also belong, the worlds invisible and intangible. Our citizenship is also in Heaven. The unseen world is only an expansion of that which is seen. There is one more contribution of his. At the time of the inauguration of the Theosophical Society, the adepts did not use the phrases 'The inner government of the world', 'The Ideas of Manu, the Bodhisattva and the Logos'. These were all later revelations. These were elaborated by the investigations of Annie Besant and C.W.Leadbeater from whom we also heard of the Monad, the Group Soul, etc.

But the cycle is not complete; if we want to complete this cycle we must be able to see the immanence as well as transcendence. It is really the summation, the integration, the climax of the group of thought-forms, the thought processes and evolution ....

And in the words of an American philosopher, adapted slightly, even the Truths of Theosophy may dust the mind by their dryness unless they are effaced each morning and rendered fertile by the dews of fresh and living truth. Otherwise, our love of Theosophy has no reality behind it. The vital principles and truths that operate in any spiritual movement are likely to become a dogma or creed when the movement settles down. Each one of us must discover his own mystery, what the *Light on the Path* calls 'final secret'. To do this is to discover something in terms of our own experience, a vital transforming experience. Until we have discovered that centre in ourselves, whatever may be the magnitude of our contribution, all that activity, all that contribution, is bound to be devoid of the unique and vitalizing factor, namely, individual inspiration. In the ultimate analysis, it is the individual that matters. Only to the extent that an individual is inspired from within himself can he contribute to the common work and thus energize what we call group activity. This process of inwardness, if I may say so, is not morbid isolationism or an ivory tower outlook. Now we cannot go deep down into ourselves except in a state of relationship with others. To the extent that we are periodically able to go deep down into ourselves can we find that inspiration which is necessary....

It is said that the Maha-Chohan has given, as it were, a charter for the work of the Theosophical Society, when he said: 'The Theosophical Society was chosen as the cornerstone, the foundation, of the future religions of humanity.' Shall we not see that day? The world needs Theosophy. The forces of the world are with us, the times and the spirit of the age are with us and I have no doubt the Truths of Theosophy which insist on a quest more than a creed would enable us to join the pursuit of the ideal.

This address was made by U.G. *ex tempore*. If one goes through this address closely, one observes that the germs of what U.G. is saying now were present even then.

U.G. continued to lecture on his own in the United States, primarily because he needed the money. He had a manager, Miss Irma E. Crumley, to arrange his lectures. She was able to get him a hundred dollars per lecture. He delivered about sixty lectures on various subjects including Politics, Education, Philosophy, Economics, Indian thought and world affairs. The lectures were held at various Kiwanis Clubs, Lion's Clubs, Rotary Clubs,

University Clubs, Women's Clubs and some universities like the University of Washington at St Louis, Missouri. Newspaper editorials commented on his lectures. Here is a sample:

INTERNATIONAL GIVEAWAY SOMETIMES BACKFIRES

Immediately following World War II and continuing down to the present, this country has spent millions of dollars in underdeveloped countries in an attempt to keep them from falling prey to the clutching hands of Russian imperialism.

Unfortunately, when the balance sheet has been drawn up it shows that this country is operating in the red and the country receiving the aid is being operated by the Reds.

The explanation for this kind of one-sided bargaining is not so simple. While we may criticize countries for taking our money and then playing 'footsie' with the Reds, who among the peoples on the earth is going to turn down financial help during a time of national distress? To refuse extended money would be going contrary to natural inclinations.

Only a few days ago a highly educated man from India—one of the countries which has received millions of American dollars and still refuses to ally herself with the Western nations—made some statements in a speech in Elgin that were freighted with truth and worthy of profound consideration.

U.G. Krishnamurti was born and has lived most of his life in India—with the exception of the months he has spent traveling and lecturing, much of it in this country.

As graduate of Madras University, he is by no means 'typical' of an Indian as only seven percent of the country's populace are literate. But as one who has traveled throughout his country and lectured at practically every college and university in that vast land, he should be able to reflect some of India's present psychology.

Krishnamurti points out that this country would be better off if she would stop spending money in India and utilize it in other directions. The masses of India—who are in the main ignorant of America's financial help to their country—would appreciate our position more if money were spent on such projects as bringing Indian patients to this country for treatment in American hospitals, and by American doctors; sponsoring Indian farmers who could get a first hand view of an American farm, or letting an Indian industrial worker see our assembly lines in action and visit the home of an American worker.

While Krishnamurti does not decry the student exchange program, he wisely points out that the Indian student is rather far removed from the common people. University graduates don't speak the language of the man in crowded streets of Bombay.

The reducing of tension among the nations of the world will not be solved overnight. If 'understanding' among the various peoples is to come about, however, it will be when they become better acquainted by person-to-person contact and not through an international giveaway program which too often has repelled rather than attracted those whom we were sincerely trying to help.

"Courier-News'Viewpoints"
in the *Courier News*, Elgin, Illinois.

Here is a sample of the newspaper reports on U.G.'s lectures in the United States in the Fifties:

LION'S CLUB HEARS LECTURE ON INDIA

Speaking at the Lion's Club here Tuesday, U.G.Krishnamurti, one of India's most accomplished lecturers, pleaded for greater understanding between India and America.

After thanking the club for the invitation, Krishnamurti paid an eloquent tribute to the Lion's International for the very valuable work it is doing here in this country and elsewhere, and added that such movements could be the greatest forces in a world which is full of misunderstanding, acrimony, discord and prejudice.

Adverting to India's place in world diplomacy, Krishnamurti said: To call Nehru a fellow-traveler with 'Krush and Bulge' or 'Mao and Chou' is a cheap device. Nehru is the most glamorous personality in world politics today. His experiment in India to work out a greater stability and equilibrium and integration in the individual is setting a great pattern for the future.

Referring to the foreign aid, he said that the country's prosperity could not depend upon foreign aid alone. To share your industrial and scientific experience with India is one thing but how far a nation can use it is a different thing. I always maintain that the prosperity of a country can only be dependent upon its own inherent strength. 'Economic recovery and industrialization were possible,' Krishnamurti said, 'only through one process, that is, collaboration between people and the Government. I am not sure that exists in

India and somehow people haven't that enthusiasm for all these first and second five year plans.'

Concluding his address, Mr Krishnamurti sounded a note of hope. 'It is said,' he went on to say, 'that America is chosen as guardian of the freedoms of the world. My prayer is that this grand land of freedom can fulfill her mission.'

Toward the end of this period of lecturing, U.G. began wondering why he was doing this, that there must be some other way of making money. He, however, had no alternatives in mind. He knew only how to 'squander' the money he had inherited. He finally told his manager that he did not want to go through with the lecture tour she had arranged for him the following year. 'You have now become a celebrity of sorts,' she said. 'You are in demand. How can you do this to me?' 'Sorry,' said U.G.

He delivered only one more public lecture in his life. This was years later in Bangalore. The auditorium was packed beyond capacity. Newspaper coverage of the lecture was so extensive that it 'scared' U.G.

4. Locking of Horns

*'Inspiration is a meaningless thing. So
many things and people inspire us
but the actions born out of
inspiration are meaningless; lost and
desperate people create a market for
inspiration. All inspired action will
eventually destroy you
and your kind.'*

-U.G.

In the late Forties, toward the ending of U.G.'s association with
the Theosophical Society, J. Krishnamurti arrived on the scene
from the United States. The countdown began. Soon the stage
would be set for the two Krishnamurtis to lock horns.

Pages from my diary which contain all the records of those
spent in Kodai, entitled "A Lonely Winter Spent Fire-watching",
flutter in my memory. A section reads:

> As we were preparing to leave for Bangalore the
> next day, quite unexpectedly one Mr Bernard Selby,
> a postman from Manchester, England, showed up.
> For a postman his mind was very agile and his
> knowledge left me in awe. He was a 'Krishnamurti
> freak'. That morning all of us went for a walk along
> the lakeside. Our conversation centred around J.
> Krishnamurti. U.G. bore down hard on him. This

was the most vehement attack on J. Krishnamurti
by U.G. that I had ever heard.

Later, as I listened to the recording of a tape of that
conversation, I found that one of the subjects that kept cropping
up in my conversations with U.G. over the years was J.
Krishnamurti. The following conversation is the most interesting
that I had recorded in Kodai:

*U.G., if I ask you to name the most remarkable man you
have met in your life, who comes to your mind first?*
Jiddu Krishnamurti. But....

(He didn't complete the sentence.) *Are you backing
out?*

Oh, no, protested U.G.

(When you are with U.G. you don't even know
what hits you. But this was shattering.) *I can't figure
you out, U.G. This morning you treated the subject of J.
Krishnamurti with disdain. Now you say that he is the
most remarkable man you have met in your life.*

I never say anything I don't mean. Do you know
the legend of Krishnamurti?

Not really.

The people from whom he sprang up—
Theosophists—looked up to him as the Buddha of
the Twentieth Century and believed that his
teaching, 'a new birth of belief ', would last five
hundred years. They founded an organization, the
Order of the Star of the East, to propagate his
teachings. When the awaited saviour of mankind
dissolved the organization and walked out, those
who had put him up on the world stage as the
World Teacher felt betrayed. Naturally
Krishnamurti's dissolving the organization had a

47

magical connotation throughout my boyhood. No doubt he has lived all that down. He is now considered to be the most outstanding religious teacher of our time. There is no question that he is immensely popular.

He is a showman par excellence and master of words. Krishnamurti's teachings may have sounded very revolutionary a century ago. But with the emergence of new revelations in the fields of Microbiology and Genetics, the ideas taken for granted in the field of Psychology will be challenged. The 'mind' (which Krishnamurti's teaching assumes), the exclusive franchise of psychologists and religious teachers and all the assumptions connected with it will also be undermined. The fashionable teachings and modern therapies they are marketing are like cabbage-patch dolls—tantalizing and sensational, unlike the old fashioned toys. They try to titillate rather than satiate their followers. They haven't got much of a future and will be outdated.

About ten years ago I accompanied U.G. to see an old friend of his in Thane. The visit was an extraordinary one. The man's name was L. V. Bhave. He was old, very graceful and handsome but sad. (This was the man who was responsible for bringing the two Krishnamurtis together. Mr Bhave used to organize J. Krishnamurti's talks in Bombay in the late Forties and early Fifties.) One could see clearly that his end was near. To use U.G.'s phrase, he belonged to Krishnamurti's 'sixty-year club.' Mr Bhave said, 'I have built a new house close by but I cannot leave this old house. How can we "die to our yesterdays", as in J. Krishnamurti's refrain?' U.G., for a change, said nothing. He hugged him and we left. A few months later Mr Bhave passed away.

Over the years of my association with U.G., I have come across people with diverse opinions about U.G.'s onslaught on J.K.'s teachings. The modern ones who are caught up in psychological jargon feel that U.G. is obsessed with J.K. The religious ones who view the relationship between these two through the portals of tradition say that U.G.'s assault on the teachings of J. Krishnamurti is in keeping with the great tradition of India in which the disciple annihilates the teachings of his guru.

When he was in his mid-twenties, U.G., who had intermittently vowed to forgo sex and marriage in deference to the life of a religious celibate, reasoned that sex was a natural drive and that it was not wise to suppress it. He said to himself, 'If it is a question of satisfying your sex urge, why not marry? That is what society is there for. Why should you have sex with some (unattached) woman? You can have a natural expression of sex in marriage.'

Three months before U.G. got married, a close friend of his happened to look at his astrological chart and said, 'If this is your chart, say what you may, you are going to marry on 15 May 1943.' The sudden death of the only surviving daughter of U.G.'s grandparents created a vacuum in their lives. He felt that he owed it to them to marry. The flipping of a coin, as was the case in all the major decisions in U.G.'s life, decided his fate.

He chose as his bride one of the three young, beautiful Brahmin women his grandmother had selected for him. Her name was Kusuma Kumari. He was to say later, 'I awoke the morning after my wedding night and knew without doubt that I had made the biggest mistake of my life.' From the very beginning U.G. wanted to get out of the marriage. But then the children came and the marriage continued. The final breakup between Kusuma and U.G. was to take place seventeen years later in the US.

For seven years, between 1947 and 1953, U.G. listened to J. Krishnamurti every time he came to Adyar, Madras. During those years U.G. never met Krishnamurti personally. The World

Teacher persona had created some kind of distance in his mind. 'How can a World Teacher be created. World Teachers are born, not made,' U.G. said to himself. He was never part of Krishnamurti's inner circle.

U.G. found the scholars, masterminds, and the 'remarkable' people he met at the Theosophical Society shallow. 'Having worked with them all, I found out there was the same hypocrisy there too, in the sense that there was nothing in their lives.'

At the end of his public talks, J. Krishnamurti always answered written questions sent to him in advance. In 1953, during one of his talks in Madras, U.G. sent him the following question: 'Sir, what kick exactly do you get out of these talks and discussions? Obviously you would not go on more than twenty years if you did not enjoy them. Or is it only by force of habit?' Krishnamurti gave the following answer to U.G.'s question:

> This is a natural question to put, is it not? Because, the questioner only knows or is aware that generally a speaker gets some kind of personal benefit out of it. Or is it merely old age? Or, whether one is young or old, is it the habit? That is all he is accustomed to; so he puts the question.
>
> What is the truth of this? Am I speaking out of habit? What do you mean by habit, force of habit? Because I have talked for twenty years, am I going to talk for twenty more years till I die? Is the understanding of anything habitual? The use of the words is habitual; but the contents of the words vary according to the perception of truth from moment to moment. If a speaker gets a kick out of it, then he is exploiting you. That is what most of us are used to. The speaker is then using you as a means of fulfilment and surely it would destroy that which is real. As we are concerned to find the truth and what is from moment to moment, in it

there can be no continuity; all habit, all certainty,
all desire for fulfilment, all personal
aggrandizement must have come to an end, must
it not? Otherwise, it is another way of exploiting,
another way of deluding people; and with that
surely we are not concerned.

—extracted from the Madras talks,
13 December 1953

The very next day, during an impasse in a discussion period,
Krishnamurti suddenly singled U.G. out and asked, 'What do
you have to say, Sir?' This was in reference to a question on
death and the death experience. Both of them became involved
in heated discussions from that day onward. Krishnamurti
never allowed others to interfere in the exchange between them.
If anyone tried to, Krishnamurti would say, 'No Sir, we have to
thrash this whole thing out between us.' The third day
Krishnamurti suddenly began talking about subconscious and
unconscious states of mind. U.G. reacted by saying, 'I don't see
any mind in me, let alone a subconscious or unconscious mind.
So why are you talking to me about these states?' Krishnamurti
replied, 'Sir, for you and me there is no such thing as a
subconscious or unconscious mind. But I am using these terms
for those people....' He was referring to the other people at the
discussion meeting. U.G. then told him that he was using him
as a sounding board for his discussions and that he was not
interested in 'that kind of a game.' Soon after that U.G. stopped
participating in the public discussions.

Mr L.V. Bhave, their mutual friend (the only one who knew
that U.G. had sent the question to Krishnamurti three days
earlier), urged him to meet with Krishnamurti personally. He
arranged a private meeting between them that afternoon.

That first meeting was very warm and pleasant. U.G. told
Krishnamurti at the outset that he had no personal problems
and that he wasn't seeking a clarification of what they had

discussed during the last three days. Then he casually mentioned his background with the Theosophical Society and his personal connection with Annie Besant, Leadbeater, Jinarajadasa and Dr Arundale. He also mentioned that his maternal grandfather had been closely associated with the leaders of the Theosophical Society, including the founder-president, Olcott. Many of these leaders had visited his home in Andhra Pradesh. U.G. told him that he had been lecturing for the Theosophical Society for the past seven years, mainly in India, and most recently in Europe and America. Krishnamurti responded saying that he had heard of his visits to Norway, Sweden and Denmark. He said that people in those countries had become confused because of his and U.G.'s common names. It seems that'. He had to write to them saying that he was not coming to those countries—that it was another Krishnamurti that they had invited.

The conversation lasted almost an hour. At the end of it, Krishnamurti asked an associate to arrange another get-together with U.G. the following day. From then on, they met together whenever Krishnamurti had free time until he left Madras.

That same evening, during his walk Krishnamurti ran into U.G.'s wife Kusuma, their two daughters and a young girl carrying their son. The next day when U.G. went to see him again, Krishnamurti told him how pained he was to see a young girl carrying a grown-up boy. He said, 'Sir, a ten-year-old girl carrying that boy....' He started admonishing U.G. who said, 'Krishnaji, he is a handicapped boy. Both his legs are affected by polio. He cannot walk without braces. That's why she was carrying him.' U.G. told him that he was considering taking the boy to the United States for medical treatment. 'They have special braces with the help of which he can flex his legs.' Then Krishnamurti suddenly said, 'Bring the whole family tomorrow.'

The next day he took his wife, two daughters and his son along to meet Krishnamurti. It was a Sunday morning. Krishnamurti didn't normally see anyone on Sunday mornings as he gave public talks on Sunday evenings. But that was the only time he could see them. This became a habit. U.G. and his family saw Krishnamurti every Sunday morning while he was in Madras.

That first morning, after the usual courtesies, Krishnamurti asked his host to bring some oranges for the children. The younger one took one of them, peeled it and threw the skin on the floor. Krishnamurti made her pick it up and then gave her a lecture on why she shouldn't throw the peel all around and that she should neatly pick the pieces up and put them in the garbage. He helped her in the process. U.G. was observing the scene. He told Krishnamurti that his words would have no effect on the child. 'Krishnaji,' he said, 'you give her another orange and she will do exactly the same thing as before. I don't trust anyone who has not raised his own children to educate them or to talk about how to raise or educate them. If you raised your own children, then you would understand.' Just as he said this, the little girl repeated her misdeed.

The subject of conversation then changed to the boy's medical treatment. U.G. told Krishnamurti, 'I calculate the cost at ninety thousand dollars. That's all that I have. But that would deprive the other children in the family of their share of the money.' Krishnamurti said in reply, 'Ninety thousand dollars is a lot of money. You know I used to heal people. Why don't you let me try?' U.G. said in response, 'I am a sceptical man. I did hear a lot about your healing work. It doesn't work in this case. The cells in the boy's legs are dead. You cannot put life into them. If you can make him walk, then I will believe you. Jesus walked on water probably because he did not know how to swim. In the story of the multiplication of the loaves of bread and fishes, he probably cut the bread into many smaller pieces.' Krishnamurti burst into laughter at this remark.

U.G.'s wife interjected, 'Why are you standing in the way of Krishnaji's wanting to help the boy?' U.G. answered, 'He is as much your son as he is mine. Personally I don't believe that he could be of any help. But I don't want to stand in the way of his healing attempts.' So, Krishnamurti tried his healing technique by massaging the boy's legs for several days.

One day, after one of those sessions, the boy went into Krishnamurti's bedroom. Krishnamurti instantly stood up and ran after him saying, 'Oh, God! I have my watch on the table.' Both of them came out of the room, the boy with the watch in his hands. As he was wont to, Krishnamurti started giving a sermon to the boy about not playing with expensive things that were not toys.

U.G. and his wife met with Krishnamurti several times. U.G.'s wife was most unwilling to gamble all the family money on the outside chance that the boy might recover in America. She didn't want to leave the girls behind. The subject of freedom to decide things for herself came up. Then U.G. gave her an ultimatum in Krishnamurti's presence, 'You have the choice to leave me and go on your own with the ninety thousand dollars or to go to the United States with me to get the treatment for the boy. In either case, I am going to the US.'

Then Krishnamurti said, 'Amma, if he gets in your way in whatever you want to do, kick him, kill him, bomb him or walk out on him.' Her reaction to his words surprised U.G. She said, 'If I could do that, why would I bother coming to you seeking your advice?' Krishnamurti was taken aback. In the end he persuaded U.G., 'Please wait for another year. I am going to Greece. From there I go to California. Why don't you put off your plans till then? I'll be back in December.' U.G. agreed.

In London, as U.G. was fixing a quick one-dish dinner in the kitchen for both of us (he is a good cook), I questioned him about his run-ins with Krishnamurti. He had anticipated my move. 'Your biography is bound to get around to my encounters with J. Krishnamurti. I have kept no systematic record of my conversations with him. But I will talk about my encounters with him as my memory allows.' I switched on my tape recorder quietly as U.G. began to talk:

One day during our conversation, I asked Krishnamurti, 'Yesterday, in answer to a question on the Masters you said, "As for the Masters, I have never denied their existence." My question to you, Krishnaji, is: Do they or do they not exist? And I want a straight answer.' He said, 'Anything I say becomes authoritative.' I said, 'I am not impressed by your diplomatic answers which neither confirm nor deny. Why do you give all these ambiguous answers? Why not hang the whole thing on a tree for everyone to see?' Instead of answering me, Krishnamurti asked, 'How is the convention going?'

I then asked him, 'Do you mean to say, Krishnaji, that the state you are in happened through the method you are indicating to your listeners? Before the war you were using utterly mystifying language. Now, after the war, you have come up with what I could call "Krishnamurti lingo". Your teaching is nothing but Freudian-Jungian-Rankian-Adlerian stuff with a religious slant. Is this just to give people a new toy? Children in my time used to play with dolls made of deodar wood. Now you are providing them with walking, dancing and talking dolls.' Krishnamurti laughed and said, 'If it works, it works. If it doesn't, it doesn't.'

At some point the conversation turned to the 'unhealthy' subject of sex. We were discussing relationships. I said, 'It's only sex.' 'There must be so much more to it,' he said. 'What, for example?' I asked. 'Love,' he replied. 'What has love got to do with it?' I queried.

Then my wife interrupted saying, 'I am not going to ask questions about sex, except one. Have you ever had sex, Krishnaji?' I was amazed at her courage. Then I looked at Krishnamurti. His eyes were glazed with stupefaction. He answered quietly, 'Amma, that's an impertinent question.'

Throughout our meetings and walks together I noticed a peculiar quality about Krishnamurti. I can only characterize it as the Boy Scout in him. For instance, one day, while we were walking together, I noticed Krishnamurti carefully observing the ground and picking up nails and thorns and throwing them to the side. In a jocular way, I pointed to a nail he had missed. He bent down and picked that nail up too.

On another occasion, when we were walking along the beach in Adyar, Madras, a small boy approached us begging for money. Krishnamurti asked me if I had any money with me. 'Sorry, no,' I said. Then Krishnamurti just hugged the boy. I told him that the boy needed money more than his hugs. The next day I brought some money, and as we were walking along the beach, the same boy came running up to us again asking for money. I handed him a two-rupee note. The boy jumped with joy and ran off with it.

Disagreement on basic issues surfaced all the time between Krishnamurti and myself. We really didn't get along well. Whenever we met we locked horns over some issue or other. For instance, I never shared his concern for the world, or his belief that his teaching would profoundly affect the thoughts and actions of mankind for the next five hundred years—a fantasy of the Theosophist occultists. In one of our meetings I told Krishnamurti, 'I am not called upon to save the world.' He asked, 'The house is on fire—what will you do?' 'Pour more gasoline on it and maybe something will rise from the ashes,' I remarked. Krishnamurti said, 'You are absolutely impossible.'

Then I said, 'You are still a Theosophist. You have never freed yourself from the World Teacher role. There is a story in the *Avadhuta Gita* which talks of the *avadhut* who stopped at a wayside inn and was asked by the innkeeper, "What is your teaching?" He replied, "There is no teacher, no teaching and no one taught." And then he walked away. You too repeat these phrases and yet you are so concerned with preserving your teaching for posterity in its pristine purity.'

The subject of my children and their education arose one day. Krishnamurti asked me, 'What school are your daughters attending?' 'Naturally, Besant Theosophical School,' I answered. 'You know, it's almost next door to us.' 'They teach religion, Sir,' he said. I retorted, 'What do they teach in Rishi Valley School? Instead of having them attend a prayer meeting, you drag those poor unwilling students to watch sunsets from the hilltop. How is that different? You like sunsets. So the children have to watch them too. You know, I spent three-and-a-half days in that Guindy National School. You will recall that you gave talks to us during that time. There is nothing marvellous about those schools. As for myself, I attended a street-side school. And what's wrong with me!'

He tried so hard to convince me to enroll my two daughters in Rishi Valley School. Furthermore, he suggested that I myself spend some time there. 'That's the last thing I would do. They have to grow up to live in this world. I do not want them to be misfits.' Then my wife volunteered to go there as a teacher with the children. But he told her, 'Amma, you have to look after that handicapped boy. It is an all-time, full-time, whole-time job.' Turning to me he said, 'Why don't you go and spend some time at the school. If you don't like it, we will tear it apart and rebuild it stone by stone, brick by brick.' Then I said, 'You stop trotting around the globe and stay at the school. Then perhaps I would consider joining you.' He replied, 'I spend one month every year at Rishi Valley School and another month at Raj Ghat School. That's about all I can do. It is my *dharma* to travel around and give talks.'

Krishnamurti always began his talks with the refrain, 'Let us take a journey together.' I asked him one day, 'Where are you? Are you *there*? Or are you actually taking a journey with us? You pick a subject and ask us to proceed step by step, logically, rationally, sanely and intelligently. There comes a point when you exclaim,. 'I got it! Somebody got it?' It is theatrics. It's a performance. To put it crudely, it is burlesque. You take off and talk of love, bliss, beatitude, immensity and so on. But we are left high and dry. You are offering us bogus chartered flights.'

The question that was uppermost in my mind every time I encountered Krishnamurti was this: 'What is there behind all those abstractions you are throwing at me? Is there anything at all? I am not interested in your poetic and romantic descriptions. As for your abstractions, you are no match to the mighty thinkers that India has produced—you can't hold a candle to them. The way you describe things gives me the feeling that you have at least "seen the sugar"—to use a familiar traditional metaphor—but I am not sure that you have tasted the sugar.'

I repeated this question time and again, one way or another, at every meeting with Krishnamurti and never received a direct or satisfactory answer. The total break came in Bombay. This was my last visit with him for a long time. Again I asked him if there was anything behind the abstractions he was throwing at me. 'Come clean for once.' Then he said with great force, 'You have no way of knowing it!' Then I said, 'If I have no way of knowing it and you have no way of communicating it, what the hell have we been doing! I have wasted seven years listening to you. You can give your precious time to somebody else. I am leaving for New York tomorrow.' Krishnamurti said, 'Pleasant journey and safe landing!'

U.G. was in America for over five years. Krishnamurti kept occasional contact with him through Mr Bhave. He wanted direct information about the medical treatment and progress of U.G.'s son. Here are two typical letters—one to U.G. and the other to U.G.'s wife—written by him during this time:

13 January '56

My dear Krishnamurti,

Thank you very much for your letter of 4 January. I had heard that you were in America lecturing. I am so glad to have heard from you about your son that there is every possibility of his being able to walk in a few years. If you are going to Ojai, you will be able to meet Mr Rajagopal who will be there. As you say, I hope we shall be able to meet in March in Bombay. Please give my best regards to your wife.

With best wishes,
Yours very sincerely,
J. Krishnamurti

11 December '56

Dear Mrs Krishnamurti,

Thank you very much for your letter of 14 November. It is very good of you to have written at some length about your family and I am very glad that your son is so very much better and I hope before he comes back, he will have completely recovered and will be able to use his legs.

I am very glad indeed that the two interviews that you had have been of some help. I do not know when I shall be coming to America and when it will be possible for us to meet. I hope everything will be well with you both and your son.

With best wishes,
Yours affectionately,
J. Krishnamurti

Years later, one day, U.G. and J. Krishnamurti were trapped in a head-on collision. They were walking on the same sidewalk in opposite directions. The sidewalk was so narrow at one place that there was room for only one person to pass. At that point U.G. saw Krishnamurti. There wasn't sufficient time to avoid him. As they neared each other, U.G.'s friends who were with him became tense. Nothing happened. As they moved closer they folded their hands simultaneously. They didn't utter a word. It was like two ships crossing in the night. They didn't even turn back. Each went his own way. The next day the talk of the town was, 'Who greeted whom first?' That was the last time that U.G. saw Krishnamurti.

My review of the book entitled, *Lives in the Shadow with J. Krishnamurti*, (written by Radha Rajagopal-Sloss and published by Bloomsbury in London) which appeared in *The Times of India* on 30 June 1991, created an uproar. To quote U.G. on the book, 'She has dumped a keg of dynamite! The story of the sex, lies and flippancy of Krishnamurti is more absorbing than his teachings. The picture that emerges from that book tells us that Krishnamurti has successfully remained an undetected hoax of the twentieth century. My hats off!' With all their claims of being more evolved, the Krishnamurtiites behaved exactly like the Rajneeshis who had written nasty letters to the editor of the *Illustrated Weekly of India*, reacting to an article I had written entitled, "The Man who Dared to Play God". I had expected them to handle their shock with delicacy and insight.

The architect of the Krishnamurti school in Brockwood visited U.G. in Gstaad. He asked U.G. what he thought of the book. U.G. replied by asking, 'Who is going to cast the first stone? Not me.' The architect's surprised reaction was, 'What refreshing modesty! On the subject of Krishnamurti you have been consistently disrespectful, disagreeable, nasty and offensive.'

Michael Longinieu who was present along with Alan Rowlands, the pianist, related to the architect a list of descriptive words that expressed U.G.'s disdain for the teachings of J.Krishnamurti. The list contained words such as 'Balderdash', 'Hogwash', 'Hokum', 'Bunkum', 'Phony baloney', 'Drivel', 'Hooey', 'Poppycock', 'Bullshit'. 'The list certainly reads like a page from *Roget's Thesaurus of English Words and Phrases*,' the architect responded. He added, 'No one until now has dared to tear apart Krishnamurti's teaching.'

U.G. did not spare Krishnamurti even when he was on his death-bed. My article entitled, 'Two Seers' in the *Illustrated Weekly of India*, (dated 25 May 1986) relates a conversation:

Hi, U.G., this is Mahesh.
Hello Mahesh.

Did you receive the article, 'Balmy Swamy', an interview with J. Krishnamurti I mailed to you from Dubai?

Yes, I did. It is interesting. At least he is finally honest enough to admit that he too has become part of the entertainment industry, like a footballer. I don't think he has really taken off his mask. You know the cancer has spread from the liver to the pancreas. Krishnamurti is dying. It is a matter of days, if not hours. Sorry, the death watch has begun.

But the Foundation has denied it.

Maybe they want to build a myth around his death. You know the tradition asserts that religious teachers do not die in an ordinary way as we mortals do.

Two days later Jiddu Krishnamurti died of pancreatic cancer. On 20 February, U.G. arrived in Bombay. My arrangement to speed his exit through the V.I.P. lounge was ignored by him. He came through the Immigration and Customs as he has always done. During the car ride to Vijay Anand's Pali Hill flat, I asked U.G., 'U.G., be serious. Tell me how you really felt when you heard of J. Krishnamurti's death.' U.G. remained silent. When I urged him to speak, he talked about the weather. His lack of response was unusual. He had always treated the subject of J. Krishnamurti with extreme distaste and hostility. His silence intrigued me. I was determined not to let him get away with his 'better-left-unsaid' attitude toward the event that had shaken one and all.

'Say something,' I insisted. His response:

> What do you want me to say? Do you want me to
> send my sympathy to those Krishnamurti freaks?
> Or do you want me to join the chorus of praises
> heaped upon him by those ardently devoted
> Krishnamurti enthusiasts? I am not beholden to
> Krishnamurti in any way. There is not much for
> me to say that has not already been said by me
> before. Why whip a dead horse? To strike a
> discordant note at a time like this, when glowing
> tributes are being paid to him and when he is being
> hailed as the foremost teacher of our times, would
> be an apotheosis of vulgarity.

I wasn't impressed. His words sounded too lame and evasive.
And then one day I walked into U.G.'s place with a book in my
hand, entitled, *The Ending of Time*—J. Krishnamurti's
conversations with Dr David Bohm. I had walked into a field of
mines. When I told U.G. that in the book Krishnamurti says, 'I
am not talking about lasting forever, though I am not sure if it
(the body) can't last forever.... If the body remains in one quiet
place, I am sure it can last a great many years more than it does
now....', U.G. lashed out:

> This joke is priceless. Isn't he getting too ridiculous,
> carrying things to the ultimate limit of absurdity,
> in his insistence that the body can live forever? To
> make such a statement in this day and age one
> must be in the valley of green and vigorous senility.
> Those who are not certain of the soul and its
> immortal nature are the ones who swallow the
> drivel of the immortality of the body. To have
> reverent affection for the man is one thing and to
> slur over such statements and feign agreement is
> another. How can you swallow that? You don't

even seem to have the basic intelligence. If you accept it, you must be a low-grade moron. Certainly it is the gerontologists, those dealing with the aged and with the process of ageing who are the ones to make that possible in not too distant a future.

'What do you consider Krishnamurti's contribution to mankind?' I asked. His reply:

Because of the seductive pull of his teachings he may have been more attractive and convincing than others in the market-place. It is not for me to say what his rightful place is in the world of religious thought. If the historians of human thought want to place him alongside the Buddha, Jesus and Mohammed, it is their affair.

5. Adrift in London

*'Experiences of others, much less our
own experiences do not help us to
change anything at all. If it were not so
all our lives would be one sweet song.'*

–U.G.

In the year 1961, U.G. landed in London, alone and penniless. 'There was no will to do anything. I was like a leaf blown here, there and everywhere.' His friends saw him going headlong on a downhill course. But, according to U.G., all that he did at that time seemed perfectly natural to him. The mystic phrase, 'the dark night of the soul' has been used to describe those years of U.G.'s wanderings. U.G. disagrees. In his view, 'There was no heroic struggle with temptation and worldliness, no soul-wrestling urges, no poetic climaxes but just a simple withering away of the will.'

To escape from the English winter cold, U.G. spent his days in the London city library sitting on a chair next to the one in which Karl Marx sat and wrote *Das Kapital*. The only book that interested him was the *Thesaurus of American Underground Slang*. During the nights he wandered the streets reading the names and telephone numbers of call-girls written on the trees.

One day U.G. said to himself, 'This kind of life is no good. I have practically become a bum living on the charity of people. This is a shoddy life. I have gone insane.'

Another day, after a night of wandering in the streets, U.G. was sitting in Hyde Park when a policeman confronted him. He warned him to leave and threatened to lock him up if he didn't. U.G. had only five pence in his pocket. 'Go to the Ramakrishna Mission,' said a voice in his head. U.G. took the tube as far as the five pence could take him. Then he walked the rest of the way to the Mission. It was ten o'clock at night when he got there.

'You can't see him now,' said the staff members of the Mission in answer to U.G.'s request to meet the Swami. As luck would have it, the Swami himself emerged. U.G. placed his scrapbook of newspaper cuttings on his background and lectures before the Swami. 'This was me and this is me now,' said U.G. to the Swami. 'What do you want?' the Swami asked. U.G. only wanted his permission to enter the meditation room for the night. The Swami explained that he could not allow that as it was against the Mission's policy. However, he gave U.G. some money and offered him a room for the next day. 'Stay in a hotel tonight and come back tomorrow,' he said.

U.G. returned to the ashram at noon the next day. He was invited for lunch. 'For the first time in a long time I had a real meal. I had lost even the appetite for food. I didn't know what hunger was or thirst was,' said U.G., describing the state he was reduced to at that time.

'I am singularly incapable of doing any literary work. I will wash your dishes or do something else. But I can't write anything,' said U.G. when the Swami asked him to help him in bringing out the Vivekananda centenary issue. The Swami said that he was looking for a man with a background in Indian philosophy. His assistant, who used to do the editorial work, had ended up in a mental hospital. The Swami declared that he was in a fix. U.G. desperately tried to drive home the point that he had a problem with writing. But the Swami did not yield.

While working on the centenary issue, U.G. was paid five pounds, as were the Swamis in the Mission. U.G. had lost the sense of the value of money. There was a time when he could write a cheque for a hundred thousand rupees. With those five pounds U.G. decided to see every film that was on in London. He stayed at the Mission, worked in the morning, ate at 1 p.m., and then went off to a film. Soon he exhausted all his money and had seen every film in and around London.

'Why are they doing all those silly things?' U.G. used to wonder, seeing people meditate at the Ramakrishna Mission. He himself was through with the entire game. Then one day, he had a very strange experience in the meditation room.

> I was sitting doing nothing, looking at all those people, pitying them. 'These people are meditating. Why do they want to go in for *samadhi*? They are not going to get anything—I have been through all that—they are kidding themselves. What can I do to save them from wasting all their lives, doing all that kind of thing? It is not going to lead them anywhere.' I was sitting there and in my mind there was nothing—there was only blankness—when I felt something very strange: there was some kind of movement inside my body. Some energy was coming up from the penis and out through the head, as if there was a hole. It was moving in circles in a clockwise direction and then in a counterclockwise direction. It was like the Wills cigarette advertisement at the airport. It was such a funny thing for me. But I didn't relate it to anything at all. I was a finished man. Somebody was feeding me, somebody was taking care of me, there was no thought of the morrow. Yet inside of me something was happening....

Then after three months U.G. said to the Swami, 'I am going. I can't do this kind of thing.' When U.G. left the Ramakrishna Mission in London, the Swami gave him fifty pounds. Here is an interesting letter which U.G. wrote to the Swami shortly before he left the Mission:

7 September '63

My Dear Swamiji,

I have just been told by Maharaj that the eye operation has been a success and that you are well on your way to complete recovery, and that you will be returning to the Center in a week or so. This is very good news. And we are all looking forward to seeing you back at the Center ere long.

I would like to pay you a visit, but certainly not if this will in any way cause strain to you. If it isn't too much of a strain, it would give me great pleasure to see you at the Hospital, and you may be assured that it will be a very short one.

I wish to God I knew what hidden hand led me to the Center. When you suggested helping you out with some kind of editing work, I did not for a moment hesitate to fall in with your kind suggestion. What I did not know was that I would be having the most Blessed Moments of my life here at the Center. It is needless to add that it has been a great privilege to have associated myself with you, and I feel greatly refreshed both in mind and body.

That, however, apart, my continued stay here at the Center and the necessary atmosphere for alert and strenuous discernment in meditation have helped me tremendously. The hidden agony of my life which no human being could understand has dissolved itself into thin air, as it were, and this has awakened me to what may loosely be called a kind of spiritual sleepwalking. I have pulled myself out from what looked like the edge of an abyss.

You know that there are very rare occasions in the lives of most of us when we have brief experiences of existing beyond time. I too have had several such moments. But this has been more than fleeting and has indeed become an abiding certainty. Nevertheless the strains and stresses of adjusting myself to a whole new way of life resulted in a peculiar state of mind hedged with some kind of indolence, maybe a form of conceit, which only meant greater and greater sorrow but left with a kind of empty expectancy. I may have achieved a certain calmness, but that calmness was of deathproducing languor. But I have always felt and still feel that one has to haul oneself out of one's own swamps by one's own bootstraps.

However, all my strenuous and directed attention hasn't helped me much to break the vicious circle. Well, now, through the touch of the inscrutable Divine power of Sri Ramakrishna, I have been blessed beyond words with the clarity of perception. And this calmness is a calmness without a trace of languor or contentment or watchful expectancy but one of completeness and wholeness. Need I say that when I burst forth into the world—the joy which overflows the heart is indeed bursting forth—I will be a new man?

With deep and affectionate regards,
Ever yours,
U.G.Krishnamurti

The news of U.G.'s wanderings had travelled to India. This is when Mr Bhave wrote to him in London urging him to meet Krishnamurti. All those years Krishnamurti had been asking Bhave about U.G. and his family. He was eager to know about U.G. personally and about his son's condition after the treatment in the United States. U.G. was not particularly anxious to meet him. Yet he wrote to him. The next day Krishnamurti phoned him saying, 'You may come over. We shall go for a walk in Richmond Park and talk things over.'

When U.G. went there that evening, it began raining heavily. Instead of going for a walk, they sat near the fireplace and talked. U.G. told him that his son's recovery had been astounding. He was now able to walk. 'What are you doing here?' Krishnamurti asked U.G. 'You don't look well. Why don't you go back to India?' U.G. answered, 'I am adrift here in London. I have nothing to do and I don't want to go back to India. My family will try to reconnect with me, which I don't want. I am finished with them.' Then Krishnamurti said, 'If your family tries to see you, tell them that you are not available.' His answer amused U.G. He smiled and asked, 'Have you ever had any family?' Krishnamurti ignored the question.

They sat there in silence for some time. All of a sudden Krishnamurti asked, 'Why are you trying to detach yourself from your family?' U.G. looked at him. Evidently he had no understanding of what was happening deep within him. 'I am not trying to detach myself. You can't understand me,' he said. 'Shall we go into the subject of why you are not attached to your family, Sir?' Krishnamurti persisted. That was too much for U.G. 'Sorry,' he said, 'I haven't come here to discuss my family affairs with you. To quote a Telugu proverb, you seem to have the same medicine for "both being struck by lightning, and being choked by rice". I am not here to seek any help from you.' Before U.G. left, Krishnamurti persuaded him to attend the twelve talks he was giving in Wimbledon.

Reluctantly, U.G. attended the first three talks. At the end of each talk Krishnamurti came to U.G. and gripping his hand, asked, 'How was it? Has it helped you, Sir?' U.G. replied saying that he hadn't paid any attention. 'Mahesh, actually, he bored me stiff with the same old stuff,' he told me. That was U.G.'s last visit with Krishnamurti.

The following is the last letter which U.G. wrote on 30 December 1961, to his wife, ending their relationship:

> I have received today on my return here your letter of 11 September, 1961.
>
> It's quite obvious that I have failed to open your eyes and make you understand the reality of the situation. It hurts me to hear, from time to time, the suicide attempts of yours. But my detachment from you and my passive acceptance of your actions is a solid piece of fact. It is not apathy. There isn't a whiff of apathy in me. The bond of the family relationships has simply fallen away from me.
>
> I have thought long and hard about this matter. You know I am not the sort of person to be persuaded in these matters and I do not act on impulse. Let the marriage wither on the vine. Neither of us can bear to see the ravages of pain in the other. Let us prefer to cling to the memory of the past. You have not, perhaps, much of a sweet memory to live with or cling to. Maybe you have a lot of things to cry over. Yes, I am quite as mentally broken down as you are, but it manifests itself in a different way in me. In the past, I may have beaten you and used insulting language toward you. All that is over and done with now. If you feel the agony about me which you say in your letters you feel, I can well understand your feelings. I know you love me deeply. And I loved you dearly too in spite of our many bickerings and constant battles. But this 'broken wing fixation' will destroy you. You can't base your life on sentiment alone and that cannot be the basis of any marriage.
>
> We have known each other for eighteen years. It is impossible to forget the ties of those eighteen years.

71

Old habits and memories have a strange way of
surviving. I can never forget you, and I know
nothing else will ever equal my feelings for you in
intensity. When we first met I liked you very much.
That impression will continue, unchanged by
anything that has happened since then. In the
nature of things, it cannot be otherwise. The bond
between us is a 'subtle inner force', which the
Sanskrit poet says is the essence of love. It is not
'erotic sentiment'. What happened to 'the feeling
that you feel when you have a feeling you never felt
before'? I wouldn't know. But we are now at the
end of our tether. Tears and torment may have been
your lot, but continued angry words, bitterness and
rancor, however justified they may be, do not take
us anywhere. This sustained nastiness for long
periods is neither desirable nor useful. Anger is a
terrible corrosive. It may seem advantageous to use
'blackmailing weapons', which is the chief
ammunition in the arsenal of your family, and it
may bring temporary relief to you, but in the long
run it is our children who will suffer.

We cannot blame anybody for the mess we have
made in the lives of the young ones. I may have
laid a harvest of woe for our children, and I know
that it will be laid up at my door that I have left my
own children bewildered, with nothing in life to
look forward to but sadness. I do not see any reason
why things should be any more difficult than they
have been. Your stubborn unwillingness to admit
the facts of our situation is also responsible for the
anguish of our situation.

Why is it, with all the will in the world, I cannot
understand what is so obvious to you? Well,
anyway, I would rather let things go to the devil in

their own way than try to go back to the past. Since we get exactly what we ask for, no more and no less, there is no question of any atonement on my part for the way things have turned out. Everyone weaves his own destiny. If our children take beatings at the cruel hand of fate, I feel that I am not wholly responsible. They are as much your children as they are mine. Let not the idea that I have left you destitute overwhelm you. You have your own name, your degrees and your own properties. Why I acted the way I did and still act is difficult to grasp. But if they are held up against the mirror of my own peculiar interpretation, my actions show a logic of their own. For all I know, life may not run on logic. Whether it is right or wrong, it in no way changes the pain of the situation. But there is nothing that I can do to change the course of events.

One more thought. Postponing a problem of course does not solve it. There is a way out of an unhappy marriage. When one partner breaks the law of commitment, the right accrues to the other of breaking the bond. The woman is not the husband's bond slave but his companion, and as an equal partner is as free as the husband to choose her own way of life. Since the new Hindu Code Bill provides for divorce, why don't you find some grounds either for divorce or legal separation? That would save a lot of mental anguish for us both. Do not for a moment think that I am asking you to do anything I would not do myself. But, personally, it does not matter to me one way or the other.

There is no reason for me to return to India. Be happy and stay happy. I wish you the best and the finest.

U.G.

U.G. never heard from her again.

If there is any significance to the number seven and cycles of multiples of seven I do not know, but U.G.'s married life lasted twenty-one years, even if they did not live together all those years.

U.G.'s wife died in 1963.

No one knew where U.G. was at that time. One of his cousins who lived in England at that time sent a letter addressed to a friend of U.G.'s in London informing him of his wife's death. His friend did not know of U.G.'s whereabouts. Six months later, when U.G. happened to visit him, he handed him the letter. He did not see any reaction on U.G.'s face when he read the letter. He asked him, 'What does the letter say?' U.G. replied, 'It says my wife died six months ago.' That's all he said to his friend. But he wrote a letter to his children expressing his sympathy for their loss. The younger daughter wrote back telling him about her mother's last years after the breakup with U.G.

U.G.'s wife had gone into a deep state of despondency and depression and had to be hospitalized. She received electric shock treatment. She came out of the hospital within a few weeks of the treatment and died in an accident in which she had slipped and broken her neck.

U.G. did not return to India. He lost contact with his children. In 1967, when he returned after almost fourteen years, his daughters were married and had children of their own.

When I think of U.G.'s children, I am reminded, in particular, of Vasant Kumar. That name brings back memories of perhaps the most intense days spent with U.G. in that summer of 1982 in Bombay. Vasant was one of India's leading copywriters. His face flickers on the screen of my mind. He was a handsome boy, soft, sweet, quiet. I was there one evening when he complained to U.G. about the pain in his back. Little did any one of us know then that in a few days he would die of sarcoma (galloping cancer). He was only thirty-two then. U.G. was in Bangalore when he received a telegram which stated that Vasant had cancer. His reaction, it is said, was not remotely close to that of a father. He was 'abnormally' casual. Our friends in Bangalore insisted that U.G. spend the remainder of his time in India with his son in Bombay.

U.G.'s flight to Bombay arrived late in the evening. I was waiting to pick him up and to take him to Vasant who was by then in hospital. 'How is your newborn son?' asked U.G. warmly as soon as he saw me. I searched his face for traces of anxiety. But U.G. looked normal—absolutely normal. I was certain that it was not pretended. As we drove to the city hospital he said, 'So the death watch has begun. I only hope that the cancer does not spread to the brain.'

In the last days of his life, Vasant had U.G. visiting him everyday. U.G. was a peculiar blend of a friend, a nurse and a comforter. How concerned he was about Vasant's prognosis! To make matters worse, Valentine fell ill suddenly. She contracted tuberculosis. She too had to be hospitalized. U.G. and I now had to shuffle between two hospitals at opposite ends of the city.

'How can U.G. be an enlightened man? He is behaving like any ordinary father. Look at the way he hangs around the hospital all the time....' No matter what U.G. did in that situation, people criticized. His calmness on receiving the news had infuriated the people in Bangalore. 'He is being callous, heartless. He should be with his dying son. What kind of a *jivanmukta* is this?' they screamed. When he heaped all his attention and affection on his dying son, they said, 'He is just an ordinary guy.' All this talk left U.G. unaffected.

'He is dead,' said U.G., in a matter-of-fact tone over the telephone. He asked me to meet him at the hospital to make arrangements for the funeral. We had known that Vasant's end was near. One of my friends had hoped that U.G. would perform a miracle. As we walked to the hospital after hearing the news of Vasant's death, my friend believed even then that U.G. would bring his son back to life. What actually happened at the hospital took us totally by surprise. U.G. wanted the body to be removed

75

and cremated immediately without any ceremonies. The hospital would not release the body until all the bills were paid. It was 6 a.m. and our total combined resources were nowhere near the amount needed.

Then U.G. laughed and said, 'You can forget about your sentiments and solemnity surrounding death. In the end it all comes down to money.' We were shocked. We found his conduct quite lacking in the decorum that such an occasion demanded. The expected miracle did not occur. We were amazed at U.G. There was no trace of emotion in him. He attended to the legal formalities that were necessary for the cremation and walked away from the scene.

As I watched the corpse reduced to ashes, what U.G. had said earlier flashed through my mind: 'If medical technology cannot save this boy who is dying of cancer, no power in the world can help him. If some of you feel that the *avatar* Sai Baba who is in town now can save him, seek his help by all means. He can't do a thing.' Vasant's friends did see Sai Baba. Vasant died the very next day.

I was shattered by Vasant's death. It formed the basis of a film that I made in later years. The film was called *Saransh*. It won the Critics Award in Moscow in the year 1985.

It was during one of our drives to the lawyer's office downtown Bombay, where Vasant's estate matters were being sorted out, that I asked U.G. an uncomfortable question: 'Do you have any regret, any remorse for doing what you did to your wife and kids?' 'No,' he said. 'Tell me, U.G., if you have to live your life again, what would you do?' His reply: 'If I have to relive my life all over again, things would not be any different. Experiences of others, much less our own experience, do not help us to change anything at all. If it were not so, all our lives would be one sweet song.'

6. Endings

'Death and birth are simultaneous processes. There is no space in between birth and death.'

–U.G.

Our stay in London has come to an end. As we take off for San Francisco I replay in my head the incidents of the past week. Someone said, 'Any story told twice is fiction.' U.G. agrees with this someone. He says, 'All autobiographies are lies. And biographies are double lies.' At times I feel that listening to U.G. can really wreck all the work I have done so far on this biography.

We are flying over the Atlantic Ocean. The aircraft bumps. 'Fasten your seat-belts,' announces the hostess. 'We are passing through some turbulence....' These bumps send a little shudder through the aircraft. They wake me up or rather, make me aware that I am awake. U.G. is sleeping through all this. The flying time from London to San Francisco is eleven hours. The very thought of flying over these long stretches of water scares me. Wanting to get away from the scare, I hasten to pick up the threads of U.G.'s life from the time he left London.

He still had an airline ticket to return to India. He turned it in at Paris and since it was paid for in dollars, he made 350 dollars. Now he had altogether about 250 pounds. For ninety days U.G. lived in Paris in some hotel, wandering in the streets as he had done before in London. The only difference was that now he had some money in his pocket.

While in Paris, U.G. heard of a comment which Charles de Gaulle had made: 'It is difficult to rule a nation which makes 360 varieties of cheese.' For those ninety days that U.G. stayed in Paris he ate a different variety of cheese each day. (Even today cheese is a favourite food of his.)

When U.G. found himself slipping into the old pattern of living, he quit Paris. But he resisted returning to India because that involved seeing his family and children. The prospect of that frightened him. He left for Geneva with a hundred and fifty francs or so to spend. He continued to stay in a hotel even after he ran out of money to pay his bill. After two weeks, the hotel management produced the bill. U.G. had no money. He threw up arms. The only recourse left to him was to go to the Indian Consulate.

'Send me to India. I am finished, you see,' he said to the officials of the Consulate. As he said this, U.G.'s resistance to return to India dissolved. He took out his scrapbook and presented it to the Vice-Consul: 'One of the most brilliant speakers that India has ever produced.' It contained, among other things, the opinions of Norman Cousins and Radhakrishnan about his talents. The Vice-Consul was impressed but said, 'We can't send you back at the expense of the Government of India. Try and get some money from India and in the meantime come and stay with me.'

It was here that U.G. met Madame Valentine de Kerven who was witnessing the exchange between him and the Vice-Consul with great interest. Valentine was a translator at the Indian Consulate. As destiny would have it, that day she happened to be there at the desk because the receptionist was absent. She and U.G. started talking and soon became close friends. She said, 'If you want I can arrange for you to stay in Switzerland. If you don't want to go to India, don't go.' After a month the Consulate turned U.G. away but he somehow managed to get by with the help of Valentine. It was Valentine who created a home for him in Switzerland. She eventually gave up her job.

She was not a rich woman. But the little money she had along with her pension was enough for both of them to live on.

Madame Valentine de Kerven was a remarkable woman in her own right. Born in Switzerland in August 1901, she was the daughter of a famous brain surgeon whose books have been translated into twenty languages. Her father is also cited in the medical textbooks for his discovery, named 'de Kerven Syndrome' after him. Her grandfather was a clergyman. Valentine left Switzerland for Paris at the age of eighteen, to lead an independent life. She was never a believer in any religious doctrine and was a revolutionary in more ways than one. U.G. never saw her shed a tear in all their years together.

Valentine belonged to a group of artists and writers. She was interested in photography and modern art and was an active member of a French experimental theater group. She became closely associated with the poet-philosopher, Antonin Artaud, an anarchist. With Dullin she gave a presentation of a play written by Artaud. She used to design costumes as well. She was a trained nurse too and worked with the Red Cross in Switzerland during and after the War.

Valentine lived openly with a male friend, which in those days was considered a social offence. She and her friend were the first to cross the uncharted Sahara desert on motorcycles. She was also the first woman to wear pants in Paris. She made a documentary on gypsies and was the first female film producer in France. Her production company was called 'de Kerven Films'. She also made documentary films on her father's medical research.

She made an unsuccessful attempt to join the fight against Franco and the Fascists in Spain. In the Fifties, she drove from Switzerland to India, a trip which turned out to be the first of many she would make.

Since this chance meeting at the Indian Counsulate in Geneva, U.G.'s and Valentine's lives melded. They remained 'travelling companions with no destination' till the sunset of her life.

At eighty-five, Valentine was struck by Alzheimer's disease. She began to slow down; her memory began to fade. But somehow the glow in her eyes continued to twinkle till the very end. Toward the end of her life she lived with friends in Bangalore, a South Indian family, whom she had met in 1969.

On 20 January 1991, as the Allied forces persistently bombed and battered Iraq, a telephone call announced, 'Valentine is dead...She passed away peacefully this evening.' She was ninety. Her death was contrary to astrological predictions, which gave her a hundred years to live.

At the time of Valentine's death, U.G. was in California. When the news of her death was conveyed to him he gave the friends, who had been looking after her, instructions for the last rites in a quiet and unemotional manner: 'She is a foreigner. You need the permission of the police to cremate her body. The Swiss Consulate in Bombay should also be informed of her death. Her body may be cremated without any ceremony since she had no religious belief of any kind. What will you do with the ashes?' he asked. 'They will be placed in the waters of the sacred river, Kaveri,' replied the friends.

Valentine, who had created the Fund for the Travels of U.G.Krishnamurti from her inheritance, was often asked by people all over the world why she had dedicated her life and her entire fortune just to be with U.G. She never responded to such queries.

A small paragraph from her diary, written in French (translated here) says it all: 'Where can I find a man like him. I have at last met a man, a man the like of whom can be met very rarely.'

In 1953, while U.G. was travelling through the beautiful valley of Saanen in the Alps, something in him said, 'Get off the train and spend some time here.' He did exactly that. While he was there for a week he said to himself, 'This is the place where I must spend the rest of my life.' He had plenty of money then but his wife did not share his inclination. She hated the climate.

Ever since, living in Saanen had remained an unfulfilled dream for U.G. And now, just like that, it had materialized. Valentine set up a house for U.G. in Saanen.

And then, one day, J. Krishnamurti arrived there. He started holding talks and meetings in the Saanen Valley every summer. U.G. at that time was not interested in Krishnamurti, or for that matter, in anything. Not once, till his forty-ninth year, did he ever discuss with Valentine his interest in truth or reality, etc. Though there was no trace of any search left in him, nor the desire to seek after anything, he felt that something strange was happening to him.

During that time (he refers to it as the 'incubation period') all kinds of things were happening inside him—constant headaches and terrible 'pains in the brain.' He consumed huge quantities of aspirin to relieve himself, with no success. One day Valentine said to him, 'Do you know the amount of money you are spending on your aspirin and coffee? You are drinking fifteen cups of coffee every day. Do you know what it means in terms of money? It is three or four hundred francs per month. What is this?' U.G. could not explain to anybody the nature of the headaches he suffered in those days.

> All kinds of strange things happened to me. I remember when I rubbed my body like this, there was a sparkle, like a phosphorus glow, on the body. Valentine used to run out of her bedroom to see— she thought there were cars going that way in the middle of the night. Every time I rolled in my bed there was a spark of light. It was so funny. It was electricity—that is why I say it is an electromagnetic field. At first I thought it was because of my nylon clothes and static electricity; but then I stopped wearing nylon. I was a very sceptical heretic, to the tips of my toes. I never believed in anything. Even if I saw some miracle happen before me, I didn't

accept that at all—such was the make-up of this
man. It never occurred to me that anything of that
sort was in the making for me.

Since the whole 'spiritual business' was out of his system,
U.G. did not relate whatever was happening to him to liberation
or *moksha*. But somehow, at the back of his mind, the question
about 'What is that state called *moksha* or enlightenment?'
persisted.

In the year 1963, it was impossible to walk on the streets of
Gstaad without bumping into J. Krishnamurti. U.G. always tried
to avoid him, as he no longer saw any reason for both of them to
meet. One day, when he was returning home, it started raining
heavily. U.G. was soaking wet. At that moment, Krishnamurti's
Mercedes came to a screeching halt. The door flung open and he
shouted to U.G., 'Hop in, quick!' 'Thanks,' U.G. said, 'but I
haven't insured my life. And I don't trust your driving.' 'Suit
yourself,' said Krishnamurti and drove away.

In April 1967, U.G. happened to be in Paris with Valentine.
Some of his friends suggested, 'Why don't you go and listen to
your old friend, Krishnamurti? He is here giving talks.' As
Valentine had never heard Krishnamurti before, U.G. thought
that they should go. When they got there, they found they had to
pay a two-franc admission charge to go in. U.G. was not ready
for that. He said, 'Let's do something foolish. Let's go to Casino
de Paris.' Even though it cost twenty francs they went there.
While watching the show, U.G. had a strange experience. 'I
didn't know whether the dancer was dancing on the stage or I
was doing the dancing. There was a peculiar kind of movement
inside me. There was no division. There was nobody who was
looking at the dancer.' This experience, which lasted till they
came out of the theater, puzzled U.G.

The last time he had a dream was a week after this incident.
In the dream he was bitten by a cobra and died instantly. His
body was carried on a bamboo stretcher to the cremation ground.

It was placed on a funeral pyre. The flame from the fire awakened him with a start. He found that his electric blanket was on high. This dream was a prelude to his 'death'.

Even though U.G. no longer dreams, he continues to have what can be called 'death experiences'. To call them 'death experiences' is misleading because death cannot be experienced by him or anybody. As U.G. says, 'It is not something poetic and romantic, like "dying to all your yesterdays". Death and birth are simultaneous processes. There is no space in between birth and death.'

This death that U.G. undergoes occurs in all kinds of situations and places. Once in Rome he had gone to see a James Bond film along with some of his friends, including Dr F. Leboyer, the well-known authority on natural childbirth. In one scene, gun shots were fired. Leboyer found U.G. collapsing on the floor. He was alarmed. A few seconds later, U.G. revived. Leboyer said, 'The way you fell, U.G., was exactly like a man who has been shot.' Leboyer went on to say that as U.G. was recovering, his movements were similar to those of a newborn baby. U.G. said, 'Those movements were the origin of Yoga. The movements bring the body back to its natural rhythm. What is called Hatha Yoga today is nothing but acrobatics.'

Each time, this 'death' happens to U.G. in a different way. It cannot be anticipated. There is no way of knowing how and when it will occur. It is one of those 'strange, unexpected happenings.' For U.G., it is a renewal of the body. He says that once the body cannot renew itself through this process, what we call 'final death' will occur. U.G. describes the process in this way: 'It is quite similar to actual death—cold feet and hands, stiffening of the body and gasping for breath.'

An observer of this process said that U.G. appeared to him like a corpse. U.G. is unable to describe what actually happens during this condition. He says: 'This is totally unrelated to what people call the "near-death experiences".' He adds, 'They are only useful for writing books, conducting seminars and making money.' He says that the process is not something that happens only to him. It happens to every living organism on this planet including the planet itself. He says the reason people are not aware of this process is that they are blocked by their thought.

The events in the Casino de Paris followed by the dream in which U.G. saw his body burning, was just the beginning of a series of even stranger events that were to occur later.

7. What is that State?

*'If a heap of rice chaff is ignited it
continues burning inside; you don't
see any fire outside but when
you touch it, it burns you.'*

–U.G.

'His name is Douglas Rosenstein. He was there in Saanen when this calamity occurred. He knew me even before the calamity,' answered U.G. as we drove into Carmel, California. I had asked him if I could meet someone who had known him before the events of 1967 so that I could find out for myself if there was any major change in him because of the event. 'Don't worry, you'll meet him during your stay here....'

The house that we live in here in Carmel is like a palace, perhaps a little too silent for my liking. Tranquillity kills creativity. Work starts tomorrow. A sense of apprehension overtakes me. I stare into the night, fighting this feeling of inadequacy. Will I stand up to the task?

Finding a co-sufferer can be comforting. The visit of Scott Eckersley brought me the much-needed relief. It worked like a balm. Scott and I had spent a great deal of time together in the year 1978-79 in Mahabaleshwar, along with U.G. It was there that he had narrated to me his first encounter with U.G.

Scott, now a craftsman and a builder, was once a Director of Live Oak School in Ojai, California. The school's educational philosophy was based on the teachings of J. Krishnamurti. In

June 1969, at the end of the academic year, the board of directors of the school sent Scott and his entire staff to Switzerland to have daily discussions on education with Krishnamurti. Krishnamurti and Scott were locking horns more often than not. They were getting nowhere. Scott stopped going to these discussions. A few days later he was fired from his job as Director. Thus began a period of the most profound loneliness in Scott's life. He was isolated from his friends and abandoned by the Krishnamurti community. Broke and alone, he took refuge in a tiny tent in a waterlogged camp-ground near Saanen. Here an acquaintance dropped by and said that he wanted Scott to meet another Krishnamurti:

> I cannot describe nor do I remember anything that we talked about on our first meeting. However, soon after leaving his chalet, I realized that things were quite different. My despair was gone. In its place an odd sort of peace and calm descended upon me in just a few hours. I felt happy and secure.

Scott had, however, no idea of the terrifying pain that was about to visit him a short while later. The next day he woke up with a 'flu'like ache in his spine and an awful headache. His condition deteriorated over the next few days and he could not even crawl out of his tent. One evening around sunset, he had a very real feeling that he might die that night. He asked his friend if she would carry him out of his tent so that he could watch the sunset 'one last time.' Desperate, the next day he asked his friend who had introduced him to U.G. to ask him if he ever did any healing. U.G. sent a message back saying that he could do no such thing. Later that day, however, U.G. showed up at his tent.

> U.G. was alone. And it was raining. This was only the second time that I had seen him. He crawled into the tent and asked if we could just sit quietly together. I remember feeling honoured by his visit. Whether or not U.G.'s visit affected my recovery I

don't know. Two days later, exactly seven days after it began, my torment disappeared.

This illness was to recur again and again in my life.

About every other year and only after a visit with U.G. It took several years for me to connect my illness with U.G., and when I did, he would always brush it off with his favourite phrase which he uses several times a day, 'Just forget it!'

Nine years later when this illness occurred once again in Frankfurt, on his way back from Bombay where he had spent an intense period with U.G., Scott realized that whatever was going on between U.G. and him had to stop. He wrote to U.G. explaining everything and thanked him for his help in clearing away the many cobwebs in his mind. Scott didn't hear from him or write to him for almost three years. Ever since then Scott and U.G. reconnected many times, and his illness, he says, never returned.

That evening I asked him how he would sum up what U.G. meant to him, having known him for so many years. He had this to say:

He is a festering splinter that never goes away. The pain and the blister are always there. It would be worse when he dies. That's when the infection will set in, because when he dies he will become immortalized. That's when the whole thing will really start. Then people will get together and start discussing, 'What did U.G. really say? What did he really mean by that ...? What *was* he saying?' J. Krishnamurti was easy to get rid of after his death, Mahesh.... There is enough positive stuff in this world. There is enough real philosophy out there. But there is no antiphilosophy. U.G. is really calling it like it is. How many people take away your hope? How many people pull out the rug under your feet? Nobody does that.

Sometimes being with U.G. gets to be overwhelming. You just have to go away. Sit in the woods for a while. Because there are things that you need as you get older. And one of them is the sense of self that isn't there. A little bit of self-esteem. I didn't need it when I was young. But now I find that there is some remnant self that really needs something to go on. If you are staying with what U.G. is saying, there is nothing to go on. And that's tough. Really tough. Especially when you age. You know when you are younger, you deal with these things in a haphazard way.

With U.G. I have been going around for some twenty years with this hope issue. He's always said that there is no hope but that it is not hopeless. There is a hint of something there that I am missing. I want to get my hands on that. But U.G. said that there is nothing to get. You know, if you face that, if you are really entrenched in that, it is not something you can joke about. It hurts. Sometimes I have to run away from him. Really run from him, put my mind on something else. But he comes on you like a shadow.

...U.G. is a man of many moods. And I always enter his domain with caution. There is so much that I don't understand about him and I have given up thinking that I ever will.

He can be very cruel to some people—I mean verbally. Most people eventually get blasted if they hang around him long enough. And yet he has never blasted me or even so much as raised his voice at me in all these twenty-two years. He will verbally mop the floor with his closest friends to the extent that they will want to walk out and never return. But with me he is always tender, soft and forever humorous.

You cannot express affection to U.G. It obviously bothers him and he simply will not allow it. He has always gently pushed aside my expression of love for him as just so much sentimental nonsense. And so it may be. But in my heart I cannot believe it. The world is a lonely place and I just can't accept the fact that I will grow old and die without U.G.Krishnamurti, the most profound influence in my life, ever returning my love, or even acknowledging that he ever cared.

Later in a note he mailed, Scott implored me to conclude his account with the following sentiment:

One last thing, Mahesh. I want to close this out with a personal sentiment for U.G. that will no doubt rattle his cage, ruffle his feathers and get stuck in his craw. He is sure to instruct his biographer to edit it out of the story. Don't do it Mahesh! If any of this story is used in your biography, then what I am about to say must remain unedited as my summation. *So, U.G., are you listening? For fear of your rejection, I have never told you directly: I love you.*

In July 1967, U.G.'s life went through another phase. The question, 'What is that state?' had tremendous intensity for U.G. But it had no emotional overtones. The more he tried to find an answer and the more he failed to find one, the more intense the question became in his mind. 'It's like rice chaff. If a heap of rice chaff is ignited, it continues burning inside; you don't see any fire outside, but when you touch it, it burns you, of course. In exactly the same way, the question was going on and on: What is that state? I want that state.'

U.G. was a finished man. Krishnamurti had said, 'You have no way—' but still U.G. wanted to know what that state was, the state in which the Buddha was, Sankara was and all those teachers were.

That year J. Krishnamurti was again there in Saanen giving talks. One day U.G.'s friends dragged him to one of those talks saying, 'Now at least it is a free business. Why don't you come and listen?' When U.G. listened to him he had this peculiar feeling that Krishnamurti was describing U.G.'s state and not his own. 'Why did I want to know his state? He was describing something, "movements", "awareness", "silence"—"In that silence there is no mind; there is action." I said to myself, 'I am in that state. What the hell have I been doing these thirty or forty years, listening to all these people and struggling, wanting to understand his state or the state of someone else, Buddha or Jesus? I am in that state. Now I am in that state.' Thus U.G. walked out of the tent and never looked back.

However, that question— 'What is that state?'—transformed itself into another question, 'How do I know that I am in that state, the state of the Buddha, the state I very much wanted to be in and demanded from everybody? I am in that state but how do I know that?' As destiny would have it, this question would resolve itself the following day.

8. Calamity

'The search must come to an end before
anything can happen.'

–U.G.

20 September 1991. Carmel, California. The time is 4.30 a.m. I am up and I am here at my desk writing. This has been my work pattern for almost a fortnight now. These hours and hours of silence get into one's bones. I ask why I have sentenced myself to such isolation. Writing is indeed a lonely job. I guess anything one does deeply leads to loneliness. Every creator experiences the painful chasm between his dream and its final expression. The chasm is never completely bridged. We all have this certainty, perhaps illusory, that we have much more to say.

This birthday of mine appears to be a long one. The calls from India began last evening and went on right through the night. 'What do you mean it is not your birthday yet?' asked my nine-year-old son Rahul, unable to comprehced the time difference between California and Bombay. I tried to explain but failed. When I mentioned to Rahul about the three mild-to-moderate earthquakes I had experienced here in Carmel over the past few days he was thrilled. 'How lucky, papa! You are having a great time, aren't you?' Suddenly we were cut off...

U.G. has not been feeling well. It is his usual 'plumbing problem' (a cardio-spasm). He has not been able to keep any food or drink in his stomach. He looks emaciated. For the first time since 1939 he has lost three kilos of weight. (His weight has never fluctuated much.) There is an unspoken anxiety about his health amongst us all. But U.G. himself seems unaffected. He is his usual self. Narayana Moorty has been successful in making U.G. take some homoeopathic medicine. Watching U.G. popping pills is a funny sight! He looks like a baby. These pills make him sleep for long hours. 'If he doesn't respond to these pills, we should ask him to see a doctor,' says Moorty. 'The only time I will see a doctor is when I need the death certificate,' says U.G., meaning every word of what he is saying. I am sliding into a swamp of depression.

As I sat down to write what can be termed in film jargon, the climax of U.G.'s life, the earth beneath our feet shook. It was another earthquake. 5.1 on the Richter, reported the newsreader on television.

On his forty-ninth birthday (according to the Indian moonbased calendar), the day after he walked out of J. Krishnamurti's tent, U.G. was sitting on a bench under a tree overlooking one of the most beautiful spots in the whole world, the seven hills and seven valleys of Saanenland:

> I was sitting there. Not that the question was there; the whole of my being was the question: 'How do I know that I am in that state?' I asked myself. 'There is some kind of peculiar division inside of me; there is somebody who knows that he is in that state. The knowledge of that state—what I have read, what I have experienced, what they have talked about—it is this knowledge that is looking at that state, so it is only this knowledge that has projected that state.'
>
> I said to myself, 'Look here, old chap, after forty years you have not moved one step; you are still there at square one. It is the same knowledge that projected your mind there when you asked this question. You are in the same situation, asking the same question,

"How do I know?" because it is this knowledge, the description of the state by those people, that has created this state for you. You are kidding yourself. You are a damned fool.' But still there was some peculiar feeling that this was the state.

U.G. didn't have any answer to the second question—'How do I know that this is the state?' It was like a question in a whirlpool. It went on and on. Then suddenly the question disappeared. Nothing happened—*the question just disappeared*. U.G. didn't say to himself, 'Oh, my God! Now I have found the answer.' Even that state disappeared—the state he thought he was in, the state of the Buddha or Jesus—even that disappeared.

> The question disappeared. The whole thing was finished for me and that was all. From then on, never did I say to myself, 'Now I have the answer to all those questions.' That state of which I had said, 'This is the state'—that state disappeared. The question disappeared; finished. It is not emptiness; it is not blankness; it is not the void; it is not any of those things; the question disappeared suddenly and that's all.

The disappearance of his fundamental question, on discovering that it had no answer, was a physiological phenomenon, U.G. says: 'It was a sudden "explosion" inside, blasting, as it were, every cell, every nerve and every gland in my body.' And with that explosion, the illusion that there is continuity of thought, that there is a centre, an 'I' linking up thoughts, was not there any more. U.G. further says of this state:

> Then thought cannot link up. The linking gets broken and once it is broken, it is finished. Then it is not once that thought explodes; every time a thought arises, it explodes. So, this continuity comes to an end and thought falls into its natural rhythm.

93

Since then I have no questions of any kind because the questions cannot stay there any more. The only questions I have are very simple questions like 'How do I go to Hyderabad?'—questions necessary to function in this world. And people have answers for these questions. But for those ('spiritual' or 'metaphysical') questions, nobody has any answers. So there are no questions anymore.

Everything in the head had tightened—there was no room for anything there inside my brain. For the first time I became conscious of my head with everything 'tight' inside it. These *vasanas* (past impressions) or whatever you call them, they do try to show their heads sometimes, but then the brain cells are so 'tight' that the *vasanas* have no opportunity to fool around there any more. The division (created by past impressions in the form of thought) cannot stay there. It's a physical impossibility. You don't have to do a thing about it.That is why I say that when this 'explosion' takes place (I use the word 'explosion' because it is like a nuclear explosion), it leaves behind chain reactions. Every cell in your body, the cells in the very marrow of your bones, have to undergo this 'change'—I don't want to use the word—but it *is* an irreversible change, an alchemy of some sort.

It's like a nuclear explosion. It shatters the whole body. It's not an easy thing; it's the end of the man. Such a shattering blasts every cell, every nerve in your body. I went through terrible physical torture at that moment. Not that you experience the 'explosion'; you can't experience the 'explosion'— but only its after-effects. The 'fallout' changes the whole chemistry of your body.

The after-effects of that (the 'explosion') are the way the senses are operating now without any coordinator or centre—that's all I can say. Another thing: the chemistry has changed—I can say that because unless that change in the whole chemistry takes place, there is no way of freeing this organism from thought, from the continuity of thought. So, since there is no continuity of thought, you can very easily say that something has happened but what actually has happened, I have no way of experiencing at all.

This is a thing that has happened outside the field, the area in which I expected, dreamed and wanted change. So I don't call this a 'change'. I really don't know what has happened to me. What I am telling you about is the way I am functioning. There seems to be some difference between the way you are functioning and the way I am functioning but basically there can't be any difference. How can there be any difference between you and me? There can't be. But from the way we are trying to express ourselves, there seems to be some difference. I have a feeling that there is some difference and what that difference is, is all that I am trying to understand.

U.G. noticed, during the week following the 'explosion', some fundamental changes in the functioning of his senses. On the last day his body went through 'a process of physical death' and the changes became permanent features.

Ending: The changes began. For seven days, every day a change occurred. U.G. discovered that his skin had become extremely soft, the blinking of the eyes had stopped and his senses of taste, smell and hearing had undergone a change.

On the first day he noticed that his skin was so soft that it felt like silk and also had a peculiar kind of glow, a golden glow. 'I was shaving and each time I ran the razor down my face, it slipped. I changed blades but it was no use. I touched my face. My sense of touch was different.' U.G. did not attach any significance to all this. He merely observed.

On the second day he became aware for the first time that his mind was in what he calls a 'declutched state.' He was upstairs in the kitchen and Valentine had prepared some tomato soup. He looked at it and didn't know what it was. She told him it was tomato soup. He tasted it and then he recognized it: 'This is how tomato soup tastes.' He swallowed the soup and he was back to that odd frame of mind. Rather, it was a frame of 'no mind.' He asked Valentine again, 'What is that?' Again she said it was tomato soup. Again U.G. tasted it. Again he swallowed and forgot what it was. 'I played with this for some time. It was such a funny business—this "declutched state".'

Now that state has become normal for U.G. He says he no longer spends time in reverie, worry, conceptualization and other kinds of thinking that most people do when they are alone. His mind is only engaged when it is needed, as, for instance, when someone asks questions or when he has to fix a tape recorder. When it is not needed, there is no mind there, there is no thought. There is only life.

On the third day, some friends of U.G. invited themselves over for dinner. He agreed to cook for them.

> But somehow I couldn't smell or taste properly. I became gradually aware that these two senses had been transformed. Every time some odour entered my nostrils it irritated my olfactory center in just about the same way—whether it came from an expensive scent or from cow dung, it was the same irritation. And then, every time I tasted something, I tasted the dominant ingredient only—the taste of

the other ingredients came slowly, later. From that moment on, perfume made no sense to me and spicy food had no appeal for me. I could taste only the dominant spice—chilli or whatever it was.

On the fourth day, something happened to his eyes. U.G. and his friends were at the Rialto restaurant in Gstaad. It was here that U.G. became aware of a tremendous sort of 'vista vision', like a concave mirror.

Things were coming toward me, were moving into me, as it were. And things going away from me seemed to move out from inside of me. It was such a puzzle to me—as if my eyes were a gigantic camera, changing focus without my doing anything. Now I am used to the puzzle. Nowadays that is how I see. When you drive me around in your car, I am like a cameraman dollying along. The cars in the other direction go into me and the cars that pass us come out of me. When my eyes fix on something they do it with total attention, like a camera.

That day, when U.G. returned home from the restaurant, he looked in the mirror to find that there was something odd about his eyes—they were 'fixed.' He kept looking at the mirror for a long time and observed that his eyelids were not blinking. For almost forty-five minutes he stared into the mirror—still no blinking of the eyes! 'Instinctive blinking was over for me and it still is.'

On the fifth day, U.G. noticed a change in his hearing. When he heard the barking of a dog, the barking seemed to originate inside him. All sounds seemed to come from within him and not from outside. They still do.

The five senses changed in five days. On the sixth day, U.G. was lying down on a sofa. Valentine was in the kitchen.

And suddenly my body disappeared. There was
no body there. I looked at my hand.... I looked at
it—'Is this my hand?' There was no actual question
but the whole situation was somewhat like that.
So I touched my body: nothing. I didn't feel there
was anything there except the touch, the point of
contact. Then I called Valentine and asked: 'Do
you see my body on this sofa? Nothing inside of
me says that this is my body.' She touched it and
said, 'This is your body.' And yet that assurance
didn't give me any comfort or satisfaction. I said to
myself, 'What is this funny business? My body is
missing.' My body had gone away and it has never
come back.

Now, as regards his body, the points of contact are all that
U.G. has, nothing else, because the sense of vision, he says, is
independent of the sense of touch. So it is not possible for him to
create a complete image of his own body because, in the absence
of the sensation of touch, the corresponding points are missing
in his consciousness.

And finally, on the seventh day, U.G. was again lying on the
same sofa, relaxing, enjoying the 'declutched state.' Valentine
would come in and he would recognize her as Valentine. She
would go out of the room. Then, finish, blank—no Valentine. He
would think, 'What is this? I can't even imagine what Valentine
looks like.' He would listen to the sounds coming from the
kitchen and ask himself, 'What are those sounds coming from
inside me?' But he could not relate to them. He had discovered
that all his senses were without a coordinating mechanism inside
himself; the coordinator was missing. And then...

I felt something happening inside me: the life
energy drawing to a focal point from different parts
of my body. I said to myself, 'Now you have come
to the end of your life. You are going to die.' Then I

called Valentine and said, 'I am going to die, Valentine, and you will have to do something with this body. Hand it over to the doctors; maybe they will use it. I don't believe in burning or burial. In your own interest you have to dispose of this body. One day it will stink. So, why not give it away?' Valentine replied, 'U.G., you are a foreigner. The Swiss government won't take your body. Forget about it.'

The frightening movement of U.G.'s life force had come to a focal point. Valentine's bed was empty. He moved over and stretched out, getting ready to die. Valentine, of course, ignored what was going on. She left. But before she left she said, 'One day you say this thing has changed, another day you say that thing has changed and a third day you say something else has changed. What is all this? And now you say you are going to die. You are not going to die. You are all right, hale and healthy.' Saying this, she left the room. U.G. continues his account:

Then a point arrived where it looked as if the aperture of a camera was trying to close itself. It is the only simile that I can think of. The way I am describing this is quite different from the way things actually happened at that time, because there was nobody there thinking in such terms. All this, however, must have been part of my experience, otherwise I wouldn't be able to talk about it. So, the aperture was trying to close itself and something was there trying to keep it open. Then after a while there was no will to do anything, not even to prevent the aperture closing itself. Suddenly, as it were, it closed. I don't know what happened after that.

This process lasted for forty-nine minutes—this process of dying. It was like a physical death. U.G. says that even now it happens to him:

> My hands and feet become so cold, the body becomes stiff, the heartbeat slows down, the breathing slows down and then there is a gasping for breath. Up to a point you are there, you breathe your last breath, as it were, and then you are finished. What happens after that, nobody knows.

When U.G. came out of this, his landlady said that there was a telephone call for him. He went downstairs in a daze to answer the phone. He didn't know what had happened. He had been through physical death. What brought him back to life, he didn't know. How long it lasted, he didn't know. 'I can't say anything about that because the experiencer was finished: there was nobody to experience that death at all....

Here the account of Douglas Rosenstein, the only eye-witness to this thing called the 'calamity', will be most appropriate. In fact, portions of what follows were written by him prior to his visit to Carmel. The rest he relates to my video camera. For a moment I was filled with envy. Here was a person who could boast of having witnessed the most extraordinary breakthrough of U.G.'s life:

> Twenty-four summers ago I was a witness to that rarest of all transformations, arguably the only real one—the death and rebirth of an ordinary human being. This was an ordinary man rather than a godman, a chosen one or a world teacher. It all began in the summer of 1966 when I went to Saanen to listen to the talks of J. Krishnamurti. I was camping by the river with some friends. One day someone told me he had bumped into an intense Indian man whom he described as very unusual.

He encouraged me to go and meet this man who lived in a three-hundred-year-old chalet called Chalet Pfynegg (which means 'windy') in the Saanen Village.

I remember vividly the first time I laid eyes on U.G. He was the first Indian I had ever seen. He was arguing vehemently with an American musician who played the organ in a Saanen church. U.G. was denouncing J. Krishnamurti. I had recently heard J. Krishnamurti's talks and I was very impressed. My very first thought was that this guy was way off base. But I didn't wish to intrude. So I watched the heated debate go back and forth for some time. Something other than my judging mind was attracted to U.G. Even while I was intellectually offended, I was drawn to him. That battle in myself raged for many years.... but that is another story.

That summer of 1966 was preparatory for what happened the following summer. I frequently lunched with U.G. There were times when U.G. would come to our tent with Valentine and my friends and I would do our best to fix a vegetarian meal for them. My best memories revolved around the talks and lunches we had at Chalet Pfynegg. We would come back from the talks of J. Krishnamurti and would sit around discussing his abstractions. There would be U.G., one moment tearing apart Krishnamurti's arguments, while paradoxically praising the man in the next breath. So the summer passed. U.G. and Krishnamurti both encouraged me to go to India and study Yoga.

On my return from India, I spent the summer again in Saanen. I remember that U.G. seemed much the same as he had the previous summer, only the amperage was up on his attacks on Krishnamurti. Often before the talks, I would see him standing alone looking absorbed, while everyone else was socializing.

The talks ended in mid-August with a surprise announcement that Krishnamurti was extending the talks. On the last day of the talks I saw U.G. again. He didn't appear to be very involved in what Krishnamurti was saying. The next day I was having lunch with Valentine and U.G. U.G. began telling the story of how on the previous day he was lying on a couch and had asked Valentine where his body was. And she had answered that his body was there on the couch. Valentine admitted that this crazy conversation had indeed taken place. We were talking about all this between bites of our lunch. The conversation took place in the past tense. U.G. went on repeating how his body disappeared. I asked him, 'What about now? Is your body there for you now?' And with more certainty than I have ever seen in anyone, he said, 'No, it's gone for good. It can't come back.' I asked, 'How can you be sure?' And he switched emphatically into the present tense and for the next twenty-five years I have never again heard him use the past tense in reference to how he is functioning.

That day I was at my apartment in Gstaad. It was evening time. The moon was just coming up on the horizon. Something told me that I should call U.G. at his chalet. I did. The landlady answered the phone. I could hear her yelling, 'U.G. Krishnamurti, phone for you.' Valentine came on the phone. She sounded upset. 'Something is going on with U.G. His body is not moving. He may be dying.' I said, 'Go and get U.G., I'll talk to him.' Valentine said, 'I don't think he will come.' I insisted. And then U.G. came to the phone. His voice sounded very far away and he said, 'Douglas, you better come over and, see this.' It was an invitation to see a 'dead' man. So I ran. At that time the trains weren't running. The distance between Gstaad and Saanen is about three kilometres. I entered the chalet and went up to U.G.'s room. I remember the scene very vividly: Valentine was looking white with terror and U.G. was lying on the couch. His body was in an arched position. In Yoga you would call this posture *Dhanurasana* (the posture of the bow). The full moon was just coming over the mountain. I asked U.G. to come to the window and look at the moon. He got up. I will never forget the manner in which he looked at the moon. There was something strange going on in that room. I asked him, 'What was all that?' He said, 'It's the final death.'

Moorty, who had been listening to Douglas's account, at this point butts in and asks, 'You mean he said that he was *going* to die?' Douglas replied, 'No, it had already happened. U.G. said that it was my phone call that had brought him back.' Moorty asks, 'What was your response, Douglas?' 'I was absolutely delighted; I was so happy for him.'

'Were there any noticeable changes in him?' I asked. 'His personality hadn't changed. He was the same difficult person that he always was. But there was an absence of tension. The doubt was gone. But the personality was the same. I remember very distinctly something he said to me then that has remained with me all these years. He said, "Douglas, there is one thing that I know for certain: the search must come to an end before anything can happen".'

Before he left for Mill Valley that evening, this is how Douglas summed up U.G.:

> He is the most subversive human being that ever walked on this planet earth, much more subversive than all those religious leaders mankind has been following for 2,600 years to no purpose. Yes, I am including the Buddha too. U.G.'s subversiveness is so complete that nobody wants to believe it. Everything that you believe in, everything that you put your faith in, your hope in—your desire for continuity, of not only yourself but of your family, your civilization—all that will go. You won't believe any of it any more. Nothing will have any meaning. And when all this meaning goes, then you will really make it. Only then you will hear what U.G. is saying.... That takes courage.

9. Aftermath

'The uniqueness of the individual cannot express itself because of the stranglehold of the experiences of others.'

–U.G.

U.G. refers to the events that happened to him during the summer of 1967 as the 'calamity':

> I call it 'calamity' because from the point of view of one who thinks this is something fantastic, blissful and full of beatitude, love, or ecstasy, this is physical torture; this is a calamity from that point of view. Not a calamity to me but a calamity to those who have an image that something marvellous is going to happen.... I can never tell myself or anybody that I'm an enlightened man, a liberated man, or a free man or that I am going to liberate mankind.

On the eighth day he was sitting on the sofa and suddenly, in his words:

> There was a tremendous outburst of energy— tremendous energy shaking the whole body and along with the body, the sofa, the chalet and the whole universe—shaking, vibrating. You cannot cause that movement.... Whether it was coming from outside or inside, from below or above, I didn't

> know—I couldn't locate the spot. It lasted for hours
> and hours.... There was nothing I could do to stop
> it; I was totally helpless. This went on for days.

Then for three days U.G. lay on his bed, his body contorted with pain—it was, he says, as if he felt pain in every cell of his body. Similar outbursts of energy occurred intermittently throughout the next six months, whenever he lay down or relaxed.

> It's a very painful process. It's a physical pain—it
> has a form, a shape of its own. It is like a river in
> spate. The energy that is operating there does not
> feel the limitations of the body; it is not interested;
> it has its own momentum. It is not ecstatic, blissful
> beatitude and all that rubbish!

U.G. explains that thought had controlled his body to such an extent that when that control loosened, the whole metabolism went agog. Then the movement of his hands changed. They started turning backwards. 'That is why they say my movements are *mudras* (mystical gestures).'

Certain hormonal changes started occurring in his body. Now he didn't know whether he was a man or a woman. Suddenly there was a breast growing on the left side of his chest. It took three years for this body to finally fall into a new rhythm of its own.

Here U.G. questions the value of this description for the world. Reading about it may be dangerous because people may try to mimic the outward manifestations of the process. People . have a tendency to simulate these things and believe that something is happening to them.

His friends observed swellings up and down his torso, neck and head, at those points called *chakras*. These swellings of various shapes and colours came and went at regular intervals. On his lower abdomen, the swellings were horizontal, cigar-

106

shaped bands. Above the navel was a hard, almond-shaped swelling. A hard, blue swelling, like a large medallion, in the middle of his chest was surmounted by another smaller, brownish-red, medallion-shaped swelling at the base of his throat. These two 'medallions' were as though suspended from a varicoloured, swollen ring—blue, brownish and light yellow—around his neck, as in the pictures of some Hindu gods. There were other similarities: his throat was swollen to a shape that made his chin seem to rest on the head of a cobra, as in the traditional images of Shiva. Just above the bridge of the nose was a white lotus-shaped swelling. All over the head the small blood vessels expanded, forming patterns like the stylized lumps on the heads of some statues of the Buddha. Like the horns of Moses and the Taoist mystics, two large and hard swellings periodically appeared and disappeared. The arteries in his neck, blue and snake-like, expanded and rose into his head.

U.G. says that his body is affected by everything that is happening around it:

> Whatever is happening there is also happening here—there is only the physical response. This is affection. You can't prevent this, for the simple reason that the armour that you have built around yourself is destroyed; so it is very vulnerable to everything that is happening.

In his discussions with medical doctors, U.G. learnt that the ductless glands are located in exactly the same spots where the Hindus speculated that the *chakras* were. The thymus gland, it is said, is very active when one is a child. Therefore, children have extraordinary feelings. When they reach the age of puberty, the gland becomes dormant—at least that's what the scientists say. When this sort of an explosion takes place within the body, which the scriptures refer to as being born again, that gland is automatically activated so that all the extraordinary feelings are there again. 'Feelings are not thoughts, not emotions; you feel for somebody. If somebody hurts himself there, that hurt is felt here—not as a pain but there is a feeling. You automatically say, "Ouch!"'

There is an incident in U.G.'s life which illustrates this. He was once staying at a coffee plantation in South India. For some reason a mother started beating her child. She was angry and she hit her child so hard that the child almost turned blue. Somebody then asked U.G., 'Why did you not interfere and stop her?' U.G. answered, 'I was standing there. I was puzzled: "Whom should I pity, the mother or the child?" Both were in a awkward situation: the mother could not control her anger and the child was so helpless. Then I found all marks corresponding to the marks of the beatings, on my back. So I too was a victim of that beating.' U.G. says that this was possible because consciousness cannot be divided. 'With this affection, there is no question of your sitting in judgment on anyone.'

Here is another incident: It was some time during the mid-Seventies that U.G. was visiting the hill country in North Goa. Many of his friends from Bombay were with him. One morning a group of people visited him. They were sitting together at the foot of a hillock. Valentine came to join the group. But when she found that the path was steep and slippery, she decided to return to her cottage.

Then a discussion arose among the people there about what each would have done if Valentine had slipped and fallen. U.G. said nothing. After a while Valentine came back and ventured down the path to join the group. She did indeed slip and fall. No one got up or did anything to help her, not even the person behind her. U.G. pointed out to them that they did nothing even though each of them had said they would help her. One of the members of the group asked U.G., 'How come you yourself did nothing to help then?' U.G. replied, 'I never said that I would give her a helping hand. If, however, you want to see for yourself how I myself was involved in that event...' and he rolled up the leg of his trouser. They found scratches on his knee similar to those found on Valentine's knee. Everybody was stunned. U.G. said that there was no significance to these occurrences.

U.G. says that the 'third eye', also called the *ajna chakra*, is the pituitary gland. When once the interference of thought is gone, the function of thought is taken over by this gland: it is this gland, and not thought, that gives the instructions or orders to the body. That is why they probably call it *ajna* (command) *chakra*. U.G. says that there is a built-in armour created by thought, which prevents us from getting affected by things:

> Since there is nobody here who uses thought as a self-protective mechanism, thought burns itself up. It undergoes combustion, ionization. Thought is, after all, a vibration. So, when this ionization of thought takes place, it throws out, and sometimes it covers the whole body with, an ash-like substance.... There is tremendous heat in the body as a result of this.

One of the major reasons why U.G. expresses the 'calamity' in pure and simple physical and physiological terms is that it has no psychological or mystical content or religious overtones. Such a thing, U.G. says, must have happened to many people. It is not something that one could especially be prepared for. There is no purificatory method or *sadhana* necessary for such a thing to happen.

Narayana Moorty says that if he had to reduce U.G.'s teaching to one sentence it would be the following: 'Consciousness is so pure that whatever you are doing in the direction of purifying that consciousness is adding impurity to it.' U.G. says:

> Consciousness has to flush itself out: it has to purge itself of every trace of holiness and of every trace of unholiness, of everything. Even what you consider 'sacred' and 'holy' is a contamination in that

consciousness. Yet it does not happen through any volition of yours. When once the frontiers are broken—although not through any effort or volition of yours—then the floodgates are open and everything goes out.

In that process of flushing out, you have all these visions. Suddenly you yourself, the whole consciousness, takes the shape of the Buddha, Jesus, Mahavira, Mohammed or Socrates—only of those who have come into this state; not of great men or leaders of mankind. One of them was a 'coloured man.' Then a naked woman with breasts and flowing hair. I was told that there were two saints here in India—Akkamahadevi and Lalleswari—they were women, naked women. Suddenly you have these two breasts and flowing hair. Even the organs change into female organs.

But still there is a division there—you, and the form that your consciousness has assumed, the form of the Buddha, say, or Jesus Christ, or God knows who. The situation there is: 'How do I know I am in that state?' But that division cannot stay long; it disappears and something else comes along. Probably the same thing happened to so many hundreds of people. This is part of history: so many *rishis*, some Westerners—monks—and so many women. All that people have experienced before you is part of your consciousness. I use the expression, 'The saints go marching out.' They run out of your consciousness because they cannot stay there any more because all that is impurity, a contamination there.

...This flushing out of everything good and bad, holy and unholy, sacred and profane, has got to happen. Otherwise your consciousness is still contaminated, still impure. After that you are put back into that primeval, primordial state of consciousness. Once consciousness has become pure, of and by itself, then nothing can touch it, nothing can contaminate it any more. All the past up to that point is there but it cannot influence your actions any longer.

U.G. saw these visions for three years after the 'calamity.'

He says that the most puzzling and bewildering part of the 'calamity' was when the sensory activities began their independent functioning. He says that there was no coordinator linking up the senses. That presented a problem to Valentine. 'We'd go for a walk and I'd look at a flower and ask her, "What's that?" She'd say, "That's a flower." I'd take a few more steps, look at a cow and ask, "What's that?" Like a baby, I had to relearn everything. Not actually relearn. All the knowledge was in the background and never came to the forefront.'

Valentine didn't know what to make of what was going on. She consulted a leading psychiatrist in Geneva. The psychiatrist told her that unless he saw the person he couldn't be of help. He asked her to bring U.G. over. But U.G. declined because he knew that something extraordinary had happened inside him. His difficulty was that the people who came to see him didn't seem to understand the way he was functioning and he didn't seem to understand the way they were functioning. 'How can we carry on a dialogue? Both of us have to stop. I am talking like a raving maniac. The difference is only a hair's breadth. That is why I say you either flip or fly at that moment of "calamity".'

Reproduced here are a couple of the most frequently asked questions concerning U.G.'s 'calamity'. These questions, in a way, also sum up what U.G. himself has to say on this topic:

111

Q: *Are even those who 'realized' different from one another?*

U.G.: Yes, because their background is different. The background is the only thing that can express itself. What else is there? My expression of it is the background: how I struggled, the path I followed, how I rejected the path of others—up to that point I can say what I did or did not do .... Such an individual is different, not only from you but from all the others who are supposed to be in this state, because of his background.

Q: *Although each one who is supposed to have undergone this 'explosion' is unique, in the sense that each one is expressing his own background, there do seem to be some common characteristics.*

U.G.: That is not my concern; it seems to be yours. I never compare myself to someone else.

Summing up the account of the happenings surrounding his 'calamity', U.G. says:

And that's all there is to it. My biography is over.... There is nothing more to write about and there never will be. If people come and ask me questions, I answer. If they don't, it makes no difference to me.... I have no particular message for mankind, except to say that all holy systems for obtaining enlightenment are nonsense and that all talk of arriving at a psychological mutation through awareness is rubbish. Psychological mutation is impossible. The natural state can happen only through biological mutation.

The incredible physiological changes continued to occur for years. U.G. was so bewildered by what had happened to him that he did not speak for a year after the 'calamity.' He had to practically learn to think and talk all over again, so complete was his mutation. After a year or so, he had regained most of his communicative powers. Yet he did not say much. 'What is there to say after a thing like this?' he asked. One day the answer came in a flash: 'I'll say it exactly the way it is.' Except for a year's break in the late Sixties, U.G. has been speaking tirelessly ever since. Of all this U.G. now says:

> I did not know what was happening to me. I had no reference point at all. Somehow I died and came back to life, free of my past. This thing happened without my volition and despite my religious background. And that is a miracle. It cannot be used as a model and duplicated by others.

10. Years After

*'It is just not possible to produce
enlightened people on an
assembly line.'*

–U.G.

Lately I have this feeling that I have spent these past few days
assembling the pieces of an impossible puzzle called U.G. This
quiet dawn echoes my desperation. My inability to sum up U.G.'s
life becomes sharper as the daylight seeps into this pitch dark
room. 'You don't know me. You think you know me,' said U.G.
to a friend during the course of a telephone conversation. These
words, like bullets, ricocheted to me and before I could blink,
they exploded all my claims of knowing U.G. intimately. Despite
spending endless hours on this biography, I am still miles away
from my goal of giving a fair account of this man and his life.

Talking about the myth of Icarus and using it as a device to
romanticize defeat is one thing. Staring at one's charred self-
esteem after it has taken a thrashing and knowing very well that
there are no spiritual payoffs, is quite another story.

In a quest-adventure story, usually the central character sets
out to find or learn or do something. Passing through trials along
the way, the character finally succeeds or at least survives, often
at great personal cost. But that is not the end. Having won
through, the character returns home, in part to be rewarded,
and also to share the benefits of the experience with the family,
tribe, nation or mankind, whether these benefits be tangible
treasures or intangible insight and wisdom.

The history of mankind gives us a blow-by-blow account of scores of individuals who, having gone through such quest-adventures, have come back and used their insight and wisdom for the benefit of mankind. Their insight has become the bedrock of so many religious movements all over the world.

So, after his quest of forty-nine years and his extraordinary physiological transformation, what does U.G. have to offer to the world which is desperately looking for something to keep it from falling apart? U.G., when asked about what had happened to him as a result of the 'calamity', usually has recourse to the 'Peanuts' cartoon and says:

> I don't know why it happened
> or when it happened
> or how it happened.
> I don't even know what happened.
> Did something happen?

U.G. also illustrates his point with the following Indian parable:

> Once, twelve children were playing in an uninhabited part of a village. There they discovered an image of Ganesh, the elephant god, the god of beginnings, the deity that makes all your wishes come true. They started dancing and singing around this image. The pot belly of the god's image attracted the attention of one of the boys; out of curiosity he stuck his finger in its navel. He felt something sting his finger. Instantly he withdrew his finger from the navel. Instead of crying out in pain, he pretended to his playmates that something extraordinary had happened to him. The boy closest to him followed suit. One after another the rest of the boys tried the same. Except for the last—the youngest. 'It's a scorpion!' he cried. Everyone

115

nodded their heads and they all joined him in crying.

U.G. is like the little boy in the above story who is screaming to the world that he has been 'stung by a scorpion.' Excerpts from the book, *Thought is Your Enemy*, replay that 'scream':

... Whatever has happened to me has happened *despite* everything I did. Whatever I did or did not do and whatever events people believed led me into this are totally irrelevant. It is very difficult for me to fix a point now and tell myself that this is me and look back and try to find out the cause for whatever happened to me. That is why I am emphasizing all the time that it is *acausal*. It is something like, to use my favourite phrase, lightning hitting you. But one thing I can say with certainty is that the very thing I searched for all my life was shattered to pieces. The goals that I had set for myself, self-realization, God-realization, transformation, radical or otherwise, were all false. And there was nothing there to be realized and nothing to be found there. The very demand to be free from anything, even from the physical needs of the body, just disappeared. And I was left with nothing. Therefore, whatever comes out of me now depends on what you draw out of me.

I have actually and factually nothing to communicate, because there is no communication possible at any level. The only instrument we have is the intellect. We know in a way that this instrument has not helped us to understand anything. So when once it dawns on you that that is not the instrument and there is no other instrument to understand anything, you are left with this puzzling situation that there is nothing

116

to understand. In a way it would be highly presumptuous on my part to sit on a platform, accept invitations and try to tell people that I have something to say.

What I am left with is something extraordinary—extraordinary in the sense that it has been possible for me not through any effort, not through any volition of mine. Everything that every man thought, felt and experienced before has been thrown out of my system.

There is no teaching of mine and never shall be one. 'Teaching' is not the word for it. A teaching implies a method or a system, a technique or a new way of thinking to be applied in order to bring about a transformation in your way of life. What I am saying is outside the field of teachability. It is simply a description of the way I am functioning. It is just a description of the natural state of man. That is the way you, stripped of the machinations of thought, are also functioning.

Your natural state has no relationship whatsoever with the religious states of bliss, beatitude and ecstasy. They lie within the field of experience. Those who have led man on his search for religiousness throughout the centuries have perhaps experienced those religious states. So can you. They are thought-induced states of being and as they come, so do they go.... The timeless can never be experienced, can never be grasped, contained, much less given expression to by any man. That beaten track will lead you nowhere. There is no oasis situated yonder. You are stuck with the mirage.

117

'Doesn't an encounter with you help people in any way in their quests?' I asked U.G. in the kitchen as he was teaching me to fix the washing machine. 'Look, during your stay here, you have learned to make coffee, toast your bread, use the washing machine and wash your dishes like anybody else. These are the only things you will learn from me,' he said laughingly. 'Jokes apart, tell me. I have a deadline to meet, damn it! What can people get out of you?' I persisted.

> My way of life and what I am saying will not help people to face the difficult situations in their lives. If there is any potential in them, it will surface. But this doesn't apply to spiritual progress or potential because that doesn't exist. If you are a murderer, you will murder with finesse. This doesn't mean that I condone murder but whatever there is in you will bloom.

When I look back at my life with its successes and its failures and its endless errors, I know for certain that had it not been for U.G., I wouldn't be here today. Whenever I am with U.G. I find a mighty current of strength coursing through my heart. The few words I speak and write are only through the force of that current gained by coming in contact with him. I do not for a moment think that I have any greatness of my own. Inhaling the memory of the times spent with him fills me with vigour and courage.

I often ask myself what value all that he says has for me. In fact, it has none. I still am and perhaps will always remain what I am. Though I am a 'somebody' now, deep down inside I know I am ordinary—a somebody who is in fact a nobody. I have tried every creed and they have all failed to comfort me. Where do I go from here? U.G. says, 'Get up and go.'

What he says is unacceptable and how he says it is revolting. No wonder a philosopher of great repute christened him a 'cosmic Naxalite'. Never have I seen or met a man who is so certain about what he is saying. It is this certainty which plays havoc with our attitudes and platitudes. U.G. says, 'As long as "you" are there, you are dead. And if by some chance or accident this "you", as you know yourself, is absent, even for a trillionth of a second, that is when you will touch life. But you will never know what is there.'

Bernard Selby, the English postman I had met in Kodai in the year 1979, who is now a Labour leader in Manchester and aspiring to be a member of Parliament, once gave voice to my feelings:

> I know U.G. for fourteen years and there again I don't know U.G. I know him and I don't know him at the same time. I think that with him, the more you get to know him the more you discover that in a sense you don't know a great deal about him....
>
> When I see U.G., he affirms in me a negative sense. He deepens my ignorance.

How does this living quality operate in U.G.'s life—his day-to-day life? U.G. says, 'I sit, I eat, I walk, I talk and I travel.' But there is a lot more to the story, a never-ending story, and now I will let the story tell itself.

After the 'calamity', U.G. returned to India. His visits to India are now regular. Every year while he is in India, he divides his time between Bombay, Bangalore and, of late, Delhi.

Though U.G. says that he does not discuss personal problems, the fact is that hundreds of people all over the world have undergone a total change after coming into contact with him. I have observed that for some reason people who are 'mentally ill' get U.G.'s very special attention.

'Why do all the crazy people come only to you, papa,' my daughter Pooja once asked. 'So that I can drive them completely mad and then hand them over to U.G.,' was my reply.

Some of U.G.'s friends who believe in the doctrine of Karma say, 'Since U.G. abandoned his wife, who was then mentally ill, he has had to pay now by caring for all the maddies.'

'Why are you talking to all these people? Do you know that only the four walls of this house are benefited by what you are saying?' said Kalyani, cutting into a conversation that a group of leading psychiatrists were having with U.G. one evening in Bangalore. 'Do you know the difference between a schizophrenic and a paranoid?' she asked the doctors. And then without even waiting for their response she started explaining: 'The difference is very thin. Take the example of a girl who comes out of a midnight movie. She is apprehensive and anxious that the driver of the autorickshaw she got into would molest her, as she is alone. This is a schizophrenic. Now the paranoid believes that she is actually going through an experience of being raped.'

Kalyani was one of the most fascinating women I came across around U.G. in Bangalore. She must have been in her late fifties when I first saw her. That was ten years ago. Her presence was dazzling. She had a history of mental illness and had spent some time in a mental hospital in Delhi. She hailed from a cultured South Indian family. Her husband was a bureaucrat; so was her son-in-law. At one time Kalyani also taught mathematics in a high school. Kalyani suffered from the mania of showering all her money, jewellery and other valuables on the temple priests and holy men. It was because of this that her family members committed her to a mental hospital. Ironically, it was the testimony of those priests to whom she gave all the money that led to her being institutionalized.

Kalyani used to wander aimlessly on the streets of Bangalore before she met U.G. For the remaining years of her life, U.G. became her anchor. He gave her some money every month for her expenses and also helped her to find a place to live. I can hardly get over those exhilarating moments of exchanges between the 'mad woman and the sage.'

'After I met U.G., any difference between the street and the home has disappeared,' Kalyani remarked. She had once healed a lady friend of severe neck pain by a mere touch. When the friend thanked her, Kalyani said, 'You must thank U.G. I am just a surrogate.' Her singing and dancing and her begging for money kept everybody enthralled. U.G. always put a little money in her hands each time she visited, even though he knew that she would give all that money away or drop it in a mail box.

Even when Kalyani was dying of breast cancer, she refused to receive any medical help. She looked like an open wound when I saw her for the last time. The cancer had eaten into her chest. Despite her condition, she came out into the street to greet U.G. when he paid her a visit. 'Help me to die, U.G.,' she cried, 'you are the only one who can....' U.G. held Kalyani's hand and for a while they both stood in silence. A few months later Kalyani died, leaving behind all her earthly belongings to U.G. They consisted of a few torn saris and other clothing and seven thousand rupees. As always, U.G. passed this money on to others.

The story of the role U.G. played in Parveen's battle with insanity has never been told. Perhaps the time has now come to tell it all.

"Back to normal! I am fit to work without a break now!—Parveen Babi—" screamed a headline of the number one gossip magazine, *Stardust*. With that Parveen Babi was back 'forever' from her trip to Europe, U.G. and insanity. Back in the world of films, ready to run in the race once again...

> ... But I could not be with U.G. forever. I have to live my life myself. U.G. cannot live my life for me, just the way I cannot live his life. And now that I am back, I miss him but I am not lost without him.
>
> Parveen Babi
> —to *Stardust* on her arrival in Bombay in 1980.

After her first breakdown, Parveen had accompanied U.G. to Bali. At that time she was limping back to what is called 'functional sanity'. While they were away, a news item appeared in *India Today* announcing that U.G. and Parveen were married and were honeymooning in the exotic Bali islands. This news created an uproar. When the media confronted U.G. on his arrival in Bombay about the authenticity of the report, U.G. said, 'I wish it were true. What more does an old man like me want? Parveen is a famous actress—rich, young and beautiful. What more can I ask for?' The reporters were aghast at U.G.'s answer. Later, when U.G.'s friends suggested that he should file a legal suit against *India Today* and claim damages for defaming him, U.G. laughingly said, 'If it is true, it should not hurt me. If it is false, it should not hurt me—in any case it should not hurt me at all.'

Behind Parveen's 'all is well' exterior loomed the terror of sinking once again into the abyss of madness. U.G. had tried to get her out of the 'dog-eat-dog'world of the Bombay movie industry. But soon he gave up. He knew that a relapse was inevitable. It was just a matter of time.

She told U.G. while she was spending some time with him and Valentine in Switzerland, 'If I stay here, I will go mad. If I return to Bombay, I will go mad there also. I don't know what to do.' To which U.G. said, 'Better go to Bombay and go mad there....' He thought her only way out of the impending doom of insanity might be to lead a sort of protected life, like that of a nun.

Later, in July 1983, Parveen once again had a breakdown.

The following excerpts are reproduced from an article which appeared in the *Illustrated Weekly of India* dated 29 January 1984.

> This time U.G.'s attitude was not protective or patronizing like the last time. He told me he would not be able to give me any advice, that I was well enough to make my own decisions.... For me it has come to this. If I stay in the film industry I lose my head. So I am staying out. Sorry, but I just can't take it any more.
>
> For the first time in my life, I am finished. Done with it all: my fame, my success, my identity as an

actress and my old life. I have come to U.G. because I feel he is the only man who can help me bridge over to whatever fate has in store for me.... I am now in America with U.G. and Valentine resting, doing everyday chores like cooking, cleaning, watering plants, etc. I have never felt more secure, peaceful and happy.

One year later, on 4 April 1984, on her birthday, Parveen suddenly disappeared from U.G.'s house in London. 'She could be flying down to India,' said U.G., informing me of her disappearance. He asked me to keep a vigil at the Bombay airport. I immediately contacted Parveen's former secretary and passed the news on to him. For two whole days there was no news about Parveen. In a letter dated 4 April 1984, written from London, U.G. explains how and why Parveen ran away from his house:

> ... As I told you, Parveen's present condition has been a great drain on my time, patience and energy ever since we left California. I have been making it crystal clear to her for some days that her idea of digging in her heels here and wanting to be with me forever is very unrealistic and that it is time that she started living her own life.... She has looked after Valentine so well that Valentine is already missing her. Isn't it an eternal shame that she can't make anything of her talent and of her life now? What lies ahead of her can never be clearly sign-posted by anybody.
>
> Babi girl's exit is as sudden and as theatrical as last time. She just got up from her chair and said, 'I don't want to be a burden on you. I am going to India right now.' She left all her things here and walked out.

123

> But I gave her some money to take care of her tickets,
> etc., for aught I know she may still be somewhere
> in London. Maybe she is already there in India....'

New York, 7 April 1984. A disturbed and distraught Parveen
Babi landed at the New York International Airport. She was
asked to show her identification papers by the airport authorities.
Something in her snapped. She is said to have acted difficult
and was handcuffed. When she put up a frantic struggle, she
was also ankle-cuffed and carried by four policemen to a public
hospital. An Indian doctor recognized Parveen and came to her
aid. He got U.G.'s telephone and address from Parveen and
called him to tell him of her whereabouts.

U.G. informed me about the tragedy that had occurred in
New York. We spoke at great length over the telephone of what
could be done to get her out of the mess she had got herself into.
Finally, I convinced U.G. to go to New York and bring Parveen
back.

When U.G. landed in New York, he found Parveen in a
general ward with thirty other mentally disturbed patients. The
Indian Consul General, who had been informed of the
unfortunate incident, had personally come to visit Parveen at
the hospital. During U.G.'s visit, Parveen smiled and chatted
with the Consul as though nothing had happened. In his letter
dated 12 April 1984, U.G. wrote to me explaining in detail what
exactly he was going through with Parveen.

In a letter dated 25 April 1984 (U.G.'s final letter to me on the
Parveen crisis) he wrote from the Shelburne Murray Hotel, New
York:

> Well, I am afraid my usefulness has come to an
> end. Every time she reached out for help I found it
> hard to let her down. My determination to prevent
> her from ending up in a mental hospital worked. I
> couldn't let this happen to her. Now she is
> spiralling toward disaster. This seems to be the

final breakdown. She is plunging herself into her final manic-depression. She is doing things which I thought she never would do. I am sure she will completely and totally fall apart with no hope of ever putting herself together without medical care.

As I sit here in California writing this piece on Parveen Babi, she is back for the past few years in Bombay leading a life of a recluse. Recently she mailed a set of pages written on U.G. to K. Chandrasekhar in Bangalore, portions from which are reproduced here:

> U.G. is the most perfect human being I have ever met in my life. There is nothing apparently extraordinary about him. It is when you spend some time with him that you see the perfection operating. I have lived and travelled with U.G. And after being with him for a substantial period of time I have realized that U.G. treats human beings as human beings should be treated—with respect, consideration, understanding and compassion. I also realize that he treats everybody as his equal—whether the person is younger, poorer, richer or older. We all treat people as relations either above us or below us. We do not treat them as our equals. His behaviour comes naturally to him. He does not make a deliberate effort to act this way, nor is his behavior accompanied by the feeling that he is a special person, that his behavior is special and that he is doing people a favour.
>
> Another most special quality about U.G. is that he never uses people for his personal gain. U.G. usually gives back much more than he receives. And his giving is the purest kind of giving. He gives without expecting anything back in return.

He gives so silently and so selflessly that oftentimes even the receiver does not realize that he has received. If he feels it is necessary to state the bitter truth for a person's good, he states it. He can state the bitter truth because he does not mind losing the person's friendship, if it helps the person.

I have never seen U.G. take advantage of anybody, cheat anybody, mislead anybody, use anybody, or take advantage of a person or situation for his personal gain even in the most insignificant way. Apart from U.G., I am afraid I cannot say this of anybody else I have come across in the world.

11. The Never-ending Story

'What is left there is the pulse, the beat
and the throb of life.'

–U.G.

For U.G. there is no distinction between day and night. He takes only catnaps. All in all, he says, he sleeps about four to five hours.

He eats like a bird, a morsel of food, three times a day. For a vegetarian he does not eat many vegetables and hardly any fruit. He eats practically the same thing every day. His breakfast consists of oatmeal with double or triple cream and a glass of orange or pineapple juice. Sometimes he eats the same food for lunch and dinner, when he is alone. For lunch, here in the US, he generally makes couscous with (frozen!) broccoli heads, or 'Angel Hair' with a touch of canned tomato (never fresh!) and at night he eats the same with a bit of cheese. Heaven only knows how he survives with such a small quantity of food! He says, just to let the body function he 'throws' a morsel of food three times a day into his body! 'You have made eating into a pleasure movement. As far as I am concerned, there is no difference between looking for varieties of food or looking for varieties of girls (or men, as the case may be).'

The only exercise he has is walking from the bedroom to the living room, to the kitchen and sometimes to the toilet and back to the bed! He says riding in a car is his only constitutional— that that's a lot of exercise to every part of the body because the whole body is moving with the movement of the car at the speed of sixty miles an hour! If this exercise is not enough, he goes 'malling' in the shopping malls, i.e. window-shopping.

Wherever he is, people come to meet him and it is from these informal talks that several books have been compiled. More than one of these books has been translated into French, Russian, Italian, German, Chinese, Japanese and Polish.

The very first book entitled, *The Mystique of Enlightenment*, was the brainchild of two former Rajneesh sannyasis. Out of sheer gratitude for the role that U.G. had played in their lives, they wanted to share what they had learned from U.G. with the general public. This book, along with the others, has paved its way all over the world without any fanfare. 'If there is anything to whatever I say, it stands or falls on its own,' says U.G.

Although he says he has nothing to say, and cannot help anyone at all, multitudes of people come to see him, some out of curiosity and some out of the hope that he will help them in some fashion. 'U.G. is not a teacher. He is a friend to you when your own teacher has become your enemy,' says Vijay Anand, film director, who was in the inner circle at Rajneesh's ashram for eight years before he met U.G.

> U.G. says that you should stay with your misery and that you don't need a teacher. And you don't know how to do that. It is too severe. You can't cope with the misery. You want to get rid of it. And then U.G. comes along and says, 'I can't help you. It's your misery. Go to hell.' It is difficult to understand. It's easier said than done.

Vijay Anand, who has been through the gamut and has considerable knowledge of the world of spirituality and meditation, describing the predicament of the aspirant, adds:

> There are moments in our lives when we go through a crisis—not an intellectual crisis but an emotional

128

crisis, when you cannot cope with the suffering. Since no help is coming and you cannot help yourself, that is when you turn to the religious books like the *Koran*, the *Gita* or the *Bible*. You suddenly feel that you get solace. But that solace does not last. You read the books again. They give you exhilaration for an hour or so. Again it wears out. This goes on. And then you feel that probably these are dead words. That's why the books are not working. So when these books fail, that is the time when you start looking for a teacher. If there is a crisis in your profession, you go to an expert. If there is a problem with your health, you go to your doctor. When you have a crisis of this kind, you are likely to go to people like Rajneesh, Da Free John, and J. Krishnamurti. You do find initially that they help. These people give you a way of life. Certain meditation, certain philosophy which fills you up for a short while. You feel as if you have got an answer. As long as you do the meditation, it seems that the crisis has passed away. But the moment you stop and you are with yourself, you are back to the crisis. So you really have found no solution. Here the teacher tells you that you have not done enough of whatever you are supposed to do. So you go back and put in double the effort. This is a kind of forgetfulness like drinking. If you are honest with yourself, you will find that you are not getting anywhere. You are stuck. This is when you should meet U.G....

At times these informal conversations become heated. People are provoked into fighting desperately to latch on to whatever they believe in, while U.G. is negating practically everything they say. They might feel their very existence is threatened. Yet seemingly masochistically, they keep returning to see U.G. This indeed is a sort of fatal attraction. Or it is as if the moth cannot avoid the fire.

'I don't know and I don't give a *paisa* for what he says on matters religious, much less his teachings. Yet there is something in him that drags me to him,' laments Brahmachari Sivarama Sarma, a former professor of chemical engineering and Indian Administrative Service officer, who was also once nominated to be the Shankaracharya of the Kudli Math but who didn't make it for political reasons.

> U.G. shuns religious persons, ridicules social reformers, condemns saints, speaks with disgust about *sadhakas* (spiritual aspirants), detests the chanting of the Vedas or the recitation of the Upanishads and is full of rage when one speaks of Sankara or Buddha. He becomes furious at the very mention of Sai Baba or Rajneesh. The height of his rage could only be seen when 'J.Krishnamurti freaks' approach him.

> He doesn't give any solution to any of the problems raised and avoids questions about 'enlightenment.' Whenever he gets entangled in a controversy he says, 'It is so. Take it or leave it.' Whenever he is confronted with arguments he becomes violent and says, 'Who asked you to come here? You may get up and go. That's fine with me....'

> He is against morality but refrains from preaching immorality. He gets wild when somebody speaks of honesty though he is not dishonest himself. He is a bundle of contradictions. His statements are devastating. His ideas are shocking. His expressions are bewildering. His utterances are irritating.

Yet, I am pulled toward such a person! Is it my weakness? No. Or is it because of my passivity or cowardice or incapacity to stand on my own? No. Not at all. Then what? I don't know! I made up my mind not to think about him any more, nor bother to visit him; and yet the moment he is anywhere near Bangalore my nerves reverberate. I become restless and find no peace till I run to him. Why? Why? Why?

U.G. and Brahmachari have for more than twenty years shared a volatile relationship. Brahmachari apparently had the world at his feet when U.G. stepped in and prevented him from getting it. The story goes that before dying, the pontiff of the Kudli Math nominated Brahmachari as his successor. This meant being heir to a property worth hundreds of millions of rupees, a fleet of cars and a residential palace in the heart of the city of Bangalore. A contest for the throne began when a rival stepped in, challenging Brahmachari's succession. This was the beginning of a long-drawn legal battle for the throne. Obviously both sides had much to gain. Little did Brahmachari know that even his life was in danger. Had it not been for U.G. who for three months, till the appointed day of coronation, sheltered him, Brahmachari's life would have ended in a tragedy.

Every day, from dawn to late night, U.G. kept him under his guard, preventing him from venturing out, dissuading him from entertaining the idea of becoming a pontiff of the *math*. Brahmachari was permitted to go back home every night only when it seemed safe. On the day of the coronation, when his dream of sceptre, throne and crown came tumbling down and his rival ascended the throne, Brahmachari was with U.G. The next day Brahmachari took him to see a piece of land granted to him by the Karnataka government. That same evening U.G. dropped him off at his residence, which happened to be a garage, and handing him two rupees, the remainder of the cab fare, said, 'With this, start your own ashram....'

Months later, with the assistance of the Karnataka government, Brahmachari set up a huge ashram on the outskirts of Bangalore, in which he also built a school, a temple, a guest house and cottages for the elderly.

Conversations with U.G. are not always of a serious nature. One of the visitors who came all the way from Rio de Janeiro in a Concorde, was shocked and disappointed when he heard U.G. discussing monetary exchange rates and the stock market. 'Have I come all the way to listen to money, power and sex, instead of mystical experiences, truth or enlightenment?' To this U.G. replied, 'I have not asked you to come here. You will do well to take the next available flight to Brazil.' But the gentleman came back the next day and every day for almost a month.

Wherever U.G. happens to be, his friends gather around him. They tease each other, joke, and a party-like atmosphere prevails. 'I feel so comfortable in his physical presence,' says Paulo Marrusic, an Italian film maker. 'The atmosphere around him is very informal, easy, like flowing water. We entertain ourselves with games, like horoscopes and financial matters.' Even in India, U.G. is always surrounded by people who are either looking at his horoscope or getting some palmist to comment on his future. Everybody knows that all this is sheer entertainment for U.G.

While we are in the area of astrology and palmistry, a look at the Nadi reading of U.G. done in 1988 may be of interest. Nadi, as a type of astrology, is practised in different parts of India. In one form (Kaumara Nadi), the astrologer carries volumes of palm leaf manuscripts which he inherited from his ancestors, which were presumably written hundreds of years ago in somewhat archaic dialects and which contain astrological charts and readings on all the people who would visit the astrologer in future (including their names, backgrounds, their past and their future destiny).

This particular Nadi consisted of two bundles of palm leaves, one of large and long leaves that looked ancient and the other of smaller leaves that appeared to be some sort of index to the text in the larger volume. On the leaves are astrological messages written in archaic Telugu and Tamil. The Nadi astrologer's job is to locate the appropriate leaf in the manuscript for the person in question and interpret the contents to him or her.

Mr Nagaraj, the Nadi reader, began the proceedings by lighting an incense stick and passing it around the books with great veneration. He then held out one end of a string, the other end of which is attached to the bundle of palm leaves, and offered it to U.G. He asked U.G. to part the stack of leaves at random with his end of the string by passing it through the stack. The astrologer opened to that leaf where U.G.'s string divided the stack and began reading what was written on it. These ancient scribblings, set down so long ago by some unknown astrologers and mystics, astounded all those present. The accuracy and insight with which those ancient ones were able to describe the man in question were, to say the least, mind-boggling.

The Nadi astrologer himself had no knowledge of U.G. whatsoever. He was visibly perplexed when the Nadi started singing praises of this man:

> What is there to say about this recluse who lives totally unattached like a droplet on a lotus leaf? This man lives like Bharata in the epic *Ramayana*, completely disinterested in the midst of all the royal comforts and pleasures. The combination of the planets Mercury and Saturn enabled him to understand the essence of life. He is well-read and experienced.

Mr Nagaraj stopped reading for a moment, looking doubtfully at U.G., wondering if he perhaps hadn't turned the wrong leaf. U.G. reassured him quickly that the reading was indeed accurate. So, the Nadi reading resumed:

This man will rise to prominence in his *Ravidasa* (the phase of the Sun) like the rising Sun. Having been displaced from his native place, he never stays in any one place long. He does not go through initiation of any kind: he is born with it. His teaching is not like the teachings of hermits and jungle-dwellers. The light of his teaching keeps spreading everywhere. But he thoroughly disappoints those who come to him hoping to get somewhere. This person should be addressed as '*Atma*' (the Self) and not as 'man' (implying that individuality is absent in him).

Then, as if the ancient mystics needed a break at this point, they wrote: 'We shall continue with the reading after a break of a *ghatika* (24 minutes).' Mr Nagaraj closed the book. He and his colleagues were evidently eager to know more about U.G. U.G. obliged them by explaining for the next fifteen or twenty minutes how events in his life clearly reflected this and other astrological readings. He said:

I cannot make a definitive statement as to whether there is anything to the predictive part of astrology but if anyone wants to do an intensive case study, my chart would provide a good example. The events that I have mentioned paralleled exactly the predictions of the astrologers. Take it or leave it.

Meanwhile, those who were present at the reading were all anxious to know what else the Nadi had to say regarding U.G. We implored the reader, Mr Nagaraj, to go on with the reading. He consented. But, to the utter amazement of everyone present, when he opened the book a blank leaf greeted him, as if the ancient seers had anticipated our undue haste! 'The blank leaf means that my future is blank,' quipped U.G., chuckling.

Then the book was closed and after half a minute was opened once again with the string. Writing did appear on this leaf. It said:

> You still have a minute and a half to complete the 24-minute break we have in the previous reading. This reading is of no use to such a man. Nevertheless, we shall continue just for the fun of doing it. You need not pay respects to us but would do better to offer your *namaskarams* (salutations) to the one sitting opposite you and proceed with the reading.

The Nadi went on:

> For eleven years from now, he will be haunted by the Spirit of Good Luck wherever he goes. It will not leave him.... This man, whether he is eating, drinking, walking, sleeping, or doing anything, he always remains in *Sahaja Samadhi* (the 'Natural State of Union', i.e., the state of liberation).... During the final phase of *Chandradasa* (the phase of the Moon) his very look would suffice to initiate a person spiritually....For such a man what use is this reading?

With that rhetorical question, the Nadi ended its reading. K.Chandrasekhar, who was present at the time of the reading, recorded the above account.

At times, suddenly out of nowhere, a cloudburst hits the people present. Every word is charged with tremendous energy and the atmosphere becomes electrified. Unfortunately, just these moments are the ones that have never been recorded. For some reason, if anyone anticipates such a moment and arranges for a recording, the moment never happens. The situation leaves the participants dazed. They may even have trouble recalling what was said and heard. Such moments can happen when one goes for a walk with U.G., or when U.G. is cooking or when one is driving in a car with him.

Sometimes people come and just sit around U.G., not necessarily participating in any conversation. The general feeling they get is one of peace, security, comfort, intimacy and communion. My friend, one of India's greatest actresses, the late Smita Patil, often spoke to me about this feeling of great ease in U.G.'s presence. Nevertheless, you are never off your guard when you are with him as you feel that you and your being are always under question in his presence.

Even strangers are attracted to U.G. The incidents below will illustrate my point:

Robert Carr was a sort of guru himself. He had a modest following before he ran into U.G. twenty-five years ago. After meeting U.G., Robert, closed shop and is now running a small restaurant near San Francisco. One day in this restaurant, a middle-aged couple, who were watching U.G. all through the evening from a few tables away, made an interesting comment to Robert: 'Who is this man? Is he a guru?' they asked. 'No, he is an anti-guru. In fact, he is just a regular guy,' answered Robert. The couple were not satisfied with the answer. One of them said, 'It seems your friend knows what the rest of us don't know. But he wouldn't tell us....' Robert smiled.

I was looking for a black panther to cast in one of my films which dealt with the theme of the supernatural. The search took me to Rome. It was a pleasant coincidence that in those days U.G. too happened to be in Rome. I still savour the memory of that picturesque dawn when I wandered with U.G. through those cobblestoned, pigeon-filled, narrow streets of Rome reverberating with the bells from the Vatican. 'Belief is an industry. Every church, every temple, every mosque is built brick by brick on the gullibility of man. If Jesus had all this security, there would be no Christianity at all,' said U.G., pointing to the guards who were shielding the Vatican.

I found a black panther in a private zoo owned by an Italian trainer named Daniel, on the outskirts of Rome. Being a stranger to Rome, I sought U.G.'s assistance to get to this zoo. What happened there that day remains a mystery to me till now. Daniel took us into the zoo and showed us the black panther. The animal looked untrained. The chances of using this panther for the film were slim-to-none. Daniel sensed this. He tried to swing our attention to a magnificent looking nine-foot tiger which, according to him, was the best trained animal in all of Europe. Just then the black panther began growling. U.G. turned to the panther and gesturing to it said, 'Quiet, sit down.' The animal obeyed. Daniel and his wife seemed surprised at first. But since U.G. repeatedly managed to make the panther quiet every time he grew agitated, they were spellbound. 'This is a black panther. It is very difficult to control him. Is your friend an animal trainer?' asked an astounded Daniel.

On a Sunday morning in Paris outside a church where Rue Bonaparte crosses Boulevard St Germain, U.G. was taking a stroll. 'Do you want this picture of yours?' asked the photographer, showing U.G. a Polaroid shot which he had taken without asking him. 'No,' said U.G. Just then a voice from behind said, 'I'll take it.' She was a young, well-dressed, pretty girl with an intelligent face. 'Why should *you* pay 200 francs for my picture?' asked U.G. 'I like the face,' said the girl, paying the photographer. Two weeks later, U.G. happened to be at the same spot when he ran into this girl again. She invited him to her house saying, 'I want to show you something, come.' She lived on the seventh floor of a building which had no elevator. As they spiralled upstairs, U.G. observed the residents of the building casting strange glances at him. The girl was a prostitute. Inside her apartment, the girl showed him an enlargement of his picture on the wall opposite her bed.

Later, she told U.G. why she was leading the life she was. The story was that she had broken away from her parents and wanted a degree from the Sorbonne. Since she had no money for that, she had no choice but to become a prostitute. U.G. just listened to her story silently. When he got up to leave, the girl said, 'You know, you are the only person who has not advised me about changing my life after listening to my story. Even my clients whom I pick up on their way out of the church on Sundays don't spare me a sermon.... Who are you?' U.G. did not answer. He smiled and walked away.

U.G. seemingly leaves places even before he arrives there. The first few hours in Bombay, immediately after his arrival, are inevitably spent in arranging his future travels. 'Why do you travel so much, U.G.?' asked a friend, curious. U.G. said, 'My travels are always influenced by the climate. I am like that bird, the golden plover. I travel with the changing seasons. That bird travels South with the sun and returns North with the sun. That's the only way the bird and I can stay comfortable. The bird builds no nest. And I have no home.'

This has been U.G.'s way of life ever since he was fourteen years old. He has been everywhere in the world except China and now divides his time between India, Europe, the US and Australia.

At any given point in his life, U.G.'s worldly belongings did not exceed twenty kilos. They have now come down to five kilos and he seriously plans to reduce their weight further. He travels all over the world with just one handbag. At the end of every year, that is, on 31 December, he gives away any unspent money. What his pattern of travel in the years to come will be is anyone's guess. With Valentine's death and that of Terry Newland in the US (in whose studio apartment in Mill Valley, California, he used to stay when he visited there), his pattern is sure to undergo a change.

30 September 1991. Autumn is here in Carmel. In the hush of this moonlit night I sit here in the living room, leafing through the manuscript, trying to wrench out of myself as much as I can to pour into these pages.

I have come a long way through this book. On my desk I have a few beginnings. Someone once said, 'From one lunch with U.G. a whole book could be written. Even libraries could be filled with books about this man called U.G. But books have to end just as films finally fade out. U.G.'s story, however, does not seem to have a finale. Superimposing an end on U.G.'s life is like freezing the upsurge of lava from an erupting volcano. So how does a storyteller end a story that has no beginning or end? He just doesn't....

Just as I am wrapping up, patting myself on the back for a job done, U.G. adds a postscript: 'This is just a fairy tale!'

A sign reading, "Welcome to Carmel, U.G. and Mahesh!" put up by our friends here in California is coming off the wall. 'Time to leave, time for us to part,' says U.G., pointing to the wall.

There is a kind of release and a kind of sadness every time I say goodbye to U.G. There is no way I could be like that dunlin bird that follows the golden plover. As U.G. and I drive toward the San Francisco International Airport, the after-image of our house in Carmel in which I have spent almost a month glistens in my memory.

'Where do you go from here, U.G.?' I ask as I get out from the car. 'I'll spend some time here in the Bay Area and then on to Australia,' he answers. 'I will call you from New York or from London,' I say, trying my best to make my farewell seem casual.

'By the time you know where I am, I may very well be somewhere else,' says U.G. as he drives away, leaving me with my words and my emotions in my mouth.

Part II

Conversations

The following conversations, based on recordings,
were held over an extended period of time
between U.G. Krishnamurti, the
author and several others.

- *Being a film maker let me begin with that word 'creativity'. Much has been said on the subject. What do you have to say about it?*

There is no such thing as creativity at all. All that people do is imitate something or the other that already exists. Only when you do not use anything as a model, what emerges can be called creativity and that cannot be used again as a model for future acts of yours. And there it ends. If you look at human faces or even those leaves—no two faces are the same, no two leaves are the same.

- *Behind the changes in nature, there seems to be some kind of plan or purpose, don't you think?*

I don't see any plan or scheme there at all! There is a process—I wouldn't necessarily call it evolution—but when it slows down then a revolution takes place. Nature tries to put something together and start all over again, just for the sake of creating. This is the only true creativity. Nature uses no models or precedents and so has nothing to do with art per se.

- *Do you mean to say there is nothing to the creativity of artists, poets, musicians and sculptors?*

Why do you want to place art on a higher level than craft? If there is no market for an artist's creation, he will be out of business. It is the market that is responsible for all these so-called artistic beliefs. An artist is a craftsman like any other craftsman. He uses that tool to express himself. All human creation is born out of sensuality. I have nothing against sensuality. All art is a pleasure movement. Even that (the pleasure) has to be cultivated by you. Otherwise you have no way of appreciating the beauty and art that artists are talking about. If you question their creation, they feel superior, thinking that you don't have taste. Then they want you to go to a school to learn how to appreciate their art. If you don't enjoy a poem written by a so-called great poet, they forcibly educate you to appreciate poetry. That is all that they are doing in the educational institutions. They teach us how to appreciate beauty, how to appreciate music, how to appreciate painting and so on. Meanwhile they make a living off you. Artists find it comforting to think that they are creative: 'creative art', 'creative ideas', 'creative politics'. It's nonsense. There is nothing really creative in them in the sense of their doing anything original, new or free. Artists pick something here and something there, put it together and think they have created something marvellous. They are all imitating something that is already there. Imitation and style are the only 'creativity' we have. Each of us has our own style according to the school we attended, the language we were taught, the books we have read, the examinations we have taken. And within that framework again we have our own style. Perfecting style and technique is all that operates there. You will be surprised that one of these days computers will paint and create music much better than all the painters and musicians that the world has produced so far. It may not happen in our lifetime but it will happen. You are no different from a computer. We are not ready to accept that because we are made to believe that we are not just machines—that there is something more to us. You have to come to terms with this and accept that we *are* machines. The human intellect that we have developed through education, through all kinds of techniques is no match for nature. They (creative activities) assume importance because they have been recognized as expressions of spiritual, artistic and intellectual values. The drive for self-expression is born out of neurosis. This applies to the spiritual teachers of mankind too. There is no such thing as a direct sense-experience. All forms of art are nothing but an expression of sensuality.

- *Is there something more to self-expression, U.G.? Having had a tremendous experience of some kind you want to relate it to somebody or maybe just replay it to yourself. Is there anything to this overriding need to express oneself?*

There is no such thing as my experience and your experience. When you experience something, you think it is something

U.G. in 1945, with his wife Kusuma and daughter Bharti

U.G. 's children–Bharati, Vasant and Usha

th his son and his family in Virginia

Before the 'calamity'

Soon after the 'calamity'. Note the change

With the author

Carmel, USA, where the book was written. On the right is Narayana Moorty

...th the author

Valentine de Kerven

Valentine as a young woman

In Gstaad, with Parveen Babi

U.G. and Valentine in Bangalore

U.G. and Valentine in 1985, in Amsterdam

In Gstaad

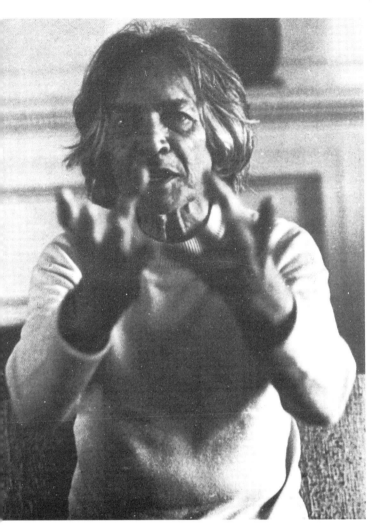

A portrait

In California, with Terry Newland, Robert Carr, Douglas Rosenstein and Paul Ly

In New york, in 1983, with Parveen Babi and Valentine

'Malling' in New york (above) and Hong Kong (below)

The author, seated on the bench where U.G. sat just befor the 'calamity

extraordinary and naturally the need arises to share that experience with somebody else. When you and I go out for a walk, you naturally look at something that you have not looked at before and it is something extraordinary for you. And when you say to yourself this is something extraordinary that you have not seen before, there is a need for you—which is a part of your self-fulfilment—to share that pleasure with somebody else. Whatever you experience has already been experienced by someone else. Your telling yourself, 'Ah! I am in a blissful state,' means that someone else before you has experienced that and has passed it on to you. Whatever may be the nature of the medium through which you experience, it is a second-hand, third-hand and last-hand experience. It is not yours. There is no such thing as your own experience. Such experiences, however extraordinary, aren't worth anything.

- *We want to know what truth is. We want to know what enlightenment is.*

You already know it. Don't tell me that you don't. There is no such thing as truth at all.

- *So, does all this (U.G.'s search and his 'calamity') mean that there was a certain programming?*

If there was, you have to rule out all such things as mutation and radical transformation. I ruled those out because I didn't find anything there to be transformed. There was no question of mutation of mind, radical or otherwise. It is all hogwash. But it is difficult for you to throw all this stuff out of your system. You can also deny it and brush it aside, but this, 'Maybe there is something to it' lasts for a long time. When once you stumble into a situation that you can call 'courage', you can throw the entire past out of yourself. I don't know how this has happened. What has happened is something which cannot but be called an act of courage because everything, not only this or that particular teacher you had been involved with, but everything that every man, every person, thought, felt and experienced before you, is completely flushed out of your system. What you are left with is the simple thing—the body with extraordinary intelligence of its own.

When I went to school I studied everything, including Advaita Vedanta. Vedanta was my special subject for my Masters in Philosophy. Very early during my studies, I arrived at the conclusion that there is no such a thing as mind at all.

There was a well-known professor of psychology at the University of Madras—Dr Bose. Just a month before my final examinations, I went to him and asked him the question, 'We have studied all these six schools of psychology, this, that, and the other, exhaustively, but I don't see in all this a place for the "mind" at all.' (At that time I used to say that 'Freud is the stupendous fraud of the twentieth century.' The fact that he has lasted for a hundred years does not mean anything.) So my problem was that I did not see any mind. So I asked my professor, 'Is there a mind?' The only honest fellow that I have met in my life was not any of those holy men but that professor. He said that if I wanted my Master's degree I should not ask such uncomfortable questions. He said, 'You will be in trouble. If you want your postgraduate degree, repeat what you have memorized and you will get a degree. If you don't want it, you explore the subject on your own.' So I said, 'Goodbye.' I did not take my examination. I was lucky because at that time I had a lot of money and I told him that I had four times the income of what he had as professor of psychology. I told him that I could survive with all this money and walked out of the whole business.

But my suspicion (about the mind) persisted for a long time. You see, you cannot be free from all this so easily. You get a feeling, 'Maybe the chap (whoever is talking about the mind) knows what he is talking about. He must have something.' Looking back, the whole thing was a stupendous hoax. I told J. Krishnamurti that he was a stupendous hoax of the twentieth century along with Freud. I told him, 'You see, you have not freed yourself from this whole idea of messiahs and Theosophy.' He could not emerge clean from the whole thing.

If you think that he is the greatest teacher of the twentieth century, all right, go ahead. You are not going to have all these transformations, radical or otherwise. Not because I know your future but because there is nothing there to be transformed, really *nothing*. If you think there is and think that plums will fall into your stretched palm, good luck to you. What is the point of my telling you this? There is no such thing as enlightenment. So whether Rajneesh was enlightened or someone else is enlightened is irrelevant. It is you who assumes that somebody is, whoever he is. Good luck to you! Somebody coming and telling me, 'That I am', is a big joke. There is nothing to this whole nonsense. I have heard that there is a course in the United States: If you want enlightenment in twenty-four hours they charge you one thousand dollars and if you want it within a week, five hundred dollars and so on.

- *So you say that the mind doesn't exist. What does exist?*

This (pointing to himself) is just a computer.

- *What difference does it make whether you call it a computer or the mind?*

If you want to use that word, it is fine with me. The mind is (not that I am giving a new definition) the totality of man's experiences, thoughts and feelings. There is no such thing as your mind or my mind. I have no objection if you want to call that totality of man's thoughts, feelings and experiences by the name 'mind'. But how they are transmitted to us from generation to generation is the question. Is it through the medium of knowledge or is there any other way, say for example, through the genes? We don't have the answers yet. Then we come to the idea of memory. What is man? Man is memory. What is that memory? Is it something more than just to remember, to recall a specific thing at a specific time? To all this we have to have some more answers. How do the neurons operate in the brain? Is it all in one area?

The other day I was talking to a neurosurgeon, a very young and bright fellow. He said that memory, or rather the neurons containing memory, are not in one area. The eye, the ear, the nose, all the five sensory organs in your body have a different sort of memory. But they don't yet know for sure. So we have to get more answers. As I see it, everything is genetically controlled. That means you don't have any freedom of action. This is not what we have been taught in India—the fatalistic philosophy. When you say that there is no freedom of action, it means that you have no way of acting except through the help of the knowledge that is passed on to you. It is in that sense, I said, no action is possible without thought. Any action that is born out of thought which belongs to the totality of knowledge is a protective mechanism. It is protecting itself. It is a self-perpetuating mechanism. You are using it all the time. Every time you experience anything through the help of that knowledge, the knowledge is further strengthened and fortified. So every time you experience greed and condemn it you are adding to its momentum. You are not dealing with the actual greed, anger or desire. You are only interested in using them. Take, for example, desirelessness. You want to be free from desire. But you are not dealing with desire—only with the idea of 'how to be free from desire.' You are not dealing with something that is existing there. Whatever is there or happening there *cannot* be false. You may not like it and may condemn it because it doesn't fit into your social framework. The actions born out of desire may not fall into the society's framework which accepts certain actions and rejects others as antisocial. But you are concerned only about values. You are concerned about grappling with or fighting that which you condemn. Such a concern is born out of culture, society, norms or whatever. The norms are false and they are falsifying you....

148

- *Say there are two cities and a river in the middle. These two cities have to communicate and we have to build a bridge.*

Yes, you already have the technical know-how.

- *No. We don't.*

Someone else can give it to you.

- *Suppose no one gives it?*

Then, you don't bother about that. We don't discuss hypothetical situations. Who the original man was, how he got this idea—whether it was by trial and error—we don't bother about all that. The demand to cross over to the other side because there is a rich land... there is a kind of drive—the drive for survival. That drive is an extension of this survival mechanism that already exists in nature. You don't have to teach dogs, cats, pigs and other wild animals how to search for food, how to eat and survive. All our activity is nothing but an extension of the same survival mechanism. But in this process we have succeeded in sharpening that instrument. With the help of that instrument we are able to create everything that we are so proud of—progress, this, that and the other. You may be able to put this record player together and take it apart. This kind of knowledge can be transmitted from one person to another. But the problems which we are interested in solving—the day-to-day problems, living with someone else or living in this world—are the living problems. They are different every time. We would like to treat them on a par with mechanical problems and use that knowledge and experience (coming from dealing with the mechanical problems) to resolve problems of living. But it doesn't seem to work that way. We cannot pass these experiences on to others. It doesn't help. Your own experiences don't always help you. You tell yourself, for example, 'If I had this experience ten years ago, my life would have been different.' But ten years hence you will be telling yourself exactly the same thing, 'If I had this experience ten years ago....' But we are now at *this* point and

149

your past experiences cannot help you to resolve your problems. The leaning concerning mechanical problems is useful only in that area and not in any other. But in the area of life we don't learn anything. We simply impose our mechanical knowledge on the coming generations and destroy the possibility of their dealing with their problems in their own way.

The other day I met somebody, a leader. He had come straight from some university. He said, 'We have to help the coming generation.' He said that the future belongs to the young generation. I told him, 'What the hell are you talking about? Why do you want them to prepare to face their future? We have made a mess of this world so far and you want to pass this mess on to the younger generation. Leave them alone. If they make a mess of the whole thing, they will pay the price. Why is it your problem today? They are more intelligent than us.' Our children are more intelligent than us. First of all, we are not ready to face that situation. So we force them into this mould. But it doesn't help them.

The living organism and thought are two different things. Thought cannot conceive of the possibility of anything happening outside the field of time. I don't want to discuss time in a metaphysical sense. By time I mean yesterday, tomorrow and the day after. The instrument which has produced tremendous results in this area is unable to solve problems in the area of living. We use this instrument to achieve material results. We also apply the same thing to achieve our so-called spiritual goals. It works here but it doesn't work there. Whether it is materialistic goals or spiritual goals, the instrument we are using is matter. Therefore, the so-called spiritual goals are also materialistic in their value and in their results. I don't see any difference between the two. I haven't found any spirit there. The whole structure which we have built on the foundation of the assumed 'self' or 'spirit', therefore, collapses.

What is mind? You can give a hundred definitions. It is just a simple mechanical functioning. The body is responding to stimuli. It is only a stimulus-responding mechanism. It does not know of any other action. But through the translation of stimulus in terms of human values, we have destroyed the sensitivity of the living organism. You may talk of the sensitivity of the mind and the sensitivity of your feeling towards your fellow-beings. But it doesn't mean a thing.

● *But there must be some sensitivity without a stimulus.*

What I am talking about is the sensitivity of sensory perceptions. But what you are concerned with is sensuality. They are different things. The sensory activity of the living organism is all that exists. Culture has superimposed on it something else which is always in the field of sensuality. Whether it is a spiritual experience or any other experience, it is in the field of pleasure. So the demand for permanence is really the problem. The moment a sensation is translated as a pleasurable one, there is already a problem. The translation is possible only through the help of knowledge. But the body rejects both pain and pleasure for the simple reason that any sensation that lasts longer than its natural duration is destroying the sensitivity of the nervous system. But we are interested only in the sensual aspect of the sensory activity.

● *But we have to understand.*

What is there to understand? To understand anything, we have to use the same instrument that is used to understand this mechanical computer that is there before me. Its workings can be understood through repeatedly trying to learn or operate it. You try again and again. If it doesn't work, there is someone who can tell you how to operate it, take it apart and put it together. You yourself will learn through a repetitive process— how to change this, improve this, modify this and so on and so forth. This instrument (thought) which we have been using to understand has not helped us to understand anything except that every time we are using it, we are sharpening it. Someone asked me, 'What is philosophy? How does it help me in my day-to-day existence?' It doesn't help you in any way except that it sharpens the intellect. It doesn't in any way help you to understand life. If that (thought) is not the instrument and if there is no other instrument, then is there anything to understand? 'Intuitive perception' or 'intuitive understanding' is only a product of the same instrument. The understanding that there is nothing to understand, nothing to get, dawned on me. I was seriously wanting to understand. Otherwise I would not waste forty-nine years of my life. But when once this understanding that there is nothing to understand somehow dawned on me, the very demand to be free from anything, even from the physical demands, was not there any more. But how this happened to me I really wouldn't know. So there is no way I can share this with you because it is not in the area of experiencing things.

- *How do you place those people who don't have this burden of trying to understand life—those who are just existing in the world?*

Whether you are interested in moksha, liberation, freedom, transformation, you name it, or you are interested in happiness without one moment of unhappiness, pleasure without pain, it's the same thing. Whether one is here in India or in Russia or in America or anywhere, what people want is to have one (happiness) without the other (unhappiness). But there is no way you can have one without the other. This demand is not in the interest of the survival of this living organism. There is an extraordinarily alert quality to it (the organism). The body is rejecting all sensations. Sensations have a limited life; beyond a particular duration, the body cannot take them. It is either throwing them out or absorbing them. Otherwise they destroy the body. The eyes are interested in seeing things but not as beauty; the ears hear things but not as music. The body does not reject a noise because it is the barking of a dog or the braying of an ass. It just responds to the sound. If you call it a response to

152

the sound, then we get into trouble. So you don't even know that it is a sound. Anything that is harsh, anything that would destroy the sensitivity of the nervous system, the body cuts out. It is like a thermostat. To some extent the body has a way of saving itself from heat, cold or anything that is inimical to it. It takes care of itself for a short period and then thought helps you to take the next step to cover yourself or to move yourself away from the dangerous situation you find yourself in. You will naturally move away from the cement mixer that is making a loud noise and is destroying the sensitivity of your nervous system. The fear that you would be destroyed because the sound is bad or that you will become a nervous wreck and so on and so forth, is part of your paranoia.

● *Since there are no questions, there is no question of answers. Where then are the questions?*

All the questions are born out of the answers. But nobody wants the answers. The end of the question is the end of the answer. The end of the solution is the end of the problem. We are only dealing with solutions and not with the problems.

Actually there are no problems, there are only solutions. But we don't even have the guts to say that they don't work. Even if you have discovered that they don't work, sentimentality comes into the picture. The feeling, 'That man in whom I have placed my confidence and belief cannot con himself and con everyone else,' comes in the way of throwing the whole thing out of the window, down the drain. The solutions are still a problem. Actually there is no problem there. The only problem is in discovering the inadequacy or uselessness of all the solutions that have been offered to us. The questions naturally are born out of the assumptions and answers that we have taken for granted as real answers. But we really don't want any answers to the questions because an answer to the questions is the end of the answers. If one answer ends, all the other answers also go. You don't have to deal with ten different answers. You deal

153

with one question and that puts an end to the answer. Not that you get an answer. But there will be no questions. Yet I have to accept the reality of the world as it is imposed on me for purposes of functioning sanely.

- *When I visited a place where people who are mentally different are kept...*

Mentally different or sick or ill or....

- *I would prefer to call them mentally different because they think we are mentally different and vice versa.*

That is true.

- *The dividing line is very thin. They may be looking at us as victims. Really we don't know who is different. But biologically both of us are functioning..*

...exactly the same way...

- *... the same way. What could be the basis for calling them mentally different?*

Because we have established the so-called normal man.

- *That's what I am hinting at.*

Some people who are in the All India Institute of Mental Health at Bangalore visited me. One of them is a top neurosurgeon. I asked him the same question, 'Who is normal? Who is sane and who is insane?' He said, 'Statistically speaking, we are sane.' That was quite satisfactory to me. And then I asked him, 'Why are you putting all of them there and treating them? How much help do you give them?' He said, 'Not even two per cent of them are helped. We send them back to their homes but they keep returning.' 'Then why are you running this show?' I asked him. He said, 'The government pays the money and the families don't want to keep those people in their homes.'

So, we now move on from there to the basic question, 'Who is sane and who is insane?' Sometimes such people come to see me. Even people who are hardcore cases come to me. But the line of demarcation between them and me is very thin. The difference seems to be that they have given up, whereas I am not in conflict with society. I take it. That's all the difference. There is nothing that prevents me from fitting into the framework of society. I am not in conflict with society. When once you are—I don't like to use the word, freed from, or are not trapped in—this duality of right and wrong, good and bad, you can never do anything bad. As long as you are caught up in wanting to do only good, you will always do bad. Because the 'good' you seek is only in the future. You will be good some other time and until then you remain a bad person. So, the so-called insane have given up and we are doing them the greatest harm and disservice by pushing them to fit themselves into this framework of ours which is rotten. I don't just *say* it is rotten but it *is*.

I don't fight society. I am not even interested in changing it. The demand to bring about a change in myself isn't there any more. So, the demand to change this framework or the world at large isn't there. It is not that I am indifferent to the suffering man. I suffer with the suffering man and am happy with the happy man. People seem to get pleasure out of others' suffering. Why don't they get the same pleasure when they see a rich man throwing his weight around? They are the same. This you call pleasure and that you call jealousy or envy. But I don't see any difference between the two. I see suffering. Individually, there isn't anything that I can do. And at the same time I don't want to use this (suffering) for my self-aggrandizement, my self-fulfilment. The problem is there and we are individually responsible for it. Yet we don't want to accept the responsibility for creating the problems. The problems are not created by nature. It is we who have created the problems. There is plenty, there is bounty in nature; but we take away what rightfully belongs to everybody and then say that we should give charity. That's too absurd!

The practice of charity, started by the religious man, is what refuses to deal with the problems squarely. I may give something to a poor man because he is suffering. But unless I have something more than he has, there is no way I can help. What do I do if I don't have the means to help him? What do I do in a situation where I am totally helpless? That helplessness only makes me sit with him and cry.

- *U.G., you say that nature is not concerned with creating a perfect being but a perfect species. What do you mean by that?*

We have for centuries been made to believe that the end product of human evolution, if there is one, is the creation of perfect beings modelled after the great spiritual teachers of mankind and their behaviour patterns.

- *By great spiritual teachers you mean people like Jesus and the Buddha?*

All of them. All the great teachers—the occidental and the oriental. That is the basic problem we are confronted with. I don't think I have any special insight into the laws of nature. But if there is any such thing as an end product of human evolution (I don't know if there is such a thing as evolution but we take for granted that there is), what nature is trying to produce is not a perfect being.

- *But scientific research has revealed that there is such a thing as evolution.*

Even today some universities don't allow their students to study Darwin's *The Origin of Species*. His statements have been proved to be wrong to some extent because he said that acquired characteristics cannot be transmitted to the succeeding generations. But every time they (the scientists) discover something new, they change their theories.

Nature does not use anything as a model. It is only interested in perfecting the species. It is trying to create perfect species and not perfect beings. We are not ready to accept that. What nature

156

has created in the form of human species is something extraordinary. It is an unparalleled creation. But culture is concerned with fitting the actions of all human beings into a common mould in order to maintain the status quo—its value system. That is where the real conflict is. *This* (referring to himself) is something which cannot be fitted into that value system.

● *I began with this whole question of nature because I find in your statements a profound sense of nature, a profound sense of the absolute and primitive reality of life itself, which seems to me an extraordinarily positive force and a force for the good.*

The fundamental mistake that humanity made somewhere along the line was to experience this separateness from the totality of life. At that time there occurred in man, this self-consciousness which separated him from the life around. He was so isolated that it frightened him. The demand to be part of the totality of life around him created this tremendous demand for the ultimate. He thought that the spiritual goals of God, truth, or reality, would help him to become part of the 'whole' again. But the very attempt on his part to become one with or become integrated with the totality of life has kept him only more separate. Isolated functioning is not part of nature. This isolation has created a demand for finding out ways and means of becoming a part of nature. But thought in its very nature can only create problems and cannot help us solve them.

We don't seem to realize that it is thought that is separating us from the totality of things. The belief that this is the one that can help us to keep in tune with totality is not going to materialize. So, it has come up with all kinds of ingenuous, if I may use that word, ideas of insight and intuition.

● *Where then do we go from here? I am not going to ask you what the purpose of life is because obviously, as you were saying, that is really not a relevant question.*

No. It is a relevant question but is born out of the assumption that we know about life. Nobody knows anything about life. We have only concepts, ideations and mentations about life. Even the scientists who are trying to understand life and its origin come up only with theories and definitions of life. You may not agree with me but all thought, all thinking is dead. Thinking is born out of dead ideas. Thought or the thinking mechanism, trying to touch life, experience it, capture and give expression to it are impossible tasks.

What we are concerned about is living. Living is our relationship with our fellow-beings, with the life around. When we have everything that we can reasonably ask for, all the material comforts that you have in the West, the question naturally arises: 'Is that all?' The moment we pose that question to ourselves, we have created a problem. If that's all there is, what then is the next step to take? We do not see any meaning in our life and so we pose this question to ourselves and throw this question at all those who we think have answers.

What is the meaning of life? What is the purpose of life? It may have its own meaning; it may have its own purpose. By understanding the meaning of life and the purpose of life we are not going to improve, change, modify, or alter our behaviour patterns in any way. But there is a hope that by understanding the meaning of life, we can bring about a change. There may not be any meaning of life. If it has a meaning, it is already in operation there. Wanting to understand the meaning of life seems to be a futile attempt on our part. We go on asking these questions.

Once a very old gentleman, ninety-five years old, who was considered to be a great spiritual man and who taught the great scriptures to his followers, came to see me. He asked me two questions: 'What is the meaning of life? I have written hundreds of books telling people all about the meaning and purpose of life, quoting the scriptures and interpreting them. I haven't understood the meaning of life. You are the one who can give an me answer.' I told him, 'Look, you are ninety-five years old and you haven't understood the meaning of life. When are you going to understand the meaning of life? There may not be any meaning to life at all.' The next question he asked me was, 'I have lived ninety-five years and I am going to die one of these days. I want to know what will happen after my death.' I said, 'You may not live long enough to know anything about death. You have to die now. Are you ready to die?' As long as you are asking the questions, 'What is death?' or 'What is there after death?' you are already dead. These are all dead questions. A living man would never ask those questions.

- *Let me ask another question which is not intellectual. What should we do?*

(Laughs) For centuries we have been told what to do. Why are we asking the same question, 'What to do?' What to do in relation to what? What I am emphasizing is that the demand to bring about a change in ourselves is the cause of our suffering. I may say that there is nothing to be changed. But the revolutionary teachers come and tell us that there is something there in which you have to bring about a radical revolution. Then we assume there is such a thing as soul, spirit, or the 'I'. What I assert all the time is that I haven't found anything like the self or soul there.

This question haunted me all my life and suddenly it hit me: 'There is no self to realize. What the hell have I been doing all this time?' You see, that hits you like lightning. Once that hits you, the whole mechanism of the body that is controlled by this thought (of the 'I') is shattered. What is left is the tremendous living organism with an intelligence of its own. What you are left with is the pulse, the beat and the throb of life.

'There must be something more and we have to do something to become part of the whole thing.' Such demands have arisen because of our assumption that we have been created for a grander purpose than that for which other species on this planet have been created. That's the fundamental mistake we have made. Culture is responsible for our assuming this. We thus come to believe that the whole of creation is for the benefit of man. The demand to use nature for our purposes has created all the ecological problems. It is not such an easy thing for us to

159

deal with these problems. Again, you may say that I am a pessimist.

The point is, we have probably arrived at a place where there is no going back. What is the fate of mankind and what is one to do? Anything that is born out of thought is destructive in its nature. That is why I say very often in my conversations and interviews that thought, in its birth, in its nature, in its expression and in its action, is fascist. Thought is interested in protecting itself and is always creating frontiers around itself. And it wants to protect the frontiers. That is why we create frontiers around us: our families, our nations and then this planet.

- *Why do you speak? I pose the question to you.*

Why do I speak? (Laughter) Am I speaking? You know, it may sound very funny to you. I have nothing to say and what I am saying is not born out of my thinking. You may not accept this. But it is not a logically ascertained premise that I am putting across. It may sound very funny to you and you have put me in a very precarious position by asking me why I am talking. Am I talking? Really I am not, you see. There is nobody who is talking here. I use this simile of a ventriloquist. He is actually carrying on both sides of the dialogue but we attribute one side of it to the dummy in front of him. In exactly the same way, all your questions are born out of the answers you already have. Any answer anybody gives should put an end to your questions. But it does not. And we are not ready to accept the fact that all the questions are born out of the answers. If the questions go, the answers we take for granted also go with them. But we are not ready to throw the answers away because sentiment comes into the picture. The tremendous investment we have made and the faith we have in the teachers, are also at stake. Therefore, we are not ready to brush aside the answers.

Actually we do not want answers for our questions. The assumption that the questions are different from the questioner is also false. If the answer goes, the questioner also goes. The questioner is nothing but the answers. That is really the problem. We are not ready to accept this answer because it will put an end to the answers which we have accepted for ages as the real answers.

- *We have always been told that mankind has a certain purpose in creation. But ever since I have met you, I have begun to wonder whether this is true.*

You are the one to answer that question. We don't give a tinker's damn, to use that harsh expression, about what others have said about it. How does it matter whether what they have said is true or not. It is up to you to find out. I can say that there is no purpose and if there is any purpose, we have no way of knowing it. We only repeat what we have been told. We are made to believe that there is a purpose and that belief is what is responsible for the tragedy of mankind today. We have also been made to believe that we are created for a grander purpose, for a nobler purpose than all the species on this planet. This is not all. We are also told that all creation was created for the benefit of man. That's why we have created all these problems—ecological problems and problems of pollution. Now we are almost at a point where we are going to blow ourselves up. The planet is not in danger; we are in danger. You can pollute this planet and do all kinds of things; the planet can absorb everything—even these human bodies. If we are wiped out, nature knows what to do with the human bodies. It recycles them to maintain the energy level in the universe. That's all it is interested in. So, we are no more purposeful or meaningful than any other thing on this planet. We are not created for any grander purpose than the ants that are there or the flies that are hovering around us or the mosquitoes that are sucking our blood. I can say all this, but what do you have to say? That is more important than what I have to say. We really don't know. We have no way of knowing anything. Even the scientists—they can say what they like. How does it interest us? It does not really matter as to how this whole

161

universe was created—whether God created it or the whole thing came out of some dust and pebbles or hydrogen atoms somewhere. It is for the scientists to talk about all this and every now and then come up with new theories. They will be amply rewarded and given Nobel Prizes. But the theories don't help us to understand anything. So I really don't know if there is any purpose. I don't think that there is any. I do not see any meaning or purpose in life. A living thing, a living organism is not interested in asking the question, 'What is the purpose of life? What is the meaning of life?'

• *Does it matter if you create your own purpose?*

We are not satisfied with the daily grind of our lives, doing the same thing over and over again. We are bored. So boredom is responsible for asking the question, 'What is the purpose?' Man feels that if this is all that is there, what more is there for him to do?

• *You said that if we get bored, we invent something or the other.*

We create all sorts of things.

• *Why does man get bored?*

Because man imagines that there is something more interesting, more meaningful, more purposeful to do than what he is actually doing. Anything you want above the basic needs creates this boredom for the human being. You get the feeling, 'Is that all?'

Nature is interested only in two things—to survive and to reproduce. Anything you superimpose on that, all the cultural input, is responsible for boredom. So we have varieties of religious experience. You are not satisfied with your own religious teachings or games; so you bring in others from India, Asia or China. They become interesting because they are new. You pick up a new language and try to speak it and use it to feel more important. But basically, it is the same thing.

- *Christianity tells us to develop our talents. But you need no talent to reproduce.*

No talent is required to reproduce. Nature has done a tremendous job in creating this extraordinary piece—the body. The body does not want to learn anything from culture. It doesn't want to know anything from us. We are always interested in telling this body how to function. All our experiences, spiritual or otherwise, are the basic cause of our suffering. The body is not interested in your bliss or your ecstasies. It is not interested in your pleasure. It is not interested in anything that you are interested in. And that is the battle that is going on all the time. But there seems to be no way out.

- *We have lost touch with the original state somewhere..*

... because culture or society has placed before us the model of a perfect being. Nature does not imitate anything. It does not use anything as a model.

- *Where does it all lead us?*

It leads you to where you actually stand and therefore the questions...(Laughter)

- *Asking questions about all this is wrong?*

Don't ask this question. You have no questions and I have no questions. I have no questions at all other than the basic questions we need to ask. I am here and I want to get the bearings of this place. So I go and find out. I ask, 'Where is this station?' If I want to go to London, I ask, 'Where is the British Airways office?' These are the basic questions we need to ask to function sanely and intelligently in this world. We do have to accept the reality of the world as it is imposed on us. Otherwise we will go crazy. If you question the reality of anything that is imposed on you, you are in trouble because there is no such thing as reality, let alone the ultimate reality. You have no way of experiencing the reality of anything.

● *Well, we have invented reality...*

We have invented reality. Otherwise you have no way of experiencing the reality of anything—the reality of that person sitting there, for instance, or even (the reality of) your own physical body. You have no way of experiencing that at all except through the help of the knowledge that has been put in you. So, there may not be any such thing as reality at all, let alone the ultimate reality. I do have to accept the fact that you are a man, that she is a woman. That is all. There it stops. But what is the reality you are talking about?

● *When I was a little kid my parents and the people around told me about the bearings of my culture. I was trained not to question them.*

They don't want you to question. They force on us everything they believed in, even the things they themselves did not believe, the things that did not operate in their lives. There is no use blaming them now. We are adults. So we don't have to blame them. This is a silly idea, the Freudian idea that for everything that is happening your mother is responsible or your father is responsible. We are all grown-up people. There is no point in blaming our mothers and fathers. It is not a one-way street. Even children want to be accepted by us. We force them to fit into this framework and they want to be accepted by us. This is two-way traffic.

● *So there is no way of seeing what I think I see.*

You never see anything. The physical eye does not say anything. There is no way you can separate yourself from what you are looking at. We have only sensory perceptions. They do not tell us about that thing—for example, that it is a camera. The moment you recognize that it is a camera, and a Sony camera, at that you have separated yourself from it. So what you are actually doing is translating sensory perceptions within the framework of the knowledge you have of it. We never look at anything. It is too dangerous to look because that 'looking' destroys the continuity of thinking.

We project the knowledge we have of whatever we are looking at. Even if you say that it is an object without giving it a name, like, for example, 'camera', knowledge has already entered. It is good for a philosophy student to talk about this everlastingly, separating the object from the word, or separating the word from the thing. But actually, if you say that it is an object, you have already separated yourself from it. Even if you don't give a name to it, or recognize it as something, or call it a camera, a video camera, you have already separated yourself from it.

All that is already there in the computer. We are not conscious of the fact that we have all that information locked up there in the computer. It emerges suddenly. We think it is something original. You think that you are looking at it for the first time in your life. You are not. Supposing somebody tells you that this is something new, you are trying to relate what he calls new to the framework of the old knowledge that you have.

- *So if it is not in the computer, you cannot see it.*

You cannot. If the information is not already there, there is no way you can see. There is only a reflection of the object on the retina. Even scientists who have done a great deal of observation and research would agree. There is no way of experiencing the fact of that for yourself, because the stimulus and response are one unitary movement. The moment you separate yourself, you have created a problem. You may talk of the unity of life or the oneness of life and all that kind of stuff and nonsense. But there is no way you can create that unitary movement through any effort of yours. The only way for anyone who is interested in finding out what this is all about is to watch how this separation is occurring, how you are separating yourself from the things that are happening around you and inside you. Actually there is no difference between the outside and the inside. It is thought that creates the frontiers and tells us that this is the inside and

165

something else is the outside. If you tell yourself that you are happy, miserable, or bored, you have already separated yourself from that particular sensation that is there inside you.

- *And the cells react to what we think?*

The cells are wearing out. That's why I say that the tragedy that is facing mankind is not AIDS or cancer, but Alzheimer's disease. We are using the neurons, our memory, constantly to maintain our identity. Whether you are awake or asleep or dreaming, this process is carried on. But it is wearing you out.

You experience what you know. Without the knowledge, you have no way of experiencing anything. There is no such thing as a new experience at all. When you tell yourself that it is a new experience, it is the old that tells you that it is a new experience. Otherwise, you have no way of saying that it is something new. It is the old that tells you that it is new. And through that it is making it part of the old.

The only way it (the experience) can maintain its continuity is through the constant demand to know. If you don't know what you are looking at, the 'you' as you know yourself, the 'you' as you experience yourself, is going to come to an end. That is death. That is the only death and there is no other death.

- *That's terrifying....*

That is terrifying—the fear of losing what you know. So actually, you don't want to be free from fear. You do not want the fear to come to an end. All that you are doing—all the therapies and techniques that you are using to free yourself from fear, for whatever reason you want to be free from fear—is the thing that is maintaining the fear and giving continuity to it. So you do not want the fear to come to an end. If the fear comes to an end, the fear of what you know comes to an end. You will physically drop dead. Clinical death will take place.

- *You said that we would die if we gave up our beliefs.*

You replace one belief with another. You can't be without a belief. What you call 'you' is only a belief. If the belief goes, you go with it. That is the reason why, when you are not satisfied with one belief structure, you replace it with another.

- *Do you believe that there is nothing wrong with the world?*

I don't see anything wrong with this world because the world can't be any different. I am not interested in making a living out of telling people that the world needs some change, radical or otherwise. If you are a politician or a president of a nation, then it is a different story. Otherwise it is what it is. We being what we are, the world cannot be any different. What I say is not an abstraction. You and I living together is the world.

- *You often say, 'You are the medium through which I can express myself.'*

Yes. You are the medium through which I can express myself. There is no other way. I don't even have the impetus to express myself. You may well ask me, 'Why the hell do you talk? Why the hell do you meet people?' It is you who have brought all these people. Why do you ask me questions? That is one of the reasons why I have always avoided publicity of any kind. I don't want to promote myself, nor will I allow others to promote me.

- *What is nature?*

All of us are the same. That's what I am saying.

- *There is still a sidestepping of nature. What is that?*

Yes. That's it. That is exactly what I am saying. To sidestep the complexities of this society is one of the biggest mistakes that we are making. But there is nothing out there, you see. All these godmen, gurus and flunkies are offering us a new oasis. You will find out that it is no different from other mirages. We are

167

leaving everything for some mythical certainty offered to us. But this is the only reality and there is no other reality.

What I am emphasizing is, if your energy is not wasted in pursuit of some mythical certainties offered to us, life becomes very simple. But we end up being wasted, misled and misspent individuals. If that energy is released, what is it that we can't do to survive in the midst of these complexities created by our culture? It is very simple. The attempt to sidestep these complexities is the very thing that is causing us all these problems.

- *I get the impression that what you are proposing is in a way a revolutionary idea. When you say, 'All these flunkies and godmen,' it's a kind of revolt.*

They are giving you false comfort and that is what people want. The mainstream of the population is not interested in what I am saying. They hear what they want to hear. What I say is of no interest to them. If you say that God is redundant, it is not a rebellion against anything. You know religious thinking is outdated and outmoded. But I go one step further and say that all political ideologies are nothing but the warty outgrowth of the same religious thinking. They may call it a revolution. But revolution is only a revaluation of things. You will only end up creating another value system which may be slightly different from the value system that we want to destroy. But basically they are all the same. That is why when it (the revolution) settles down, it calls for another revolution. Even the talk of the continuous revolution of Mao Tse-tung has failed. In the very nature of things, a revolution has to settle down.

- *Coming back to what you said earlier about rejecting the whole past—experiences, thoughts, everything....*

It is not something that you can do through any effort, will or volition of yours. It has to be a miracle. Whatever has happened to me has happened despite everything I did. In fact, everything

I did only blocked it. It prevented the possibility of whatever was there to express itself. Not that I have gained anything. Only what is there is able to express itself without any hindrance, without any constraints or restraints imposed on it by society for its own reasons, for its own continuity and stability.

- *Shouldn't we have to search first?*

The search is inevitable and is an integral part of it. That is why it has turned us all into neurotics and has created this duality for us. You see, ambition is a reality, competition is a reality. But you have superimposed on that reality the idea that you should not be ambitious. It has turned us all into neurotic individuals. We want two things at the same time.

Whether he is here or in America or in Russia or anywhere else, what does man want? He wants happiness without one moment of unhappiness. He wants permanent pleasure without pain. This is the basic demand—permanence. It is this demand that has created religious thinking—God, Truth or Reality. Since things in life are not permanent, we demand that there must be something permanent. That is why these religious teachers are peddling their wares in the streets. They offer you these comforters: 'permanent happiness' or 'permanent bliss'. Are they ready to accept the fact that bliss, beatitude, immensity, love and compassion are also sensual?

- *You mean there is nothing to what Christ or Buddha said?*

Let's leave them alone. Otherwise we will all be in trouble.

- *You say that there is no individual.*

Where is the individual?

- *Well, I feel I am one.*

You are not an individual. You are doing exactly the same thing that everybody is doing.

169

- *Am I not separate from this body and that body?*

No, not at all.

- *How are we connected?*

If you accept what I am talking about, it's a very dangerous situation. Your wife goes, you see.

- *No relationship....?*

No relationship. Sorry....

- *I don't want it.*

You don't want it? 'How can you ask for this?' is all that I am saying. You are only trying to fit me into a framework by calling me an enlightened man. This fellow (U.G. points to a guest) is telling everyone, 'Jesus is living here. Why should I go to church?' He is crazy. (Laughter) Don't you think that they (the religious people) have all created a mess for us. They laid the foundation for destruction.

- *From what I understand, you don't have to reach for answers because all the answers are really coming from the answers that you already have.*

But is there any way you can free yourself from that activity?

- *Isn't it in a way a part or expression of that state?*

There is no other way I can point out the danger that is involved in your seeking whatever you are seeking. You see, there is this pleasure movement. I am not against the pleasure movement. I am neither preaching hedonism nor advocating any 'ism' or anything. What I am saying is a threat to 'you' as you know yourself and experience yourself. You necessarily fit me into that framework (of the Buddha, Jesus and others) and if you don't succeed, you will say, 'How can he be outside of it?' The way out for you is either to reject me totally, or to call me a fraud or a fake. You see, the feeling, 'How can all of them be wrong?' prevents you from listening to me. Or else you put it another way and say that the content of whatever has happened to U.G. and to them is the same but his expression is different.

- *Let us talk of the big-bang theory of the universe.*

I question the big-bang theory.

- *But you know that we were all atoms in the beginning.*

I am questioning even fundamental particles. We will never be able to find the fundamental particles.

- *In your first book you talk of the ionization of thought and an explosion.*

From then on, understanding is not through the intellect. We have developed and sharpened the intellect through years. So it (the intellect, in U.G.) understood in its own way that it is not the instrument, that there is no other instrument and that there is nothing to understand. My problem was in using this intellect to understand whatever I was looking for. But it didn't help me to understand a thing. So I was searching for some other instrument to understand, that is, intuition, this, that and the other. But I realized that this is the only instrument I have and the hope that I would understand something through some other instrument, on some other level and some other way, disappeared. It dawned on me, 'There is nothing to understand.' When this happened, it hit me like a shaft of lightning. From then on, the very demand to understand anything was over. That understanding is the one that is expressing itself now. And it cannot be used as an instrument to understand anything. It cannot be used as an instrument to guide, direct or help me, you or anybody.

- *Are you afraid of death?*

There is nothing to die here (in U.G.). The body cannot be afraid of death. The movement that is created by society or culture is what does not want to come to an end. How it came to an end (in

171

U.G.) I really don't know. What you are afraid of is not death. In fact, you don't want to be free from fear.

● *Why?*

Because when the fear comes to an end, you will drop dead.

● *Why?*

That is its nature. It is the fear that makes you believe that you are living and that you will be dead. What we do not want is the fear to come to an end. That is why we have invented all these new minds, new science, new talk, therapies, choiceless awareness and various other gimmicks. Fear is the very thing that you do not want to be free from. What you call 'yourself is fear. The 'you' is born out of fear—it lives in fear, functions in fear and dies in fear.

● *It is difficult to put you in a definite category.*

All those who come to see me have this problem of where to fit me. It is easy for them to call me a godman, enlightened man, guru and stick all those fancy labels on me. 'That is our difficulty,' they say. 'We really don't know where to fit you. It is a reflection on our intelligence,' they say. Even the philosophers talk of the impossibility of fitting me into a framework. But this doesn't necessarily make me feel superior or proud.

● *If the world can't find a label for you, what kind of label do you find for the world?*

I am quite satisfied with the world! (Laughter) Quite satisfied. The world cannot be any different. Travelling destroys many illusions and creates new illusions for us. I have discovered, to my dismay, if I may put it that way, that human nature is exactly the same whether a person is a Russian or an American or someone from somewhere else. It is as though we all speak the same language but the accent is different. I will probably speak (English) with an Andhra accent, you with a Kannada accent and someone else with a French accent. But basically human beings are exactly the same. There is absolutely no difference. I don't see any difference at all. Culture is probably responsible for the differences. We being what we are, the world cannot be any different. As long as there is a demand in you to bring about a change in yourself, you want to bring about a change in the world. Because you can't fit into the framework of culture and its value system, you want to change the world so that you can have a comfortable place in it.

• *What I understand from what you are saying is that we are operating under a value system, whether it is good or bad.*

You see, both good and bad, right and wrong, are not the reverse of a coin but are the same coin. They are like the two ends of the spectrum. One cannot exist independent of the other. When once you are finished with this duality, (I am using the word with much caution as I don't really like to use it) when you are no longer caught up in the dichotomy of right and wrong or good and bad, you can never do anything wrong. As long as you are caught up in it, the danger is that you will always do wrong; and if you don't do wrong, it is because you are a frightened 'chicken'. It is out of this cowardice that religious thinking is born.

• *You were saying in some context that anger is not bad and that it cannot do any harm.*

Anger is like an outburst of energy. It is like the high tide and the low tide in the sea. The question, 'What to do with anger?' is something put in there by culture, because society considers an angry man a threat to its status quo, to its continuity.

• *Well, you are not a threat then.*

I am not a threat. I am not a threat because I cannot, you see, conceive of the possibility of anything other than this. I am not interested in changing anything. You are the one that is all the time talking of bringing about a change. At the same time, everything around you and inside of you is in a flux. It is constantly changing. Everything around you is changing; yet you don't want change. You see, that's the problem. Your unwillingness to change is really the problem and you call it tradition. You dub 'unwillingness to change with the changing things' a great tradition.

- *Why does nature deliberately want to first create and then destroy?*

Because nothing is ever born and nothing ever dies. What has created the space between creation and destruction or the time between the two, is thought. In nature there is no death or destruction at all. What occurs is the reshuffling of atoms. If there is a need or necessity to maintain the balance of energy in this universe, death occurs. You may not like it. Earthquakes may be condemned by us. Surely they cause misery to so many thousands and thousands of people. And all this humanitarian activity around the world—sending planeloads of supplies is really a commendable act. It helps those who are suffering there and those who have lost their property. But it is the same kind of activity that is responsible for killing millions and millions of people. What I am saying is that the destructive, war-making movement and the humanitarian movement on the other hand— are both born from the same source.

In the long run, earthquakes and the eruption of volcanoes are part of nature's way of creating something new. Now, you know, something strange is happening in America—the volcanic eruptions. Some unknown forms of life are growing there in that very thing which was destroyed. Of course, I am not saying that you should not do anything to help those people.

The self-consciousness that occurred in the human species may be a necessary thing. I don't know. I am not claiming that I have a special insight into the workings of nature. Your question can be answered only that way. You see for yourself. That's why I say that the very foundation of human culture is to kill and to be killed. It has happened so. If one is interested in looking at history right from the beginning, the whole foundation of humanity is built on the idea that those who are not with us are against us. That's what is operating in human thinking. So, to kill and to be killed in the name of God, represented by the church in the West and all the other religious thinking here in the East, was the order of the day. That's why there is this fundamentalism here in this country now. The Chinese—what horrors they have committed, you will be surprised. They killed scholars and religious people. They burned and buried the books of Confucius and other teachers. Today the political ideologies represented by the state are responsible for the killing of people. And they claim that what they are doing is the result of some great revolution that they had started. Revolution is nothing but the revaluation of our values. It really does not mean anything. After a while it settles down and that is why they are talking of Glasnost there (in the Soviet Union). But it does not really mean anything there. Gorbachev is going to create a hundred Punjabs in that country.

- *We do seem to have a need to search and find something.*

The body does not want to learn anything or know anything because it has that intelligence—native, innate intelligence—that helps it to survive. If this body is in a jungle, it will survive; if it doesn't, it's gone. But it will fight to the last. That's just the way the human body functions. If there is some danger to it, the body throws in everything that is available and tries to protect itself. If it cannot, it gives in. But in a way the body has no death. The atoms in it are put together and what happens at death is a reshuffling of the atoms. They will be used somewhere else. So the body has no birth or death because it has no way of experiencing that it is alive or that it will be dead tomorrow.

- *We always feel that we have to improve ourselves or find a way out of our misery. Everyone thinks that he or she has to change or get to a higher level. What is your view on the matter?*

The moment we ask the question, 'Is there something more to our life than what we are doing?' we set the whole questioning

175

mechanism going. Unfortunately, what has created this interest in the Western nations is the so-called Hippy generation. When they tried drugs, the drugs produced a change in what they called their 'levels of consciousness'. For the first time they experienced something outside the area of their normal experiencing structure. When once we experience something extraordinary, which actually it is not, we look around for varieties of experiences.... more and more of the same. That has created a market for all those people from the Eastern countries—India, China and Japan. They flood into these countries and promise to provide answers for their questions. But actually they are selling shoddy goods. What people are interested in is not some answers to their problems but some comforters. As I said before, they are selling ice packs to numb the pain and make you feel comfortable. Nobody wants to ask the basic question: What is the real problem? What is it that they want? What are they looking for? And this (situation) is taken advantage of by the people from the East. If there is anything to what they claim (that they have the answers and solutions for the problems that we are all facing today) it doesn't seem to be evident in the countries from where they come. The basic question which Westerners should throw at them is: 'Have your answers helped the people of your own countries? Do your solutions operate in your own lives?' Nobody is asking them these questions. The hundred different techniques that they offer to you have not been subjected to test. You don't have any statistical evidence to prove that there is something to what they claim. They exploit the gullibility of the people. When once you have everything that you need, the material goodies, you look around and ask the question, 'Is that all there is to it?' And that situation is exploited by those people. They don't have any answers for the problems facing us today.

What is responsible for the human tragedy or the malady that we are confronted with today is that we are interested in maintaining the identities that are created by our culture. We have tremendous faith in the value system that is created by our culture or society or whatever you want to call it. We never question that. We are only interested in fitting ourselves into that value system. It is that demand from society or culture to fit us all into that value system that is the cause of man's tragedy.

Somewhere along the line there occurred in human consciousness the demand to find out the answers for loneliness, the isolation that human beings suffer from the rest of the species on this planet. I don't even know if there is any such thing as evolution. If there is, somewhere along the line in that evolutionary process man separated or isolated himself from the rest of creation on this planet. In that isolation, he felt so frightened that he demanded some answers, some comfort, to fill that loneliness, that isolation from the rest of the life around him. Religious thinking was born out of this situation and it has gone on for centuries. But it has not really helped us to solve the problems created by mankind. Even the political systems that we have today are nothing but the warty outgrowth of the spiritual, religious thinking of man. All that has failed and a void has been created. There has been a total failure of our political and economic ideologies.

There is a tremendous danger facing mankind today. The void created by the failure of all these ideologies will be taken advantage of by the church. They will preach and shout that we all have to go back to Jesus or go back to the great traditions of our own countries. But what has failed for them is not going to help us to solve our problems.

When some psychologists and scientists came to see me, I made this very clear to them, 'You have come to the end of your tether. If you want answers for your problems, you have to find them within your own framework and not look elsewhere, especially not in the ancient dead cultures of the past.' Going back or looking back to those systems and techniques that have failed us is only going to put us on a wrong track, on a merry-go-round.

● *If we have created the problems, we are also fighting them.*

Yes. But we are not ready to accept the fact that what has created the problems cannot itself solve them. What we are using to solve our problems is what we call 'thought'. But thought is a protective mechanism. Thought is only interested in maintaining the status quo. We may talk of change but when the time actually comes for us to change things, we are not ready for it. We insist that change must always be for the better and not for the worse. We have a tremendous faith in the mechanism that has created the problems for us. After all, that is the only instrument that we have at our disposal. But actually it cannot help us at all. It can only create problems, not solve them. We are not ready to accept this fact because accepting it will knock out the whole foundation of human culture. We want to replace one system with another. But the whole structure of culture is pushing us in the direction of completely annihilating all that we have built with tremendous care.

We don't want to be free from fear. Anything you do to free yourself from fear is what is perpetuating the fear. Is there any way we can be freed from fear? Fear is something that cannot be handled by thought; it is something living. So we want to put on our gloves and try to touch it, play with it. All that we want to do is to play games with it and talk about freeing ourselves from fear. Or go to this therapist or that, or follow this technique or that. But in that process, what we are actually doing is strengthening and fortifying the very thing that we are trying to be free from.

● *So we live in a society based on fear. Even our institutions—police, banks, doctors, insurance and everything we have created—are based on fear?*

Yes, fear. But what is the point in telling ourselves that we are going to be freed from fear? If that fear comes to an end, you will drop dead, physically! Clinical death will take place! Of course, you and your fear are not two different things. It is comforting to believe that you and fear are two different things. You are frightened of certain things or you do not want this or that to happen. You want to be free from fear. But there is no way you free yourself from it. If the fear comes to an end, 'you' as you know yourself, 'you' as you experience yourself, are going to come to an end, and you *are not* ready for that sort of thing.

The plain fact is that if you don't have a problem, you create one. If you don't have a problem, you don't feel that you are living. So the solutions that we have been offered by the teachers, in whom we have tremendous faith, are not really the solutions. If they were the solutions, the problems wouldn't be there at all. If there are no solutions for the problems, even then the problems wouldn't be there. We would like to live with those problems and if we are free from one problem, we create another.

• *Does meditation affect the body?*

You put your body to unnecessary torture.

• *The body suffers?*

Yes, the body suffers. It is not interested in your techniques of meditation, which actually are destroying the peace that is already there. It is an extraordinarily peaceful organism. It does not have to do anything to be in a peaceful state. By introducing this idea of a peaceful mind, we set in motion a sort of battle and the battle goes on and on. But what you feel, what you experience as the peaceful state of mind, is a war-weary state of mind created by your thought. Once you experience some peaceful state of mind, you want more and more of the same. This creates problems for the body.

• *This week I hear there is going to be an important meeting here. Scientists from all over the world, from different disciplines— people from the spiritual world and the world of industry and economics—are for the first time coming together to talk about the similarities among their respective disciplines, instead of differences. All of them now seem to feel that they should support*

> *each other instead of focusing their energies only on differences*
> *and the compartments that they create in their minds.*

First of all, the scientists, by looking or asking for help from all
these religious people, are committing the biggest of all blunders.
They have come to the end of their tether. If they have problems
in their system, they have to solve them by and for themselves.
These religious people have no answers for the problems created
by scientific thinking. I do not know if by coming together and
exchanging their views or giving speeches they are going to
achieve anything. I may sound very cynical when I say that
nothing is going to come out of it except that they will make
speeches and feel comfortable that they are trying to understand
each other's point of view. When you say something to someone,
he will say that that is your point of view. But he does not realize
that his also is a point of view. So, how can there be any
communication between those two people who have different
points of view? The whole purpose of the conversation or
dialogue is only to convert the other man to your point of view.
If you have no point of view, there is no way he can convince or
convert you to his point of view. So this dialogue is between two
points of view and there is no way you can reconcile them.

The conference would be very interesting (Laughs). They can
all come together, talk about that (what is common to their
different disciplines) and exchange their views and that would
be that. It would be something like the United Nations. (The
United Nations is the biggest joke of this century. If each one is
trying to assert his own rights there, how can there be a United
Nations?) The problem is that thought creates frontiers
everywhere. That's all it can do.

• *Do you think that the discovery of the laws of nature and the*
  enormous money that is invested in it will ultimately help mankind?

Even if we discover the laws of nature, for whatever reason we
are interested in doing so, ultimately they are used to destroy
everything that nature has created. This propaganda that the

planet is in danger is media hype. Everybody has in fact forgotten about it. Actually it is not the planet that is in danger but us. We are not ready to face this situation squarely. We must not look for answers in the past or in the great heritage of this or that nation. And we must not look to the religious thinkers. They don't have any answers. If the scientists look to religious leaders for their solutions, they are committing the biggest blunder. Religious people put us all on the wrong track and there is no way you can reverse the process.

- *What do you think we should do then?*

I am not here to save mankind or prophesy that we are all heading toward a disaster. I am not talking of an Armageddon, nor am I prophesying that there is going to be a paradise on this planet. Nothing of the sort; there is not going to be any paradise. It is the idea of a paradise, the idea of creating a heaven on this earth, that has turned this beautiful paradise that we already have on this planet into a hell. We are solely responsible for what is happening. And the answers for our problems cannot come from the past and its glory or from the great religious teachers of mankind. Those teachers will naturally claim that you all have failed and that they have the answers for the problems that we are confronted with today. I don't think that they have any answers. We have to find the answers, if any, for ourselves and by ourselves.

- *I have read somewhere, 'Your image is your best friend.'*

(Laughs) That's a sales pitch; it's very interesting. In fact, it's the other way around: the image we have is responsible for our problems. What, after all, is the world? The world is the relationship between two individuals. But that relationship is based on the foundation of 'What do I get out of a relationship?' Mutual gratification is the basis of all relationships. If you don't get what you want out of a relationship, it goes sour. What there is in the place of what you call a 'loving relationship' is hate.

181

When everything fails, we play the last card in the pack, and that is 'love'. But love is fascist in its nature, in its birth, in its expression and in its action. It cannot do us any good. We may talk of love but it doesn't mean anything. The whole music of our age is around that song, 'Love, Love, Love...'

- *Do you like television?*

Yes, I do watch television. I turn the sound off and watch the movement only. I like to watch the commercials because most of the commercials are more interesting than the programs. If people can fall for the commercials, they can fall for anything that these religious people are selling today in the market. How can you fall for those commercials? But they are very interesting. It is not the commercials nor what they are selling that interests me but the techniques of salesmanship. They are amazing and more interesting—I am fascinated by those techniques. I am not influenced by what they are selling. If they had customers like me, they would soon be out of business. I don't buy anything they are selling.

- *Soon they will have commercials in Russia and Eastern Europe.*

That's what has happened in Russia. It is not your (American) ideas of democracy or freedom that have won the country over to your side. It was Coca Cola, I think, in China, and Pepsi Cola in Russia. Why do they have to sell organically grown potato chips there in Russia? I want to know. They have also opened a McDonald's there. That's all that the West can offer to them. That is how it (commercialism) is spreading. If America survives, if we survive and if we don't destroy ourselves through our own idiotic ways of living and thinking, the American way of life is going to be the way of life. Even in the Third World countries, including India, we have supermarkets. They are very innovative, the Americans. So, it (commercialism) is spreading all over.

- *What is your attitude to money?*

Money is the most important factor in our lives. They say that money is the root cause of all evil. But actually it is not the root cause of evil; it is the root cause of our existence, of our survival. I sometimes say that if you worship that God, the money God, you will be amply rewarded. If you worship the other God— whether He exists or not is anybody's guess—you will be stripped of everthing you have and He will leave you naked in the streets. It is better to worship the money God. Tell me one person who is not thinking of money. Not one person on this planet. Even the holy ones who talk about their indifference to money are concerned about it. How do you think they will get ninety-two Rolls Royces? You try and buy one Rolls Royce car; you will know how difficult it is. For the religious people it is easy, because other people deny themselves and give their money to them. So you can be rich at another man's expense. How much money you need is a different matter. Each one has to draw his own line. But when once your goals and needs are the same, then the problem is very simple.

- *So you stay more or less here, in this moment and deal with what happens right now.*

When once that becomes a reality in your life, it becomes very simple to live in this world, the complex and complicated world created by us all. We are all responsible for this world. When once this demand to change yourself into something better, something other than what you actually are, is not there, the demand to change the world also comes to an end. I don't see anything wrong with the world. What is wrong with this world? The world can't be any different from what we are. If there is a war going on within us, we cannot expect a peaceful world around us. We will certainly create war. You may say that it all depends upon who is responsible for the war. It is simply a point of view as to who is calling another a warmonger and himself the peace-monger. The peace-mongers and the warmongers sail in the same boat. It is something like the pot calling the kettle black or the other way around: the kettle calling the pot black.

• *We are stuck in words and ideas.*

We dare not leave that 'what is' alone. It implies that you are still grappling with what you romantically phrase as 'what is'. It is like dealing with the unknown. There is no such thing as the unknown.

The known is still trying to make the unknown part of the known. It is a game that we play. That is how we fool ourselves in our approach to problems. All our positive approaches have failed and we have invented what is called the 'negative approach'. But the negative approach is still interested in the same goal that the positive approach is interested in.What is necessary for us is to free ourselves from the goal. When once we are freed from the (of solving problems) the question of whether it is a positive approach or a negative approach does not even arise.

• *So in nature, the positive and the negative don't exist at all?*

They don't exist at all. If they do, they exist in the same frame. That is what all these scientist are talking about. If you observe the universe, there is chaos in it. The moment you say there is chaos, in the same frame, there is also order. So, you cannot, for sure, say that there is order or chaos in the universe. Both of them are occurring simultaneously. That is the way the living organism also operates. The moment thought is born, it cannot stay there. Thought is matter. When once the matter that is necessary for the survival of the living organism is created, that matter becomes part of energy. Similarly life and death are simultaneous processes. It is thought that has separated and created the two points of birth and death. Thought has created this space and this time. But actually, birth and death are simultaneous processes.

You cannot say that you are alive or dead. But if you ask me the question, 'Are you alive?' I would certainly say, 'I am alive.'

So my answer is the common knowledge you and I have about how a living being functions. That is how I say that I am a living being and not a dead person. But we give tremendous importance to these ideas. We sit and them everlastingly and produce a tremendous structure of thought around them.

- *Does that mean that the scientists who are coming next week need to recognize the fact that there is no way out?*

If they could, then they wouldn't give any solutions and wouldn't offer anything. There is no way out. The solution for their problems is to accept the fact that there is no way out. And out of that (acceptance) something can come.

- *Even if you understand the right or wrong of the matter....?*

It is not a question of calling it right or wrong. There is no way out. Anything you do to get out of this trap which you yourself have created is strengthening and fortifying it. So, you are not ready to accept the fact that you have to give up. A complete, total surrender. I don't like using that word 'surrender' because it has certain mystical overtones. It is a state of hopelessness which says that there is no way out of this situation. Any movement, in any direction, on any level, is taking you away from that. Maybe something can happen there, we don't know. But even that hope that something will happen is still a hope.

- *Sometimes it so happens that when you give up everything the problem gets automatically resolved.*

Yes. This happens to all those who are working out some mathematical or scientific problem. They go to sleep when they are exhausted and that gives some time for the mechanism that is involved to give an answer. It is not some miraculous thing. You give some time for the computer to work out a solution to your problem. On its own it comes out with the answer but only if there is an answer. If there is no answer, then that is the end of the story.

- *So you let go? It is very difficult to frame questions because of the problem of language.*

Our language structure is such that there is no way you can be free from a dualistic approach to problems. Again, I'm not happy using the word 'dualistic' because it has religious connotations.

- *What is the relationship between words and reality?*

None. There is nothing beyond words.

- *Is life difficult?*

Life is difficult. So discipline sounds very attractive to people. With great admiration we say, 'He has suffered a lot.' Our entire religious thinking is built on the foundation of suffering. If not for religion, you suffer for the cause of your country in the name of patriotism....

- *For your family....*

Those who impose that kind of discipline on us are sadists. But unfortunately we are all being masochists in accepting that. We torture ourselves in the hope of achieving something... We are slaves to our ideas and beliefs. We are not ready to throw them out. If we succeed in throwing them out, we replace them with another set of beliefs, another body of discipline. Those who are marching into the battlefield and are ready to be killed today in the name of democracy, in the name of freedom, in the name of communism, are no different from those who threw themselves to the lions in the arenas. The Romans watched with great joy. How are we different from them? Not a bit. We love it. To kill and to be killed is the foundation of our culture.

- *Wherever you go people comment on your demeanour and your physical appearance. How do you keep fit? I know you don't practise yoga or any other form of exercise.*

I don't exercise at all. The only walking I do is from my place to the post office, which is about a half a kilometre or even a quarter of a mile away from where I live. But I used to walk a lot. I am afraid that I may have to pay a heavy price for all the walking that I did before. You know, I am not competent enough to offer any comments on these matters. But one thing I want to assert is that for some reason this body of ours does not want to know anything or learn anything from us. No doubt we have made tremendous advances in the field of medical technology. But are they really helping the body? That is one of the basic questions that we should ask.

- *Can we actually help the body?*

I think what we are actually doing is trying to treat the symptoms of what we call a disease. But my question is, and I always throw this question at the people who are competent enough— the doctors—what is health? What is disease? Is there any such thing as disease for this body? You know, we translate the 'malfunctioning'(of the body) to mean that there is some imbalance in the natural rhythm of the body. Not that we know what the rhythm of the body actually is. But we are so frightened that we run to a doctor or to somebody who we think is in the know of things and can help us. We do not give a chance for the body to work out the problems created by the situation we find ourselves in. We do not give enough time for the body. We do not know whether our bodies are healthy or unhealthy.

- *We do (know). We translate health into being free from any symptoms. If I don't have a pain in my knee, then I don't have a disease there. We indulge in medical research in order to gather useful knowledge that could be applied when there is a pain in the knee.*

But what is pain? I am not asking a metaphysical question. To me pain is a healing process. But we do not give enough chance or opportunity to the body to heal itself or help itself, to free itself from what we call pain.

- *You are saying that all the things we do are in some way or other probably hindering the body from living longer, healthier and happier. So we must leave the body alone.*

Yes, leave the body alone. Don't get frightened and rush here, there and everywhere. In any case, there is no way you can conquer death at all.

- *I get what you say. People are trying subconsciously to prevent death.*

Our pushing people into a value system is a very undesirable thing, you know. You want to push everybody into a value system. We never question that this value system which we have cherished for centuries may be the very thing that is responsible for our misery.

- *Yes, that may be the very thing that is generating disease.*

Disease and conflict in our lives. We really don't know. Another thing I want to emphasize is that what we call identity, the 'I', the 'me', the 'you', the 'centre', the 'psyche', is artificially created. It does not exist at all.

- *It is also a cultural phenomenon.*

Yes, it has been culturally created. We are doing everything possible to maintain that identity, whether we are asleep, awake, or dreaming. The instrument that we use to maintain this identity strengthens, fortifies and gives continuity to it. The constant use of memory is wearing you out. We really do not know what memory is but we are constantly using it to maintain that non-existent identity of ours.

- *So we keep coming back to this point that thought itself seems to be the enemy, the interloper.*

It is our enemy. Thought is a protective mechanism. It is interested in protecting itself at the expense of the living organism.

- *You are saying that thought is the thing that causes people's worries.*

It's thought that is creating all our problems and it is not the instrument to help us solve the problems created by itself.

- *You talk of a state that is entirely natural to man. I want to know if that natural state can be acquired by effort—if it can be acquired at all—or is it simply a chance occurrence?*

When I use the term 'natural state', it is not a synonym for 'enlightenment', 'freedom', or 'God-realization' and so forth. Not at all. When the totality of mankind's knowledge and experience loses its stranglehold on the body—the physical organism—then the body is allowed to function in its own harmonious way. Your natural state is a biological, neurological and physical state.

- *Then I presume that you agree with modern science, that it is the genes that control our behaviour and destinies.*

I can make no definitive statements about the part genes play in the evolutionary process but at the moment it appears that Darwin was at least partially wrong in insisting that acquired characteristics could not be genetically transmitted. I think that they are transmitted in some fashion. I am not competent enough to say whether the genes play any part in the transmission.

Anyway, the problem lies in our psyche. We function in a thought-sphere and not in our biology. The separative thought structure, which is the totality of man's thoughts, feelings, experiences and so on—what we call 'psyche' or 'soul' or 'self—is creating the disturbance. That is what is responsible for our misery; that's what continues the battle that is going on there (in the human being) all the time. This interloper, the thought sphere, has created your entire value system. The body is not in the least interested in values, much less a value system. It is only concerned with intelligent moment-to-moment *survival*, and nothing else. Spiritual 'values' have no meaning to it. When, through some miracle or chance you are freed from the hold of

189

thought and culture, you are left with the body's natural functions and nothing else. It then functions without the interference of thought. Unfortunately, the servant, which is the thought structure that is there, has taken possession of the house. But he can no longer control and run the household. So he must be dislodged. It is in this sense that I use the term 'natural state', without any connotation of spirituality or enlightenment.

- *Still, for most of us, many questions remain. We want to somehow find out what life is, if it has any meaning.*

Life is something which you cannot capture, contain and give expression to. Energy is an expression of life. What is death? It is simply a condition of the human body. There is no such thing as death. What you have are ideas about death, ideas which arise when you sense the absence of another person. Your own death, or the death of your near and dear ones, is not something you can experience. What you actually experience is the void created by the disappearance of another individual and the unsatisfied demand to maintain the continuity of your relationship with that person for a non-existent eternity. The arena for the continuation of all these 'permanent' relationships is the tomorrow—heaven, next life and so on. These things are the inventions of a mind interested only in its undisturbed, permanent continuity in a 'self'-generated, fictitious future. The basic method of maintaining the continuity is the incessant repetition of the question, 'How? How? How? How am I to live? How can I be happy? How can I be sure I will be happy tomorrow?'This has made life an insoluble dilemma for us. We want to know and through that knowledge we hope to continue with our miserable existence forever.

- *So many people in this society are interested in ....*

Society cannot be interested in what I am talking about. Society is, after all, two individuals or a thousand of them put together. Because I am a direct threat to you individually—as you know and experience yourself—I am also a threat to society. How can society possibly be interested in this sort of thing? Not a chance. Society is the sum of relationships and despite what you may find agreeable to believe, all these relationships are sordid and horrible. This is the unsavoury fact; take it or leave it. You cannot help but superimpose over these horrible, ugly relationships a soothing fictitious veneer of 'loving', 'compassionate', 'brotherly' and 'harmonious' or some other fancy notion.

• *I often ask myself, what are my obligations to my fellow-beings?*

None whatsoever.... Sorry. All you are interested in is self-fulfilment, the ultimate goal of a Nobel Prize and power. I am very sorry. Personally, you may not be interested in that kind of thing. That's all. I encourage that kind of pursuit. Of course, you scientists have made all this comfort-bearing technology possible and in that sense, I, like all those who enjoy the benefits of modern technology, am indeed indebted. I don't want to go back to the days of the spinning wheel and the bullock cart. That would be too silly, too absurd. Pure science is nothing but speculation. Scientists discuss formulas endlessly and provide us with some equations. But I am not at all taken in by the 'march of progress' and all that rot. The first trip I made to the US in the Thirties took more than a full day and we had to stop everywhere. Later, the same trip took eighteen hours, then twelve hours and even more recently, six hours and three and so on. And if the supersonic jets are put to commercial use, we may be able to make the trip in one-and-a-half hours. All right, that's progress. But the same technology that makes fast international travel possible is making ever more deadly military fighter planes. How many of these planes are we using for faster and more comfortable travel from one point to another? And how many more hundreds of planes are we using to destroy life and property? You call this progress? I don't know. As the comforts increase, we come to depend upon them, and are loath to give up anything we have.

191

Within a particular frame I say it is progress. I am now living in an air-conditioned room. My grandfather used a servant who sat in the hot sun and pulled the punkah and before that we used a palm leaf hand fan. As we move into more and more comfortable situations, we don't want to give up anything.

- *Some would argue that a humanity restored, not through science but through love, is our only hope.*

I still maintain that it is not love, compassion, humanism, or brotherly sentiments that will save mankind. No, not at all. It is the sheer terror of extinction that can save us, if anything can. Each cell of a living organism cooperates with the cell next to it. It does not need any sentiment or declarations of undying love to do so. Each cell is wise enough to know that if its neighbour goes, it also goes. The cells stick together not out of brotherhood, love and that kind of thing but out of the urgent drive to survive *now*. It is the same with us but only on a larger scale. Soon we will all come to know one simple thing: if I try to destroy you, I will also be destroyed. We see the superpowers of today signing arms-control pacts, rushing to sign no-first-strike accords and the like. Even the big bully boys, who have among them controlled the world's resources, no longer talk about a successful nuclear war. Even the arrogant, swashbuckling United States has changed its tune. It no longer talks—as it did twenty years ago under Dulles and other cold warriors—of massive retaliation. If you read the *Time* magazine now, it doesn't talk about the United States as the mightiest, the richest, the most powerful and the most invincible of all nations. It refers to it as 'one of the superpowers.'

- *Somehow I do feel a responsibility to my fellow-beings, not in a philosophical or spiritual sense but in a more fundamental sense. You see someone starving and you would like to do something about it.*

As an individual you can. But the moment you start an institution and the institutions try to enlist individuals' help, then the whole thing is destroyed. You have to organize and there is no other way. That means my plan and your plan. It means war.

• *As you would say, the urge to help is a result of my culture. When you see someone sad, tears come to your eyes. We empathize ....*

We translate that as sadness and the tears follow as a sentimental effect. But the tear ducts are there to protect your eyes from going blind, to keep them lubricated and cleansed and not to respond to the suffering of others. This may be a crude way of putting things but that's the fact of the matter.

• *I would like to put to you one more question somewhat unrelated to what we have been discussing: This is a question many people would like to ask you. What is your opinion regarding the existence of God?*

Oh my God! You really want my answer? To me the question of whether God exists or not is irrelevant and immaterial. We have no use for God. We have used God to justify the killing of millions and millions of people. We exploit God. That's the positive aspect of it, not the negative. In the name of God we have killed more people than in the two world wars put together. In Japan, millions of people died in the name of the sacred Buddha. Here in India, five thousand Jains were massacred in a single day. This is not a peaceful nation! You don't want to read your own history— it's full of violence from the beginning to the end.

• *U.G., to most people, and at times to me, you sound totally absurd— I can't understand much of what you say and neither can people who have read your books at times make out what you are and yet there's something that makes us take notice of you. It's the manner in which you say whatever you say. There's a strange kind of certainty with which you say things. What have you stumbled into?*

There is no way I can tell you how I stumbled into what I stumbled into—the 'how' and 'what' are problems that confront us. You don't realize that it is the question which has created the problem

193

and you have not accepted the fact that solutions are responsible for the problems.

- *Lets talk about the Valiums that we have surrounded ourselves with. Success, the quest for moksha etc., relationships—these are our Valiums but of late, I see so many people I know heading for a nervous breakdown. What is the glue that we can get to hold us together? Is there a glue that can keep mankind together?*

What happens if the whole thing falls apart? Why are you frightened of the chaos that may not result? Why are you frightened that there will be chaos? Why do you want to hold on to things exactly the way they are? You may talk of change but you are not really interested in change. What you are interested in is change for the better but you don't realize that change is occurring all the time. Your unwillingness to change with a changing environment is responsible for the demand for a glue. There are so many people marketing all kinds of glues but they will not help you at all....

- *You see no hierarchy in the glue, religion, sexual pursuit, alcoholism. Whether you use one or the other, its okay by you but for us in society, going into a church or mosque is acceptable while going into a whore house or bar to find respite is condemned.*

To you the demand for all those things is exactly the same but the society in which we are living today considers certain actions as socially acceptable and certain other actions anti-social. You may call yourself a rebel, a revolutionary and break away, but you will certainly create another form no different and distinct from the structure in which you are caught up. There is no such thing as a revolution at all. What you call revolution is only a revaluation of your value system. The basic problem is the impossibility of fitting yourself into the framework, so you want to create another kind of a framework, a new way of thinking but basically and actually and fundamentally there is no difference between these two.

- *In the sexual act there is a possibility of experiencing that oneness. Perhaps that is why sex has such a tremendous hold on our lives...*

The idea that both man and woman can have the peak experience at the same time is false because there is no way that you can prepare yourself to have that moment of oneness in sexual activity. Probably animals have it because there is no foreplay. Whether it is sex or God, once you are stuck in it there is no way you can get out. That is the reason for the existence of tantric sex. Mankind is committed to suicide. It may sound very pessimistic to you but there is no way you can reverse it. Whatever is created has got to go. Birth and death are simultaneous processes and there is no way you can separate the two.

- *So I cannot use this man called U.G., or what he says, to make things permanent?*

It is absurd on your part to demand permanence when there is no such thing as permanence at all. Religious people sell shoddy goods in the market-place, make you believe that they have some way of satisfying your demand. Although they talk of impermanence, all the time they are suggesting that there is a way that things can be permanent. Nothing is permanent in nature.

- *It's all right to write of transience, to discuss the concept but when man is face to face with his own extinction....*

He is not ready to face the fact that it is going to come to an end. As far as the living organism is concerned there is nothing permanent. Your body, which you have taken for granted, belongs to you. It is not demanding any permanence but is, in a way, permanent. What you call death is a recycling process and that is the only way that nature can enrich energy levels....

- *So death is essential for the continuity of life....*

Not in the sense in which you think of the continuity of life. In a way we know that it is coming to an end, which is why we have invented the 'life after' reincarnation theory.

- *So first you dream, then you die and life seems like one long process of getting tired....*

Not tired....

- *To us life seems like a very long process of getting tired ....*

Because you have established a goal and all that you are doing is trying to achieve that goal when there is no goal there at all.

- *Is there is no summing up, no full stops?*

There is no way you can sum up what we have discussed.

Part III

A Taste of Death
Thirty Days with U.G. in Gstaad, Switzerland

Summer 1995

10 July 1995 ... DAY ONE

Zurich is hot, very hot. Europe is going through the worst heat wave in years. U.G. receives me at the airport with Sushma (the French ex-Rajneeshi who was once a pharmacist). We drive to the hotel which is situated in a seedy area. Our hotel is sandwiched between two sex shops. We have lunch in a vegetarian restaurant. Food there is sold by weight. Late in the evening, Mario arrives with 'Gorgeous' (Lisa). Mario and Lisa, too, were Rajneeshis not very long ago. 'I could not sell the images of the goddess Lakshmi, nor could I sell the Buddhas at the fair in Munich,' says Mario on arrival. U.G. laughs.

We're leaving for Gstaad early in the morning. 'Mahesh is a workaholic,' says U.G., 'He's lost without his work. How will he survive for a month in Gstaad?' 'I must write an article on workaholism,' I say to myself. Late in the evening, as I hear the church bells ring, I wonder what time it must be back in India. As I wander in the streets of Zurich, I find that I am looking more at kids and babies in their prams than at the so-called sexy chicks. I wonder if I am going through my mid-life crisis. What else do you expect at 46?

Sounds of prostitutes fighting in the streets mingle with the alarm of a car. I toss and turn all night. Finally, as I pass out, the words of U.G. echo: 'If you don't tell yourself where you are, how do you know that you are in Zurich?' And if I don't tell myself this is me who is sleeping in the bed, how would I know it is me?

I'm struck with fear.

11 July ... DAY TWO

As we check out of the hotel at dawn, we find there is no one to close our account. At last, a bulky drunk porter helps us out. 'For a porter he did a good job as a receptionist,' says U.G. as we step out into a cool dawn making our way through the deserted but not so clean streets of Zurich. The city's tower clock shows ten minutes to six. Zurich is waking up to a new day. The blue trams in the city square remind me of the red trams of my childhood in Bombay.

We are driving along in Sushma's car. 'There's nothing that money can't buy,' says U.G., reacting to the old Beatles' number *'Can't buy me love'* which is playing on Sushma's tape recorder. 'Look at their own lives. The Beatles could not love one another and ultimately had to split up. Singing songs of love to make money was their only creed....' True. Without the word 'love' the entire music industry would collapse. Can you imagine the world without love songs? All of us in the movie and music industries would be unemployed.

I'm reminded of what my wife, Soni, told me yesterday over the phone: 'I can't make these long calls every day to you, Mahesh. They're too expensive. You call me!' I am hurt. 'I understand,' I say, trying to appear very mature. Just before hanging up she says, 'Don't lose all the money you have as you did before.' And then mumbling a hurried, 'I love you,' she hangs up.

We are thirty-nine kilometres away from Berne. The sensuous voice of a woman emanates from the tape deck. 'Do you like music, U.G.?' I ask, pushing my head in between the two front seats of the car. 'I prefer the barking of a dog, the grunting of a pig, and the neighing of a horse. There is life in them, some vitality. Listening to music is a sensual activity.... '

'Even bhajans and hymns?' I ask. 'Yes, everything. In fact, your God is the ultimate pleasure your mind has created....' Out there in the fields the orange glow of the morning sun makes every blade of grass sparkle.

At seven in the morning, as we enter Berne, we hit a traffic jam. U.G. says, 'Human beings are the same all over the world. That Swiss guy ahead of us who is cursing the traffic is no different from the guy in Bombay or the guy in Madras.'

Gstaad

'The relationship you have with money says it all. When Valentine died, I asked Chandrasekhar to take the gold out of her teeth before cremating her. Do you know that the Catholic church paid 20 million dollars to those young boys sodomized by the priests?'

'You are individually, solely, and wholly responsible for the slum situation in Bombay. Seventy-five percent of Bombayites live in the slums because of people like you and me.'

Something tells me that this summer with U.G. is going to be hot. Don't they say the light burns brightest before it goes out?

At dinner, U.G. and I discuss with Marisa, the Italian sculptress, Bodil, the Swedish painter, and Professor Gottfried Meyer, the German painter, the theme of my new film about an ageing actress.

'Rekha is the right choice for the role, Mahesh. She is herself battling with the problem right now. The movie will have the pulse and the beat of the now,' says U.G.

The relationship between feminine beauty and power, oestrogen therapy, and man's quest for permanence are the themes at the dining table. 'Man's war against ageing will never be won,' says U.G. summing up a long, drawn-out conversation.

'Art is born out of frustration. Everything is born out of frustration.' The jet lag is beginning to hit me now.

12 July ... DAY THREE

They have a tennis competition going on in the valley, down below. This place is crowded. Many people from all over the world have come to watch the matches.

There are no rooms available for rent in Gstaad. Yehudi Menuhin is holding a series of musical concerts in the Saanen church.

This morning, after fixing me my second cup of coffee, U.G. narrated this funny incident that took place in his childhood on a railway platform: as U.G. stepped out from a comfortable first class compartment onto the railway platform in Madras, he ran into his grandfather, who had just gotten down from a crowded third class compartment of the same train. The sight of his grandson alighting from a first class compartment made the old man furious. 'How can you do this?' the old man said. 'We sweat day and night to see that you have a comfortable future, and here you are, blowing it all up!' Guess what U.G.'s reply was. He said, 'Why wait for the future? You have seen with your own eyes how comfortable I am already with your hard-earned money. Isn't that what you wanted?'

I walk towards a hotel in Saanen to meet Ajay Devgan who is shooting a film here in Switzerland. On the way I run into a pretty young girl whom at first sight I don't recognize. She's Twinkle, Dimple's daughter. She's hurrying to finish her last-minute shopping in Gstaad. The movie production unit of which she is a member is leaving for India in the evening. My meeting with Ajay is good. I like this guy; he has a charm of his own. On my way back, I run into Saroj Khan, the famous choreographer from Bollywood. She begins to complain to me, as always, about her son, Raju, who is my favourite choreographer. 'Why do you only work with my son? Why not with me? Am I not good? Give me at least some films to do,' she says. Well, here's the real-life story of a mother trying to grab a 'morsel of food' from her son. That's show business.

I'm reading the screenplay of *Tender Mercies*, the film for which Robert Duvall got his first Academy Award. This film also won an award for the best screenplay. There's a line in the movie which I loved: 'I distrust happiness.' The life-affirming climax of this movie, though low-keyed by popular Indian movie standards, is rather effective. At times, less is more.

13 July ... DAY FOUR

'A flower does not preach,' said U.G. earlier this morning.

'Your Rekha story about the ageing actress will certainly work. Your story mirrors what everyone wants. She'll be remembered for this role. But she must not make a big thing about turning her back on the show business. She must gracefully pull the lifeline out and quit.'

Ideas for 'Ageing Actress'

In the last scene, the heroine must walk up to the hero and thank him for showing her the mirror. In the climax scene, she must go out into the world without her make-up which has been her armour. As the dawn reveals her face, the audience must discover her ageless beauty. We should freeze the last image in an extreme close-up, with the voice of the hero saying, 'You're beautiful....'

At supper time, after the crowd leaves, Gottfried, Bodil, Marisa, and I talk about U.G. and death. The conversation soon gravitates towards the subject of ageing. Marisa mentions her friend who, having made all the efforts to stay eternally young, one day quit making up her face and walked into a beauty parlour and, watching all her friends who were still struggling with their make-up, announced, 'Hey folks, how do you like the new me?' I think this will make an interesting scene.

Bodil, the Swedish painter, suggests that in the movie the heroine must drop all her make-up materials one by one and walk into the sunset.

I like the guts and sense of humour of Marisa. I must put a character like her in my movie. It will work as a good counterpoint to the heroine's character.

Gottfried points out that here in the West it is not only the living who make themselves up, but even the dead are made up. This obsession with youthful looks has reached absurd proportions. Marisa says it's absurd that it is considered okay to put oneself after death into a deep-freeze, hoping that one day the cure to the ailment one dies of will be found and one will be resurrected, but one is considered a criminal when one disconnects oneself from the life-support devices and ends one's own life to escape from pain.

Today is full moon night. Lightning and thunder fill the room with dramatic light and sound effects. U.G. is sleeping. Just before he retired to his room, he said, 'See you if I'm still alive tomorrow morning.' As the night deepens and all the guests leave, I discover the place is too quiet for my comfort.

14 July ... DAY FIVE

U.G. suggests that the actress should discover the beauty that is there in those faces out there in the streets and slums of India. It has never been told to the world that the last scene of my film *Arth*, in which the heroine turns her back on her husband and her lover and walks away alone, was in fact suggested and insisted upon by U.G. U.G. did this despite the fierce opposition he faced from the film experts who prophesied that such an ending would destroy the box office prospects of the movie. Well, what happened is history. The film worked only because of the end.

'The cosmetic industry, the beauticians, the fashion designers, the garment manufacturers, and the fashion magazines, all will be up in arms against you if you paint them as villains in your movie,' says U.G. I am beginning to see the point he's trying to make to me. If you give up your struggle to stay eternally young and don't seek the help of all these people who cater to that need, what hold would they have over you? They would be out of business.

Late in the evening, as U.G. is giving his usual talk, a worn-out, haggard man walks in. He is Scotty-Scott, my friend from Ojai. I'm meeting him after years. He looks sad. After Scott leaves, I sit down with U.G. and ask him what he thinks could be bothering Scott. Why was he looking so sick? 'These Americans are paranoid people. This fellow stopped having salt with his meals and is supposedly suffering from the chronic fatigue syndrome. Salt is very important for the human body. These doctors and dieticians are taking you all for a big ride. One day they say that cholesterol is bad for the body, and then a few years later they reverse their opinion and say that cholesterol is necessary for the body. You see me every morning, don't you? How much cream do I pour into my coffee? I'm seventy-seven years old. What's wrong with me? All those doctors who suggested that I should not touch cream are dead and gone. I'm still here, alive and kicking!'

I sense there is something strange about U.G. this summer. He is tearing down every citadel of our culture, no matter how lofty it is.

Late at night, U.G. talks about the three call girls he met in Tokyo. One was a Rajneesh freak, the second, a J. Krishnamurti freak, and the third, a Bubba Free John freak. 'These girls charge $600 for spending a night with the customers. When I asked them how come they got so much, they explained that before and after the sex act they discussed religion, divinity, and mysticism with their customers. That is why they were so expensive.' 'Sex combined with religion always works at the box office,' said the great American director, Cecil B. DeMille.

15 July ... DAY SIX

'Sorrow is the glue. Art, religion and that political zeal to improve the lives of the human lot spring from the frustration and impossibility of making any sense out of life,' says U.G. Talking to him this morning is like taking off into a clear sky on a clear day. The vast expanse of the sky is less intimidating today.

I ask Gottfried Meyer, the retired German professor who once taught painting, etching, and sculpture at a university in south Germany, 'If you had to reduce all your teachings about painting and sculpture to one word, what would that word be?' Gottfried unhesitatingly says, 'Observing.... Observing life, observing nature....' Just then U.G. intervenes. 'You only observe through a veil of ideas put into you by your culture. A real artist knows that what you see out there does not tally, does not match with those precious artistic ideas that you are so proud of. But I know you guys won't listen to what I am saying. You will only be satisfied when you hear what you want to hear,' said U.G. and looked away, leaving us to our discussion.

Early in the evening, Scott comes and takes me down into the valley. He has a cup of coffee and I have a cup of Darjeeling tea. Scott opens his heart to me. He tells me about the affair his wife is having with a younger man. He tells me how her sleeping with that man tormented him for eight long years. But now he claims that he has succeeded in transcending that pain. He says that he is one guy out of a billion who allows his wife to do that without making things more difficult for her. He talks at length about the arrangement that the ménage à trois has struck, and also discusses at length about how erotic the whole thing is. As I listen to him, I'm reminded of the flames of jealousy that engulfed every pore of my body when a man made a pass at my woman. God, what a messy thing our relationships are.

At night, U.G. talks about another ménage à trois – J. Krishnamurti, Rosalind Rajagopal, and Rajagopal. '... Rajagopal put up with J.K.'s affair with his wife and looked the other way because of the money and real estate that were involved. He was a willing participant in that sordid drama. Don't exonerate these people. They may claim that they are different from us ordinary mortals, but they are exactly the same, perhaps worse....'

16 July ... DAY SEVEN

'There's nothing like joint proprietorship in the area of human relationships,' says U.G., summing up the triangular drama that is playing havoc with Scott's personal life. That's the real cause of his sickness. 'Will his wife agree to a similar arrangement of sharing him with another woman? If not, why should he share her with another man? And why is Scott putting up with the discomfort and pain of her sleeping with another guy?' 'Why?' I ask. 'You want to hear the blunt fact? It is because he unconsciously wants to hold on to her because of his failing physical health, and also because of the financial support he gets from her.' That made sense, but then I ask him, 'But why should his wife still hold on to him when she has a boyfriend?' He says, 'She holds on to him because she feels her boyfriend will dump her one day.'

'Die Broke—Forget About Inheritance—Make the most of your money in the here and now' —screams the cover page of an American magazine called *Worth*. It's a magazine on financial intelligence. The article states that the more eager people are to leave an estate behind for their offspring, the more likely they are of choosing a quality of death over a quality of life.

As the day wears on, I'm savaged by U.G. '... Do you know why you want me to keep on giving that money to your children after you're dead and gone? It means that you don't want to let go of that money even after you're dead and gone. You want to continue living through your kids after you die. You say you don't believe in reincarnation, you do not believe in after-life, you don't want to leave any footprints behind. All that is bogus. Like everybody else, you want continuity. That's all that you are interested in. You want to continue through your work, your writings, your books, your movies, or your so-called humanitarian acts.'

Today is the seventh day and it's a bad day. U.G.'s talks are getting to me. It's getting difficult to hide. I take a long walk towards the train station. I envy all those people who are unaware of their own dishonesty. 'Stop the world,' I say to myself. 'I want to get off.' When you're with U.G., you never know which wave will hit you, nor from which direction it will come. I feel like a leaf being blown by a storm.

The Swiss Tennis Open is being played in the valley below. Sounds of people cheering the winner nudge me back to my school days. I'm reminded of my cricket matches. Perhaps the evening light is making me nostalgic.

Silence engulfs the valley. As the evening deepens, I bury myself in the newspaper. It's a kind of bunker in which one feels safe. I'm wrong. U.G. turns towards me and suddenly assaults me. He is raging about his favourite topic, 'money'. I shudder and shiver as he strips me publicly. I wonder what he's trying to drive home, and I don't understand him. After a very long time, I get the feeling that I'm going to break down and cry. Why am I putting up with all this? What is it that I seek at the end of the road? Why am I here? Who is this man? What do I want from him? Nothing makes sense, nothing.

17 July ... DAY EIGHT

Woke up today a little before six. A discomforting feeling of dread shadows me. The loudest sound in the room is the ticking of the wall clock. There, from behind the cream curtains, a new day is beginning to peep in. Everything around me is unusually still. Living with U.G. is like living with the wind. All through the night, right up to this moment, I feel as if there is nobody living in that room next to me.

A hot shower in a warm tub is one hell of an experience. Now that one has been forced to slow down, one can take notice and enjoy these simple acts of life. U.G. once said, 'Having a bath is a sensual activity. The religious man makes a big thing about the importance of a bath. He turns the simple act of pouring water over one's body into a ritual. Don't you see how all you guys in your soap commercials endlessly flaunt and highlight the pleasures of a good bath?' I think of my mother. Childhood images of her locking herself for hours in a small bathroom in our tiny middle class flat in Bombay's Shivaji Park surface. Having a bath was my mother's only reprieve from the hell that she lived in.

'Good morning,' says U.G., moving toward the kitchen. He has had a late start this morning. It's almost 7 o'clock now. The usual time for him to fix his breakfast and my coffee is around 6:15 a.m. Sounds of cups and spoons, cupboards opening and shutting mingle with the hiss of the kettle. A voice within me asks, 'Are you ready for the take? Are you ready for the executioner's song?' 'Yes, I'm ready,' I say to myself, 'Today I shall stand up and get shot down.' At the sound of the gong, U.G. devours J. Krishnamurti. Within seconds he cuts him down and puts him into the slot of a philosopher. Then he unhesitatingly begins to praise Bertrand Russell. 'I have nothing against Bertrand Russell having his multiple affairs or sleeping with his best friend's wife. He had no pretensions. But what J. K. did was disgusting. Why did he take a moral posture on the platform against sex? Why did he tell the little boys who met him in the United States, "Why do you want to have sex, sirs? Why not just hold a girl's hand?" Probably that phoney used to have premature ejaculations.'

Jottings

'Trying to overtake your shadow is the problem. The tree does not try to overtake its shadow, does it? As long as you stand in the sun, there's going to be a shadow. The only way of getting rid of your shadow is to get rid of yourself. Misery goes when "you" go. As long as you are there, that misery will be there.'

'I torture you to take the torture out of me,' says Bob, acting out a scene from a 1936 Hollywood film titled *The Raven*. The line says it all.

Later in the evening, Scott and I go into Gstaad to have our daily coffee and tea. I give him William Styron's latest book, *A Tidewater Morning*. Styron is a great writer. I just love his writing.

Today the streets of Gstaad look deserted. The Swiss Open tennis match has ended. Scott mentions seeing some American actor here in this very restaurant earlier this morning. 'Which American actor?' I ask. He struggles, but cannot remember his name. He looks pathetic. 'God, this is what chronic fatigue syndrome does to your brain. The name is there in my head, but I can't bring it out,' says Scott, giving up.

The night is unusual.

18 July ... DAY NINE

'You're depending on the wrong man. I have no powers, psychic or spiritual. The critical phase of your life has lasted too long.... Bye,' said U.G. and then, putting down the phone, headed for the kitchen to attend to his pre-dawn chores of fixing his breakfast and my coffee. In the dark living room the hands of the clock read 6:20 a.m. The ninth day of my stay in Switzerland has begun. Inside me things are unusually quiet. 'That was a Ph.D. from Canada, Dr. Raghunath. He has completed his dissertation on Aurobindo. I once helped him stay away from India. Now he wants to go back. He wanted to know what kind of a future he has there,' said U.G. responding to my unspoken question.

'Why doesn't religion change people? Doing more and more of the same changes things for the better only in the fields of working and business, but not in the so-called moral world.'

There's a fly on my table. It is feeling its way around and is obviously looking for food. I notice that whenever I make a conspicuous movement, it instantly responds by flying away. Then, sizing up the situation, it flies back and goes ahead with its unfinished business. 'That's instinct. Your so-called protective instinct is not a natural thing. Don't you see, it's wearing you out by its constant demand for permanence? Your thinking mechanism which demands permanence is a dead thing. It cannot touch anything living.... Frustration produces results. Your whole world of art is built on frustration. You know the age-old analogy of the dog and his bone. The hungry dog chews on a lean, dry bone; and doing so hurts his gums and they bleed. The poor dog imagines that the blood that he's savouring comes from the bone and not from himself.... Whatever you experience is created by you; and these experiences, however intense and great they may be, do not last.'

The fly on my table taught me more about instinct than all the books that I had read. 'But,' says U.G., 'trying to look at a fly every day and replay that experience on and on would be absurd....'

But how can I throw away my precious experiences into the whirlpool of time? Isn't this act of writing my attempt to cage the living moment? Stringing together such moments in some sort of a pattern seems like a good thing to do. But what will all this achieve?

'If you put old cliches and traditional stuff into something that is contemporary and new, it dies,' says Professor Moorty. His words teach me what not to do with the script I am working on.

'Do you know who that actor was, Mahesh?' asked Scott, putting his mountain bicycle to rest against the wall. 'George C. Scott! Gosh, I couldn't think of his last name yesterday. I think I'll go up there on the snow-capped mountains today and write some poetry.... See you later.'

Today is Mario's thirty-first birthday. 'What is the meaning of life?' he jokingly asked, as we get into his car to go to the Palace Hotel in Montreux for lunch. 'To kill and get killed, and to justify that in ten different ways is the purpose and meaning of your life,' answered U.G., butting in and occupying the front seat.

19 July ... DAY TEN

Making the bed one sleeps on is a tough job. It's tougher than writing.

Someone has been trying to reach me since last night. The telephone bell has been constantly ringing and disconnecting just before I get to the phone.

'Fresh does not exist for me. The idea of fresh vegetables, fresh cream is bogus. You sell frozen vegetables and fruits and give it the label of "fresh" and fool people. How man has been conned! That is why I say that if you believe in the Virgin Mary, you will believe in anything. Your obsession for the "fresh" comes out of the fear of losing what you call "good health". The father of macrobiotic diet died at the dining table while giving his listeners a speech on eternal good health which he claimed could be achieved through his diet food. It is the most well-known secret that Jane Fonda, mother of the global fad, aerobics, has had secret by-pass heart surgery. J. Krishnamurti used to have an oil bath every day to keep his body supple and fit. Do you know that the oil came all the way from Kerala. Despite that, he died a miserable death. One eats to prolong life; one also fasts or eats less to prolong life. In short, delaying death is all that you are interested in. That is your agony. The body is not interested in this immortality game. Health itself is a definition.

'Yoga and all the exercises that you guys do reverse the flow of energy. The only exercise that animals do is to run around for food, or run away from danger. Our whole existence revolves around selling and buying, and that includes our spiritual ideas.... To confer everlasting fame on a person is to immortalize him. "Immortal" means deathless; and "soul" means an entity which is endless and everlasting,' says U.G., reading from the dictionary.

'Talking to you is like having a dialogue with Death,' I say to him. U.G. responded, 'How can you have a dialogue with Death. That "you" has to go before death occurs. It's okay to go on talking endlessly about death and dying to your yesterdays.'

'What's your message, U.G.?' I ask in exasperation.

'Drop dead!' he says, staring straight at my face.

'You cannot experience the death of anybody, not even the death of your near and dear ones. What you experience is the void created by the death of someone you love.'

Parting is painful. I guess in death it is far more painful because of its finality. I fill the void within me by making calls to my children in India. 'Do you know that Shaheen sleeps with your shirt on every night?' said Soni, 'She says she loves your smell. She's missing you very much.'

20 July ... DAY ELEVEN

Sanjay Dutt and I are walking together hand in hand on the crowded streets of Bombay. But nobody seems to take any notice of us. Why? 'Because you're dreaming,' says a voice in my head. I wake up. It's rather early. I had forgotten to draw the curtain before sleeping. The room is bright. I open the diary which U.G. has presented to me and cross out the date July 20. Today is my eleventh day in 'Paradise'. Whew!

It rained last night. The smell of wet grass reminds me of Shivaji Park in Bombay. Are you anything else but a bundle of sounds, smells, sights, and tastes? U.G. is up. He steps out into the morning light, barefoot, and heads to the clothesline to hang three pieces of freshly washed underwear. 'I go to the Master, not to hear him speak, but to watch him tie his shoelaces,' said a Zen pupil. Today I will do exactly what that monk had said.

The simple act of hanging his clothes is for U.G. the be-all and end-all of his existence. He's completely in it. All there, totally there. His face shows a sense of wonder as he clips his vest to the line, straightening out the tiniest fold. Living from moment to moment is a physical fact for this man, not a superimposed philosophical concept.

Opening the curtains, U.G. lets the morning into the living room. Then he gracefully glides in between the sofa and the cupboard, smoothes the cover on his chair, and sets the pillow right. Putting things in order is so easy for him. He's now looking for something which he is unable to find. His eyes scan the room. 'There was a pencil near the phone,' he says. Suddenly I realize: I who use the phone the most had also felt that the pencil was missing, but did nothing about it; while here was a guy who seldom uses the phone and has no use for the pencil, but who is doing something about it. 'I'm sure Julie must have taken it,' he says with certainty. Then finding a new pen for the corner, he settles down in the living room. Everything is still now. The ending of his movement is like the ending of a musical phrase.

An overpowering silence descends into the room. 'As long as there is recognition, there is no silence. That recognition is you. That is Mahesh. That noise of that train passing which you hear now is the one that is silencing you, putting you to an end. You cannot take it, so you run away. Just as you cannot stare at the sun long without going blind, you cannot listen to the sounds around you.'

Bob and Paul, the American friends from California, come down and sit and talk about their friend Connie. Connie was a seeker who, having gone through the spiritual bazaar, took to alcohol. Connie is missing in Thailand. Bob says that the American Embassy in Berne had tried to contact them. They sense trouble. 'He is probably dead,' says Bob, looking absolutely in control.

'Human frailties and foibles are not accepted by me. They are okay for a religious man because they become a source of living for him. Don't you see, these gurus, psychiatrists, and therapists live off your frailties and foibles,' declares U.G.

Tonight's movie is *Ed Wood*. It's a black-and-white comedy based on the life of a film director who at the very end of his life got the award of World's Worst Director. I loved the film. The relationship between a has-been actor and a failed young director was heart-wrenching to watch. Later, after the show, I watched Julie and Moorty playing with the Internet and the World Wide Web. U.G. is now available to the forty to seventy million people around the world who have access to the Internet. 'Gosh, look what technology has done, U.G.,' I say, fascinated. 'But don't forget that the same technology is being used to kill and destroy life,' says U.G., not looking impressed.

21 July ... DAY TWELVE

Film business just chews you up and spits you out on the sidewalk. To survive in the show business you need guts and the ability to constantly resurrect and reinvent yourself. One's character is determined by one's response to a situation. You

214

are what you do, not what you say you want to do. 'You think when you don't want to do anything. Thinking is a poor alternative to acting. Your thinking is consuming all your energy. Act, don't think!' says U.G., turning his fire in my direction. When U.G. goes for you, he does not pause, not even for a minute. 'I'm like an animal,' he says. 'I either fight till I kill you, or I just run away.'

I'm a workaholic. I am suffering from work withdrawals. I am no different from a junkie who misses his drug. Problems and tensions make me feel alive. Problems crystallize me, define me. You're right, U.G. We love problems. 'You have to pay for your attachments. You cannot have it both ways,' says U.G. to Mario. They are discussing the problems of his house and his woman. 'Harsh fact is the greatest teacher. It is that which will spur you into action.' I interrupt him, saying 'U.G. every time you state a fact, I withdraw from you, why?' He smiles and, looking straight into my eyes, says, 'You not only withdraw from me, but also from the harsh reality of the world. Why was Julie condemning the bullfight that she saw on the television last night? She said she couldn't stand it, but then why did she watch it? The torturing of the bull was unacceptable to her, but what happens then when her American government, which she supports, kills thousands and thousands of innocent people in the name of liberty?'

In the evening U.G. narrates a revealing incident. A woman once went to J. Krishnamurti and raved about the creative experience which she had had the previous day while listening to the music of Yehudi Menuhin. Krishnamurti said, 'What's so creative about horse's hair rubbing against cat's guts, madam?' During my stay here in Gstaad, I was told by an insider who once belonged to the J. Krishnamurti's camp that Krishnamurti himself used to love music. Very often he used to listen to the Ninth Symphony.

Late in the night, Bob, Paul, Narayana Moorty and I sit with U.G. under the starry sky. Suddenly, U.G. mauls me: 'Mahesh,

215

even you don't understand a word of what I am saying. Don't think you're superior to all those guys you're trying to look down upon....' This feels like a hand-to-hand combat. I struggle to match him. I fail. After the attack, I feel empty but calm. I look up into the sky and find that the stars for some reason seem brighter. It feels as if a veil within me has been lifted.

At night, I toss and turn, waiting for sleep.

22 July ... DAY THIRTEEN

Isn't this thing called the 'I' nothing but a treasured wound from the past?

I woke up very early this morning, reeling under the aftershocks of last night's attack. Yesterday my self-importance took a battering.

We go to a travel agent in Gstaad. U.G. is personally making the reservations for me to go back home. The date of my departure has been fixed. I'm leaving for London on the 8th. Only fifteen more days here in Painland! I begin to see the light at the end of the tunnel. Or maybe the tunnel at the end of the light. Please put out the light. I want my darkness back!

U.G. says, 'Good morning,' and moves toward the kitchen. He glances at the clock on the wall and announces the time. It's 6:15. Once again, those familiar sounds of pots and pans emanate from the kitchen. 'Your coffee is ready, sir,' he says. I will not talk to him today at the dining table. This morning I'll only work on my script.

Enter Scott, and suddenly there is action in the room. 'I'm very much a part of this world. What do you want me to do? Go and live in a cave? You are in conflict with this society. That is why you keep running away from it to search for peace. Why the hell do you keep running away to the top of those mountains? The world cannot be anything else but this,' says U.G. with unimaginable emphasis.

I think I now know what my problem is: wanting to be like him is my problem, my tragedy. But he does not want me to be like him. He wants me to be myself. But I don't want to be myself. I want to be like him. And I know I can never be like him. I can only pretend to be like him. The whole cultural game is an exercise in perfecting your pretensions. Can I ever gracefully accept my limitations and stop pretending? I guess never.

I'm reminded of a quote from Nietzsche: 'Show me a great man and I will show you a monkey of his own ideals.' How true. No wonder the poor fellow went mad.

Bob, Paul and I stay up and talk about this man called U.G. Paul says you must have to be born with an inclination towards this kind of stuff that U.G. talks about. Otherwise, why would you put up with the pain and discomfort it causes. Just then, Mario calls out to me, 'Mahesh, your master wants you down for lunch.' My heart skips a beat. Now what, I say to myself, and run down like an obedient child.

Harry, whose mother calls him an intellectual midget, gives a gift of $100 to U.G. for his birthday every year. Today, he has once again given him some money. U.G. says, 'Of all the guys who have given me gifts, yours is the most treasured, Harry. You know why? Because you clean toilets, wash windows, and sweep floors. My, you worked so hard to earn this money. That's why.' U.G.'s statement surprises everyone in the room. Sweet Harry is embarrassed, but very pleased, to receive this compliment from U.G.

Late in the evening, Gottfried talks about his near-death experiences during the Second World War. 'When you go through such intense experiences, you begin to see the truth that nothing belongs to you—not your wife, not your dog, not your child—nothing.'

The topic of death somehow keeps reappearing in all our conversations. My, it's hot!

Just then the phone rings. I run towards it, thinking it's a call for me from India. 'Can I speak to Bob Carr? This is the U.S. Embassy, calling from Thailand.' 'Just a moment, please. I'll call him. Bob has been expecting your call for quite some time,' I say, signaling to Moorty's son, Kiran, to go and fetch Bob.

'I tried to call earlier, but here in Thailand all the phone lines have been badly hit by a fierce storm,' says the calm, professional voice over the phone. Moments later, as I watch lots of people in the living room laugh as they chat with U.G., I couldn't help noticing the usually pleasant and self-contained Bob sitting in the corner like a helpless child listening intensely to the voice on the phone. I notice that he is getting progressively shaky. I can see that the finality of his friend's death is hitting him now. I learn from his conversation that Connie's body is not yet cremated. They have been waiting for Bob's 'go-ahead'. He gives it. This call has done the job of the proverbial 'last straw'. As Bob puts down the phone, he breaks down and begins to cry. U.G. is surprised to see Bob cry. Endings are tough.

23 July ... DAY FOURTEEN

There are still 270 'waking hours' to go. I'm halfway through my stay here in Gstaad. I've been walking a lot here. The phone calls to India have kept me busy. Talking to my folks down in Bombay is my only link with sanity. People say I have lost weight. 'Food is the number one enemy of man. We eat too much and we eat for pleasure. The body does not require so much food. Less food will not harm you, but more will certainly kill you faster,' says U.G. over breakfast.

'U.G., you are harsh on marriage,' says Julie, daring to walk into the kitchen. 'What else is that piece of paper for, except for property and security, tell me?' he asks. She is speechless.

Snatches from U.G.'s Conversations

... The world's problems are nothing but extensions of our personal problems.

... Insights mean nothing. In a living situation, the man with insight behaves just like anybody else. Has the psychologist solved for himself the problem that he's trying to analyse?

... Death is a release for the person who is suffering. But even here, you would rather maintain your permanent relationship with the suffering man and keep him going with the help of all those life-support systems, rather than face the void created by his death. Do you see how selfish you are?

... In most situations you want two things at the same time. That's your tragedy.

... All your feminist talk isn't worth anything. I know a woman who says she cannot bear to live with her husband. She says she finds him disgusting, but she is still hanging on shamelessly. Why? Simple, because of money, because of security.

... You cry when your best friend dies, but you're petrified of having to pay for his funeral. Now do you see what money means to you?

... You say, 'I love you, I miss you,' but you think twice before you make a long-distance call. That's why, folks, I always talk about money. That's the thing that reveals where you are really at.

... By giving money they control you, and by not giving money they control you.... As long as you want something from someone, there will always be someone out there to control you.

For U.G., anything that is left is not a saving. On the first day of every New Year, U.G. gives everything away. This he learned from Annie Besant who in turn picked this trait from King Ashoka. He used to give away everything every five years.

The heat wave is over.

24 July ... DAY FIFTEEN

My bed says it all. The manner in which the edges of the bed cover have been tucked in reveals the half-hearted attitude with which the job was done. You are what you do. You cannot separate yourself from your actions. The actions reveal you, I say to myself, looking at my clumsy bed.

'Your actions are very graceful, U.G. I love to watch you eat your oatmeal every morning,' I say to him across the dining

219

table. 'All my actions are mechanical, just like the movements of a machine,' says U.G., untouched by my compliment. 'But a machine is not graceful,' I argue. 'Of course, there is tremendous grace in a machine. Have you looked at the hands of a clock? By calling it a machine, you are preventing yourself from seeing the grace that is present there.' I see what he is saying. There is tremendous grace in the hands of a clock. One's conclusions about things prevent one from looking at things as they really are. 'But U.G., look! Now I am looking at machines with this new concept which you have just dished out which says "Machines too are graceful," am I not?' U.G. nods, 'Yes, you are.'

Then taking a split second pause, I ask, 'How is this different from my previous conclusion that machines are not graceful?' He laughs and says, 'Not different.' Once again I've hit a dead end. 'So U.G., doesn't it mean that no matter what one does, one only looks at the world through one's ideas and concepts?' 'Yes, sir!' he says and walks into the kitchen to wash his plastic bowl. Breakfast ends.

U.G. attacks your pretensions. At first you feel stripped, naked, but later, when that armour has collapsed, you feel light.

My walk on the streets of Gstaad with Scotty-Scott uplifts my spirits. His life is simply stunning. The story of this carpenter from Ojai is more inspiring than all those inspirational books. It affirms life. Scott Eckersley was the sole survivor of the eleven hikers and campers who were swept off by the raging current and drowned in the Sespe downpour.

Paul Sempé, Mario, U.G. and I drive into Berne. I sit in the back seat of the car and work on the script of my new movie, *Tamanna*. During my stay here, the script is getting a dimension it could never have gotten in Bombay. We have lunch in a vegetarian restaurant. 'Look at what's happening in India, the country which was so proud of Gandhi and his philosophy of non-violence. It's killing hundreds of people every day in

Kashmir to protect the idea of an united India,' says U.G. looking towards Paul Sempé, who is a great admirer of Mahatma Gandhi.

On the way back we pass through Fribourg. The first university in Europe was founded here. U.G. dismisses all universities, calling them concentration camps. 'Knowledge is power. There is nothing like knowledge for the sake of knowledge. The quest for knowledge is to dominate your neighbour. This organism doesn't want to learn anything!' And then suddenly, once again, U.G. begins to talk about his favourite topic, money. 'Money has nothing to do with happiness. But it is better to be miserable with money than to be miserable without it. People who do not have money often say, "Look at all those guys with money, are they happy?" They say this because they are jealous. It is comforting for them to justify the lack of money with such statements,' he says.

As we drive into Saanen, I think to myself that statements like, 'You need money to get rich, but you need people to be happy,' which I used to find impressive, are nothing but creations of a jealous mind.

25 JULY ... DAY SIXTEEN

Wow! My bed looks well-done today. The results of putting oneself totally into what one does is far superior to those which come from one's half-present mind, and half-hearted, self-preoccupied deeds. One should work just like one makes love.

That carpenter from Ojai, Scotty-Scott, who came ten days ago looking like a man who was going to drop dead any moment, left yesterday lusting for life. (He's got a pretty girl for himself now. They're spending the night together in Berne before he takes off for the U.S.). I think I will certainly make a movie one day based on Scott's life.

'Wanting and not wanting are both you. That movement of wanting can never stop. Through the use of all those meditation techniques prescribed by therapists and holy men in the market place, your wants only slow down, run down a little. But they are still very much there in the background. Wanting not to want is also a want, you see. The ending of want is death. Do you want death? Continuity is all that you are interested in,' says U.G. to a large gathering of ex-Rajneeshis who have come all the way from Cologne, Germany, to listen to him.

A Conversation

Mahesh: U.G., does it ever cross your mind that I should become like you, or at least something better than what I am right now?

U.G.: Never.

Mahesh: But that is what I want all the time. I want to be you. Why do I want to be like you? Tell me. I do not understand.

U.G.: You cannot understand. That is your tragedy. The stranglehold of culture prevents your uniqueness from blooming. You always want to become someone other than what you are. That is happening in every area of human activity. That is why I repeat that all universities, all education, all schools, all colleges, all institutes that are trying to change you into a better person are like concentration camps. But you have to learn the language of this world if you want to survive in this man-made jungle. If you try to protect your children from these schools and institutions and put them into some alternative fancy educational system which talks against competition, that would certainly destroy them. Don't teach them anything against competition. Rivalry and competition are facts of life. Your children have to live here, fight here. If you say you love them, help them get a tool to make a living, and then get out of their way.... That structure is only interested in wanting everyone to fit into itself. The stranglehold of structure prevents your uniqueness from blooming.

At noon I call Bombay and speak to Mukhesh. His voice gives him away. I sense he has been drinking. I wonder how I quit drinking. He is sounding happy. *Criminal*, our latest movie about to be released, has made a lot of money even before it's out in the theaters. Lucky fellow.

On my way back from the telephone booth, I run into Bob and Paul. We sit outside of a candy shop and have a mad conversation about what is going on in Chalet Sunbeam. We all agree that nothing of what U.G. is saying is making any sense. A feeling of apprehension and dread is beginning to shadow me.

Later in Bob's room I read aloud a line from J. Krishnamurti's *Commentaries on Living* which states how this greedy thing called the 'I' wants to somehow persist and perpetuate itself by presiding over its own dissolution. U.G. storms into the room, and, pulling the book out of my hands, says, 'Whatever this guy said did not operate in his life. A guy without this thing called the "I" cannot fuck his best friend's wife, like this crook did.'

I speak to Justin Lazard, the American actor (Julie's son) over the phone. His new television series, *Central Park West*, is going on air on 13 September 1995. Justin talks to me about his dream. He dreamt that his series was a total failure. 'Listen, Justin, you're not alone. That's the nightmare of every entertainer in the world. Take it easy!' I tell him. He laughs, relieved. Show business is the same everywhere.

We are at Mario's place having Italian food cooked by him. CNN announces that there's been a bomb explosion in a Paris subway. Marisa and Paul Sempé, are upset. U.G. is totally unmoved by this tragedy. He says, 'Why are you people pretending to be concerned about human life? What happens when you guys kill? What did you do in Iraq? Why don't those leaders who are teaching you patriotism go and fight those wars? During the Gulf War, I told Julie, "I want to see your two sons and daughter sent home in a body bag. Then you will understand what dying for a cause means." The human species is the filthiest species on this planet. It is going to wipe itself out. No power can reverse that course.' There's a pin-drop silence in the room. Nobody says a word.

I'm being robbed by the public telephone at Gstaad railway station. I put five francs in the meter. It shows I have used two francs, but when I disconnect, the telephone doesn't return my three francs change. As I walk up the hill heading towards Chalet Sunbeam, I say to myself, 'Well, Mr. Bhatt, be honest. Losing three francs hurts, doesn't it? Now just imagine losing everything that you have. That's what dying means. Are you ready to die?' My entire being turns away from the question.

There's a room full of people, mostly ex-Rajneeshi sannyasis, watching a video recording which was taken by Bob and Paul. A hot discussion on the tape between U.G. and a small group of people is keeping us all riveted. It's evening and it's raining outside. I'm reminded of those days when I used to shop around for ecstasy and bliss in the spiritual supermarket. Just then I notice U.G. standing in a dark corner, quietly watching his own taped discussion. He looks like a stranger in the room. He does not seem to recognize his own image on the TV screen. Watching the simplicity of this man called U.G. is heart-breaking. I can't help remembering the pomp and grandeur of Rajneesh and J. Krishnamurti. How aware these guys were of their own greatness!

26 July ... DAY SEVENTEEN

'Attachment becomes a problem because of our wanting to be detached. What is wrong with attachment? Permanence: we cannot hold on to attachments forever. Knowing that, one gets on to the merry-go-round of detachment. All this looks very attractive to you because you feel that you now have the mantra which will help you cope with the aches and pains attachment brings you. Then you get attached to the concept of detachment and spend a lifetime trying to make the goal of being detached into a reality,' says U.G., as I smell my early morning coffee.

Flies, too many flies. The Swiss flies are fat, unlike the skinny ones we have back in India. 'The Swiss spray the grass with cow dung. They don't use chemical fertilizers. That's why you have so many flies buzzing all around you,' says U.G. 'They have more right to be here than you do.' 'Good morning, U.G., and thank you very much,' I replied. This conversation takes place in the first half hour of the morning. The clock shows two minutes past seven.

'First Communication, Global Reunion in Mexico, ONLY MASTERS, Hermetic Societies, 24 June, 1996 (San Juan Day), ego sum qui sum,' reads an E-mail message to U.G. from the Internet on Julie's computer. 'This is the beginning,' says U.G., 'of the crazy things that are still to come.'

U.G., Paul Sempé, Gottfried and I are driving to Thun for lunch. The day is bright, clear and warm.

'Picasso had the guts to break away from the artistic stranglehold of his times. That is why his work has a distinct feel of its own. But unfortunately he has become an obstacle and a barrier for the painters of today. They just can't break out of his influence. You have to reject the model in order to come into your own,' said U.G. with great animation, driving home his point.

Thun is an attractive town. We cross a bridge on foot. The bridge is paved with multi-coloured flowers. Under it gushes a blue, sparkling river inches away from one's feet. It's a rare, uplifting experience for a city boy like me.

'Bio-pic' is a vegetarian restaurant in Thun, a town in the German-speaking part of Switzerland. One usually finds more vegetarian restaurants in the German-speaking part of Switzerland than in the French-speaking part. The restaurant has a deserted look. Gottfried, Paul and I help ourselves from the salad bar, and U.G. orders rosti. His eyes fall on the paper table mat the waitress has laid before him. It has a picture of a pretty girl leaning against a bottle of sparkling water and lifting her skirt. It's an advertisement for 'Henniez', a Swiss mineral water. 'Do you see how absurd it is? Yesterday on CNN you saw all those people in America protesting against pornography which is invading homes through the Internet. Now, look here, how these guys are using sex to market water. Everybody makes money out of sex, but then at the same time condemns it. Why?'

asks U.G. 'True, even the man who condemns sex makes money out of it, doesn't he?' I say, agreeing with him.

U.G. is getting kinky in his old age. As we finish our lunch, he makes this bizarre remark: 'Thank you, Gottfried, for paying the bill; thank you, Paul, for driving us here; and thank you, Mr. Bhatt, for the pleasure of your company.' And then he comes dangerously close to me and naughtily whispers in my ear, 'And thank you, dear waitress, for the free view of your tits.' This is the last thing you expect to hear from a guy who has put seventy-seven years behind him and is now pushing seventy-eight.

Minutes later, when we spiral down the staircase, U.G. says, 'The movement of those tits drew my complete and total attention. Only when I ask myself what is it that is moving there does the knowledge that I have about it come into operation and say: "tits". That's it. It stops there. There's no build-up beyond that point. No pleasure movement is possible for me. The moment I look away, the whole thing is wiped out.' I can't figure out what he is talking about. I ask him, 'You mean to say you can't recall the image of those tits now?' 'No, I can't,' says U.G. 'Well I can!' I said. 'That's your tragedy, buddy. If that image-making mechanism goes, you go. You will drop dead physically right here, at this very moment.'

We're driving back to Gstaad. It's hot now. Paul suddenly accelerates the car at a turn. This wakes up U.G. with a start. He has dozed off for a while. 'Sorry I disturbed you, U.G.,' says Paul with his lovely French accent and a childlike smile. 'No, you didn't disturb me. You see the body just responds to the situation. It wakes up to face the possibility of danger. This organism has far more intelligence than that filthy thing called "intellect" which is created by culture. This body is only interested in protecting itself and fucking. Unfortunately, you have turned sex into a pleasure movement and messed things up there, too. This body is not interested in your art, music, painting, writing or religion.'

27 July ... DAY EIGHTEEN

Today is my eighteenth morning in Gstaad. 'You are sitting in darkness,' says U.G. stepping out of his room, and moving towards the kitchen to attend to the routine job of fixing his breakfast and my cup of coffee.

I'm sitting here at the dining table sipping my cup of coffee, listening to the sounds of plastic spoons hitting against the bottom of his plastic bowl. He's eating his light breakfast. The sound of the paper napkin rubbing against his lips punctuates the silence. Even listening is a pleasure movement. Especially listening to the sound of silence. U.G. is now in the kitchen washing his bowl and spoon. 'Each action is independent of the others. One's mind gives them continuity,' I hear U.G.'s voice whispering in my head. I begin to see the truth of this statement. He shuts the tap, cutting the flow of water and then moves. The sound of the water disappearing into the drain pipe of the sink is more invigorating than listening to the music of Ravi Shankar or Beethoven.

'Listening is talking. Even seeing is talking. You're talking inside your head all the time. There's no recognition without naming. Recognizing that movement and calling that "sound" is you,' says U.G., when I tell him about my morning experience. 'So does it mean that this you which I call the I is nothing but a sound track?' I ask. I am bewildered by what he is saying. 'That's it; and that has been put in there by culture.... You create hierarchies and force them on other poor helpless people. There's no difference between rock music and religious songs. Even through reading what do you do? You create new sounds in your own head. New sounds seem attractive to you people. New grooves on old ones—that's what you want.... Anything you write is a lie.'

Late in the day, U.G. relates an incident that took place between him and J. Krishnamurti: Krishnaji and U.G. go for a walk in Madras. They meet a poor boy who is begging for money. Krishnaji embraces him instead of giving him money.

U.G. says, 'Krishnaji, this boy does not need a love hug. He needs money.' Krishnaji says, 'This hug will stop him from begging.' U.G. says, 'You want to bet your bottom dollar? He'll be back tomorrow at the same time, in the same place, doing the same thing.' And that's exactly what happened.

I get my ticket re-routed through London today. My plan to go to Athens hunting for a shooting location has been dropped. On my way back, I find U.G., Bob, Paul and Lisa standing outside the Credit Suisse Bank. U.G. is reading aloud a letter he has just received from his brother-in-law, Dr. Seshagiri Rao. The letter is full of praise for U.G. Dr. Rao was once a U.G.-hater. For thirty years he just could not forgive U.G. for 'abandoning' his sister, U.G.'s wife.

Bob, Paul and I give U.G. the slip and go and sit on a wooden bench outside Gstaad railway station. Just giving vent to all the stuff that gets stirred up within you while talking to U.G. can be both maddening and comforting. All three of us admit that we often find ourselves staring into the face of total insanity when U.G. is saying whatever he is saying. These small breaks away from Chalet Sunbeam and U.G. do serve a purpose. Continuous exposure to this man is just impossible.

At lunch time U.G. asks Harry Deck, a janitor friend and ex-Mehar Baba devotee from Lancaster, Pennsylvania, to 'clean up' (eat) the leftover *dal*. Harry thanks U.G. and praises him for his large-heartedness. 'Ever since your "heart line" has opened up, U.G., you've become a wonderful man to be with.' U.G. cuts in and says, 'Harry I only want you to eat because I want the pots and pans to be clean. It's better that food goes into this garbage can [pointing to his stomach] rather than that garbage can in the kitchen.'

Then, just like that, he goes for Julie. 'Get out of here. And don't leave all your junk here. I don't want things to accumulate here. I throw away people. I left my wife, children, and everybody else. You think I accumulate these cheap things you keep buying? I don't want this glue and this cream to lie around here. You never leave your money lying around. Do you? When it comes to money, you behave like a bitch....' The room had just been hit by a whirlwind.

Our old friend Gottfried Meyer, the painter, and U.G. were once driving down the streets of Gstaad. 'Look at these cars, so many of them. Look at the pollution they're creating, U.G.,' said Gottfried, shutting his window to save himself from the smog. 'What about your car, Gottfried. What is it doing? Isn't it, too, adding to the pollution?' U.G.'s always calling our bluff, especially when we separate ourselves from others and pretend we are different from them, better than them, or superior to them.

Snatches from a conversation late in the evening

'You don't have the guts to stand alone regardless of consequences. I maintain that you and you alone are the moulder of your destiny and the architect of your own fortune. But when a woman arrives on the scene—or a man, as the case may be—you begin to compromise. That is the beginning of the end....'

'Good day for a hanging,' says Bob, summing up the events of the day. We laugh. His "gallows humour" doesn't work.

28 July ... DAY NINETEEN

Memory is the leftover of bygone days. It clogs you up and prevents you from inhaling the living moment. Am I nothing but the dead refuse of the past, an unending echo of a billion yesterdays of the human race?

Our 'good mornings' are simultaneous today. U.G. looks towards the window and, saying 'rainy weather today....,' proceeds to fix my nineteenth cup of coffee. Beeps from his newly-acquired pocket fax machine fills the quiet room. He is trying to learn how to use this gadget. He is taking lessons from the nine-year-old computer 'wizard', Kiran. Kiran is Narayana Moorty's and Wendy's son. 'You have to teach me how to use this,' he says in all earnestness, 'and I'm a bad student.'

One must be empty to receive. The sound of the fly buzzing near my ear invades me. I'm filled with childlike wonder. 'The

229

experience of an empty mind is possible only through the description provided by the so-called religious teachers. What you do not know you cannot experience. Don't you see there is someone there in your so-called empty mind who says you are experiencing an empty mind?' U.G. says.

Savouring the after-taste of an empty mind is no different from replaying the images of a good 'screw'.

The tranquil morning is ripped apart by the arrival of Julie. 'Why are you here, Julie,' U.G. asks as soon as she steps in. 'I just wanted to find out if anyone is going with me to Geneva,' knowing well that her lie may not work. 'Don't play those games with me, Julie,' says U.G. flaring up. She hurries into the kitchen to parry his attack. 'I don't want you to bring anything for me,' rages U.G., sensing she is trying to unpack something. 'I brought you some garbage bags....' she says trying to sound unperturbed. 'That's all you can bring, garbage bags. Money you'll never bring.... Get out of here,' he screams. 'What did I do?' she asks. 'Just get out of here, that's what I want. It's not what you have done, but what you are that is detestable to me. I don't want you to change. But a person who has such an attitude toward money has no place with me,' says U.G. shooing her away. Julie leaves. My empty mind is now reverberating with the after-shocks of this blast.

Working on new film scripts is great fun these days. It all seems so easy. 'Do you know why?' asks Bob Carr, giving me one of his warm, toothless smiles. (Bob was once connected with the entertainment industry in Hollywood. He later became a bit of a guru himself until he ran into U.G. and gave it all up.) 'Why?' I asked. 'Simply because you want to do it,' he answers.

Wanting any pleasure to last forever is pain. All suffering is caused by wanting to prolong life. We should be like the animals—ten, twenty years of life, that's it. 'You'll have a miserable death, Paul,' says U.G. 'All your jogging, all your yoga, all your walking, all your health food will not help to keep things going on forever.' Paul Sempé, the 73-year-old retired sea captain from Marseilles, is the self-appointed summer chauffeur of U.G. He is an ardent devotee of Descartes and loves Gandhi. What amazes me about Paul is how he takes the relentless battering from U.G. with a smile. But if you look closely, one can sense something shuddering within him.

'Why do you condemn a junkie and make a big thing out of the pleasure one experiences through those meditation gimmicks. The damage done to the body through the intake of drugs and alcohol can be measured and reversed. But the harm done through meditation is irreparable and irreversible. If you don't like the way I treat people, you can just go away. Julie is not my need, I am her need. All relationships you guys have with me are one-way. In your relationships game where.the two are involved in the act, the game of one-upmanship and mutual control can go on and on. But not here. You can't have a relationship with me. The relationship game gets even more sordid when sex is involved. You know that...,' said U.G. as the night descended.

29 July ... DAY TWENTY

The countdown has begun. Nine days more and I will be hopefully out of this place. Smells and sounds from a distant past race through the dark screen of my empty head.

Another day has begun. Why do humans write so much? In fact, why do they write at all? Is it because they are lonely and full of regret? Or is it because by writing the mind tries to store and keep forever things it knows it has already lost. Writing is man's quest for permanence.

Buried moments of bygone days climb out from their graves and begin to write themselves. I work relentlessly on my scripts, pouring a lot of myself into each scene.

All the meanings are yours. The act of writing disconnects you from the very world you want to connect to. 'You are mixing colours and creating new colours, but if you reduce it or break your so-called new and original colour into its constituent elements, you will find out that you are back to the basic colours which you have stolen from nature. Anyway, these are all concepts we are talking about. The fact is that the physical eye doesn't see any colours. Absence of colour is not black or white,' says U.G. 'Then what is it?' I ask, bewildered by his statement. 'That you will never know,' concludes U.G.

Later this morning, as I gaze into the multi-coloured valley of Gstaad, U.G.'s voice thunders within me. Am I willing to buy what he says? Obviously not. If I did that, the consequences thereof would annihilate me. This very act of putting my pen on paper would freeze. No white page to write on, no black ink to write with, no light, no darkness. Words prove heartbreakingly clumsy and inadequate. They fail to perform what is after all their primary function—communication.

This journal is a sort of penitential autobiography of a film maker. Perhaps it is a critical and reflective pause at midlife. At forty-six I feel I have got everything hopelessly wrong. Now when I look back at my life, I feel I cannot even read my own years. My stay here in Gstaad has provided me with an opportunity to lick my wounds and begin a process of reinventing myself. In these jottings I have tried to look mercilessly at this organic trap called life in which we humans are forever in jeopardy because of mere chemical accidents of biological insults.

... When I try to look at the phenomenon of U.G. and try to comprehend it, I feel as though I have come with a torchlight to look at the sun.

30 July ... DAY TWENTY-ONE

I'm going through the *New York Times Book Review*. There's a book titled *The Engine of Reason, The Seat of the Soul*. This book is a philosophical journey into the brain. The book is written by Paul M. Churchland. It is a philosopher's work in which the author with his scientifically up-to-date argument concludes that all of human mental life, however subjective it feels, is reducible to material activity taking place in the brain. 'This book only proves that the philosophers, having come to the end of their tether, are now seeking the support of science to read something into the activity of the brain. Whatever you see, which separates you from what you're looking at, is a projection of knowledge. This guy is just a metaphysician who is using new terminology to tell himself and the reader that he has a sparkling new insight. But, sorry, I don't buy it. As far as I'm concerned, this new scientifically-backed theory of this guy is just a fad. People buy it just like they buy a new grandfather shirt or a new model car. They do this to tell themselves that they are in sync with the times. Whatever you learn, whatever you teach, is functional. It is only for the purpose of functioning in this world which you have created. And it is this which is preventing you from understanding anything,' says U.G., shooting Churchland's book down.

Whatever you feed into this fire called U.G. 'burns'. No wonder that every comment, every insight you bring to him is shot down and reduced to ashes. What else do you expect from fire? You cannot expect to remain unscathed if you walk into a blaze, can you?

Day-long Thunderings of U.G.

'All learning, all teaching is for destructive purposes. You learn about the laws of nature to control and dominate your neighbour. It's a game of one-upmanship. I'm not saying anything against it. I'm just saying that's the way it is. All learning, all teachings are "war games". Winning all the time is all that you are interested in. Charity is the filthiest invention of the human mind: first you steal what belongs to everyone; then you use the policeman and the atom bomb to protect it. You give charity to prevent the have-nots from rebelling against you. It also makes you feel less guilty. All do-gooders feel "high" when they do good. You're still a boy scout and a girl guide.'

This guy, U.G., fixes his morning breakfast the night before he sleeps. And he fixes his lunch right after the morning breakfast.

'Tell Major not to do yoga seriously. It will make his back problem that he's trying to get rid of worse. Exercise and yoga are bad for the body. The only exercise you need is to run around for food and sex, just like the animals,' says U.G. to Chandrasekhar over long-distance phone. 'Has the money I sent reached you yet? No? What's happening, Chandrasekhar? Where is all that money sitting? In which bank? In Switzerland or in India? Someone's making money out of our money. Why should it take so many days when the money was sent by electronic transfer.... Say hello to Suguna, and ask her to call me back as soon as the money gets there....'

Saying this, he puts down the phone and goes on and on about the crookedness and inefficiency of the banking system all over the world. Back in India, as Suguna is praying to her thirty-three crore gods, goddesses, and godlets to bring U.G. back to Bangalore, U.G. is making plans to leave for the U.S. Wanting to step out of her and Chandrasekhar's lives for good so that they can lead their lives on their own, U.G., while in Europe, finalizes the arrangements for them to have a house of their own so that they can make all their decisions without him in the picture. (The lease of the house the family is living in is about to expire.)

[Note: As is always the case, U.G. later changed his plans to go instead to China, Australia, and New Zealand.]

Strange, indeed, are the ways of life: just imagine a middle class Indian family getting a boon from the estate of a deceased Swiss lady, enabled by an enigmatic Indian sage.

We're getting set to watch *Forrest Gump* tonight. Suddenly U.G. lashes out at me with a ferocity that I have never felt, seen or experienced before. 'You cannot have it both ways. You're just like Julie. You get this and get this straight. You cannot have a relationship with me on your terms. The need to have a

relationship with me is yours, not mine. You know for certain
that if I don't see you for the rest of my life, I wouldn't give a
damn....' I feel scorched and silenced. A peculiar hush descends
on the room. I can see that that intensity, though directed squarely
at me, has ricocheted to everyone else in the room. I stop. And
give up.

31 July ... DAY TWENTY-TWO

Seven days more to go. 'It takes courage and patience to be around
this guy called U.G.,' said Marisa yesterday, just after dinner. I
have no reason to disagree with her.

As I sit here in the hush of the pre-dawn light, waiting for
U.G. to emerge from his room, I feel calm. No residue, not even a
trace, of last night's storm in the body. I'm reminded of what
U.G. once told me when we were very intensely arguing about
sorrow and frustration: 'The body handles all your despair, all
your frustrations in its own way. It doesn't need any help from
your intellect. There is no pain or pleasure that can take
permanent root in this body. Your pleasures and pains have a
permanent existence only in that thing called the experiencing
structure, which is your intellect.'

We are having coffee. I am quiet. After what happened last
night, I'm afraid to make any contact with this guy. Then, just
like that, for some strange reason, he begins to speak. 'Mahesh,
the question is the questioner, and the listener is the word. They
are one, huh....? The moment I go into that room, you don't exist
for me. Why you, I don't exist for myself. When I lie down there
in my bed, I discover there is no body there between the sheets.'
I am frightened of what he is saying. Nothing makes sense, and
I get the certain feeling that I'm getting nowhere.

We are going to Zurich. U.G. is in the front seat with Paul
Sempé, and Bob, Paul and I are huddled in the back. On the way
we stop at a gas station. As we get out and stretch our legs, Bob
jokingly asks, 'What have we done to deserve this fate, Mahesh?'
U.G. butts in: 'You've done a lot, and you're doing a lot, Bob. All

that you do makes you tense and miserable. All your techniques to relax, to feel good, must stop. And only then you'll be just fine.'

Lucern. From 9:30 to 10:30 a.m. we walk through this majestic town. As we cross the old wooden bridge, U.G. points to the water birds which are diving for food in the lake. 'Look at these swans. All their energy is just absorbed in looking for food. Can you see the little one down there? That baby's on his own, independent. That's what you guys should help your children to become.'

Zurich. We all split in different directions, fixing the time and place we will meet again. I go into a book shop. I find myself flipping through the ancient Book of Changes, the I Ching. It predicts good times ahead for me. It also says that all progress that I will make will come through the association with a sage. Some comfort to my aching, burning body. The words of Nataraj echo in my head, 'The moon is going over your birth Saturn....' Later, Bob, Paul and I sit on a bench right in the centre of Zurich, replaying and reliving the events of the previous day. Bob says, 'He looks fierce. You're in for trouble, deep trouble, Mahesh!'

Berne. We are driving into the city. Suddenly there is a downpour. 'Look with your eyes, don't use your head when you drive, Paul. I don't use my head because I don't have one. All your planning made you lose all the wars that you fought. Just look, don't think,' says U.G. The rain stops and the air begins to clear. I call Bombay. Things on the work front look rather bright for a change.

1 August ... DAY TWENTY-THREE

I wake up with a throbbing head. The image of the swan looking for food with total attention flickers in my head. The single-minded quest for food made that swan look so graceful. Later in the morning, as I watch U.G. boil broccoli, I tell him about the after-image of the swan. 'That's all that is there—hunting for a living. That's all that is there. One form of life lives on another. Even your vegetables are a form of life....' That was a direct hit at the subtle sense of superiority of being a vegetarian one feels deep within.

Comments of U.G. on food and pleasure

'Man eats for pleasure. Your food orgies are not different from your sex orgies. Everything that man does is for pleasure. And for pleasure you have to use thought. This creates problems because you cannot have pleasure without pain. It's physically impossible to make pleasure last forever. So the religious man steps in and says, "You should be free from thought," and you imagine that a thoughtless state is a very pleasurable state to be in. That's why you pursue it. You cannot have pleasure without thought. You guys live in a world of ideas, and that's why your ideas are so important to you. You yourself are an idea!'

During my stay here in Switzerland, I think I have discovered the dish for me. It is the most convenient dish, and it is the one that will free me from my dependence for food on my wives and maids: a slice of bread and a glass of water. 'With hot water, the bread melts in your mouth even better,' says U.G. Millions of poor Indians live only on bread and water. They fall sick less often than all the guys who are used to having a twenty-course meal. I'm reminded of my visit to New York in the early eighties. Living for a month without *dal* drove me insane. I suffered from *dal* withdrawals. U.G. says, 'One gets addicted to spices. Food itself is also an addiction. But to give up spices, to prove to yourself that you're highly evolved, is stupid.'

The one central theme which blazes through his talks nowadays is, 'There's nothing to what the know-it-alls have said. I'm not saying anything either. There's no need to replace what they are saying with what I am saying.'

First of August happens to be Valentine's birthday. In Bangalore, Chandrasekhar and Suguna are having a small function in the school named after her, The Valentine Model School. U.G. says that Valentine, who was the granddaughter of a clergyman, never entered a church, and she hated schools.

237

Isn't it odd that after her death, there's a school with her name on it?

Mukhesh calls from Bombay saying that a publicity angle for *Criminal* which I had given an O.K. to has created an uproar in India. All the newspapers in the country which first carried the ads are now shamelessly saying that one must not indulge in cheap gimmicks to make money. 'They do the same thing in the States,' says U.G. 'The *Time* magazine carries long articles condemning smoking. At the same time, they also carry full-page, colour ads for cigarettes.'

Today is the Swiss Independence Day. It's an occasion for festivity and celebration. The dead town of Gstaad is stirring with life. 'Blood was shed to build this country. Look down there at the tennis court, how all these people are singing and dancing. Who the hell remembers your sacrifices, once you're dead and gone?'

Suddenly there's a downpour. A wave of disappointment sweeps through the gathering below. Looks like this night of celebration has been squashed by Mama Nature.

'Whenever I open my mouth, I only talk about myself,' says Dr. Leboyer as U.G. leads him into the living room. He is replying to U.G.'s matter-of-fact greeting, 'How are things?' 'Who else is there to talk about? In any case, even when you think you are talking about someone else, you are in fact talking about yourself,' concludes U.G. Dr. Leboyer is the well-known proponent of natural childbirth. By the time of his retirement he delivered 13,000 babies in Paris.

Tonight's movie is *Heaven Help Us*. It brings back memories of my childhood in Don Bosco High School in Bombay. One has seen some very good movies here. Of all the movies we have seen, U.G. prefers *The Last Seduction*. When it comes to movies, U.G.'s tastes are those of a commoner. 'Rape, murder, mayhem, and action are what I like to see, not your love stories and psychological dramas.'

Early this evening, when I told him we had run out of all the good movies and would now have to put up with the bad ones, U.G. said, 'What difference does it make? A bad movie's as good as a good one.' Ever heard a remark like that about movies?

2 August ... DAY TWENTY-FOUR

Calls from Bombay keep me awake all through the night. It's ten minutes past midnight here in Switzerland, which means that the time in Bombay should be around 3:30 a.m. Mukhesh is drunk again. He's unable to cope with the excitement *Criminal* has created. They are threatening to arrest him. He has taken an anticipatory bail. 'Use every trick in the book to succeed. Fair means if possible, foul means if necessary. But be ready to pay the price for your actions,' U.G. once said to me. The problem, sir, is we want it both ways. Don't you know we want to eat the cake and have it too?

U.G. sits on the chair in the soft glow of the morning light, looking at his own hands with childlike wonder. The grandfather shirt which Robert has bought for him makes him look good. He has found the right look for himself late in life. 'Can you imagine we two guys, you and I, who are talking all this nonsense every day in the morning, will not be here one day? This body, which is so precious to you, will one day burn and be reduced to ashes. Can you imagine that?' I nod my head in agreement. A part of me screams, 'Run, Mahesh!'

'He's a talented guy going through a rough phase,' said U.G. supporting me when I was down and out without any work fifteen years ago. His words gave me much-needed self-confidence. I narrate this incident to Mario who, like I was, is now going through a turbulent period. Mario's eyes glimmer with hope.

'I'll give you a big bag into which you can fit all your things. But you have to pay for it. Why should a poor Indian give a rich Indian like you things free?' And saying this, U.G. pulled out a good-looking coloured bag and handed it over to me. 'A hundred francs on the barrel,' he says, pushing his empty palm towards my face. I swiftly go into my corner, and, pulling out a hundred franc note, conclude the transaction. 'Actually, the bag only cost me sixty and not a hundred francs....' Now U.G. heads back into his room and returns with some money. 'There you are, sir, here are your forty francs and some extra coins bonus for you to play with.' Robert Hornkohl, the American photographer who has taken the best-looking picture of U.G. to date, watches the entire drama with utter fascination.

'Nitie-nite,' U.G. says to me, and once again disappears into his room. The moment he is gone, one feels as if there is nobody home. I toss and turn for a while, and wait for sleep. Just when I'm about to drift off, the telephone ring wakes me up with a start. 'This is Nagarjun.... Did I wake you up, sir?' 'No, not at all,' I say, trying to sound polite. 'How did the premier of *Criminal* go,' I ask. 'Excellent. I think we're out of the woods. Judging by the opening, we have, one can say, at least a B+ piece at hand.' I'm relieved. As I listen to his voice, I say to myself, 'All success is delayed failure.' I'm reminded of what U.G. repeatedly tells me. 'Mahesh, every prostitute has her day. The life of you entertainers is like the life of a prostitute. Make hay while the sun shines. Put a decent amount of money away to back your arrogance, and then quit while you are still on the top....' I hope I can achieve what he says.

3 August ... DAY TWENTY-FIVE

The life of a writer is excruciating. Facing a blank piece of paper day after day is tough. And then drawing something from deep within oneself and spreading it out on paper for the world to see is worse.

This morning not a word is exchanged between U.G. and me. We have just been sitting facing one another. His eyes are shut. He's looking gorgeous today. Since I have nothing to do, I monkey him and I close my eyes too. I begin to listen to the sounds around me—trains, cars, birds, the creaking of the sofa, the rustling of U.G.'s clothes. Momentarily, I feel calm. Then, suddenly, the buzzing of those damn flies invades my tranquility. Finding me sitting still, they descend on me and are having a field day. They have converted my body into their feeding ground. The moment I lift my hand to shoo them, they fly away but soon return to finish their job. This goes on and on till finally I give up. They just won't let me sit still. I open my eyes and notice that U.G. is looking and smiling at me. He naughtily says, 'Flies, hmm?' and laughs. I'm reminded of what he said to me the other day at the dining table: 'What makes you feel that your life is more important than the life of that fly sitting there by the plate?' 'Why don't you call this book of yours *The Fly on the Table?*' suggests Julie. 'Not a bad idea,' I think to myself.

U.G. is sitting in the living room surrounded by a large group of seekers from all over Europe. There are Germans, Italians and Frenchmen as well as an American. Suddenly U.G. looks away from them and addressing me says, 'You guys in India must stop all these Westerners from entering your country. Throw all these people out when they knock at your doors for a visa. Do you know why they come to your country? They come to your country to stretch their pounds, marks or dollars. And once they're there, they behave as if they're big shots. In any case, all these guys convert their currency in the black market. The government doesn't make a farthing from such people. You don't need the tourist money. China and Russia have survived for years without tourist money.' His statement unnerves everybody in the room.

U.G. was put off by the recent practice adopted by the European nations of denying visas to most Indians who want to visit their countries. We know that Switzerland denies visas to anybody who comes from South India, or has a South Indian name. The reason for this, they say, is the recent illegal influx of Sri Lankan refugees into their country. U.G.'s brother-in-law, Dr. Seshagiri Rao, who is an eminent medical doctor in India, found it difficult to get a visa to Switzerland this summer while he was in the U.S. He had to abandon his plans of visiting U.G. here in Gstaad. When U.G. had had his say, I felt that as an Indian I should bring this issue into focus when I get home. I don't see any reason why any self-respecting Indian should take lying down this treatment dished out by the Western nations.

'Russia baffled as life loses death race,' reads the news on the front page of the *Herald Tribune*. As I go through the column I discover that life expectancy in Russia has plummeted in recent times, and the scientists and public health officials cannot quite figure out why this is happening. What amuses me further is that on the tenth page of this very newspaper there is another article under the section of Health and Science which says: 'Life is a mystery—ineffable, unfathomable. It is the last thing on earth that might seem susceptible to exact description. Yet now, for the first time, a free-living organism has been precisely defined by the chemical identification of its complete genetic blueprint. The creature is just a humble bacterium known as Hemophilus influenzae, but it nonetheless possesses all the tools and tricks required for independent existence. For the first time, biologists can begin to see the entire parts list, as it were, of what a living cell needs to grow, survive, and reproduce itself....' Isn't it absurd that in one part of the world you have scientists unable to find out why the death rate has suddenly accelerated, while on the other side you have people claiming they have finally unravelled the mystery of life!

We have a charming visitor for lunch. His name is Donald Ingram Smith. He's an Australian in his mid-80s who was once J.Krishnamurti's secretary. He is here to give talks in the Krishnamurti camp, which have been going on for the past three weeks. Donald often sees U.G. during the latter's visits to Australia. He is also, according to U.G., an excellent palmist. After lunch, Donald did an up-date of U.G.'s palm reading, sitting under a willow tree. Our New York friend, Ellen Chrystal, who once belonged to the inner circles of the American guru, Bubba Free John, took notes.

Donald predicts that U.G. will certainly die out of the country of his birth. He says that there is something coming out of that spectacular brain of U.G. 'It flows both ways,' says Donald, 'a door you can come in and out of.' U.G. replies: 'I am a thief. Anybody who comes, I invite him to come and take everything.' He tells the story of his wife misplacing a diamond ring, and his telling her that if the police were called in, she would be out of the house. She was accusing the maid, but found the ring later on. The police are not allowed anywhere near him.... U.G. then tells the story of the pickpocket in Times Square, New York, and how he [U.G.] wanted to invite him back to dinner at a four-star restaurant because of the deftness of his work.

Donald also predicts that in U.G.'s life there is going to be another explosion. U.G. answers, 'The next time we meet, we'll see.'

Donald says that U.G. has no ego. U.G. replies: 'If I'm not an egoist, who else is? That's the most egoistic statement, announcing from housetops, that everything that every man, woman, and child has thought, felt and experienced in the history of mankind has gone out of me....'

Later, U.G. says his mission is to tear apart everything he has ever said up until this meeting.

August 4 ... DAY TWENTY-SIX

I am wearing the new silk shirt U.G. gave me last night. This has been his favourite for quite some time. 'I'm giving this shirt to you because I want to get rid of all the old stuff I have,' he says, chucking the cream-coloured garment into my hands. Today, for some inexplicable reason, the day seems to have the feel of a new beginning.

I ask U.G. to comment on the two articles I read yesterday in the *Herald Tribune*. 'The scientific world today is as muddle-headed and lost as the religious world was yesterday. We are fools to put our faith and confidence in the scientists. We imagine that these guys have a special insight into the meaning and mystery of life. What is the point in bombarding us and trying to dazzle us with all this new scientific jargon? The human organism has survived for centuries without the help of all these so-called new, revolutionary theories and self-proclaimed breakthroughs. All these theories which the scientists call 'new' are not at all new. This new dimension which they claim they are now beginning to read in nature has always existed. So what have they actually achieved? They may get a pat on their backs from the Nobel Academy. Their wonderful, revolutionary theories will be used by the technocrats to enrich technology and themselves. A small percentage of the global population will enjoy the benefits of this technology, but let me assure you that ultimately this technological know-how will be used by man to dominate his neighbour.

'Even the pharmacists, in fact the entire medical world, thrives on your paranoia. And the media, for its own survival, helps them to propagate this paranoia. Just because you give a fancy name to a disease does not mean that you have found a cure for it. You are only adding more and more to the pool of knowledge. Today we have more words in our arsenal than Shakespeare had in his time. But that does not mean that things are any the better, does it? Say what you wish, we will never know what life is.'

Down there in the town of Gstaad they are inflating a huge blue balloon. Once again, the merrymakers are getting ready to fly far away into the sky. Up here in the kitchen, U.G. is pouring cream into his coffee. I ask him why the Krishnamurti Foundation has come up with a book which, in a way, tries to justify Krishnamurti's love affair with Rosalind Rajagopal (in the Statement by the Krishnamurti Foundation of America about the Radha Sloss book *Lives in the Shadow with J. Krishnamurti*). 'They want to separate the teaching from the teacher. Otherwise, the foundation will collapse. Obviously Radha Sloss's book was affecting them. Or else, where was the need to bring out a book like this now.'

I'm reminded of the day when after my review of Radha's book appeared in the *Sunday Times of India*, Bombay, Pupul Jayakar, the Czarina of Indian Culture, threatened to take legal action against me for maligning the reputation of the 'Sage Who Walked Alone'. She and the Krishnamurtiites were furious with me and U.G., particularly with U.G., whose harsh quotes I had extensively used in my piece. When I took up her challenge head on, and invited her to wash her dirty linen in public, Pupul backed out. As I suspected even then, Pupul did not carry out her threats because she was frightened of herself being exposed. This booklet released by the Krishnamurti Foundation confirms that suspicion.

Snatches from Conversations

Pain: 'Words transform themselves into physical pain.... For the body there is no pain. Only when you translate a sensation as pain do you feel pain. Otherwise there is no pain. You guys want to get rid of pain and hold on to pleasure forever. The holy man tells you that this is possible. I know it is not. You can spend your lifetime trying to do this, but I know for certain that you will not succeed. You'll find out eventually.'

Sex: 'Having sex and running for 5,000 metres are the same thing,' says Paul Sempé. U.G., for once, nods his head in agreement and then adds, 'Falling in love and eating chocolate are the same. They both produce the same chemical change in the body.' I jump up and begin to jog in place. U.G. asks, 'What are you doing, mister?' I mischievously say, 'Having sex! You just agreed with Paul, didn't you, that having sex and jogging are the same. So here I am having sex.' U.G. laughs. He seems to be in a good mood today.

At dusk, we sit under the willow tree, gossiping. Marisa narrates a naughty incident: once a pretty Italian woman sat down right in front of U.G., feeling, to put it mildly, 'turned on' by him. This went on for some time. Then, just when the lady was about to leave, U.G. turned to her, saying, 'Lady, I feel everything that you feel. Sorry, nothing can be done.'

Since I'm on this healthy subject of sex, I might as well relate another incident: once a woman went up to U.G. and looking straight in his face, said, 'What would your response be if I tried to seduce you?' U.G. said, 'Try it, and you'll find out.' The woman apologized, fled from the room, and never returned.

Tonight's movie is *Thelma and Louise*. This Ridley Scott movie is simple, unlike *Blade Runner* which had all the visual dazzle. *Thelma and Louise* was a big hit, much bigger than *Blade Runner*. 'What good is the art of saying things well to a person who has nothing to say,' said U.G. to me way back in the 80s. This statement changed my entire perspective on cinema.

5 August ... DAY TWENTY-SEVEN

Two spiders occupy my bathtub. I don't like spiders. I'm frightened of them. So I grab the shower handle and with its spray try to frighten these creepy creatures away. So strong is the flow of the water that instead of scaring these poor creatures, I drown them. As I watch these helpless insects go down the drain, I feel remorse. The message is clear: out of fear you kill your neighbour.

There's something about bathrooms and spiders. Julie just tells me that several years ago, during the summer while she was staying here, she developed an attachment to a spider living in this same bathroom. The spider was missing one leg, but still managed to move about the bathroom. It was sometimes on the tub, sometimes on the ceiling, and sometimes in the sink. Julie liked the spider's company. At the end of the summer, however, Julie found herself in a quandary: should she leave him in the bathroom where he would be vacuumed by the landlord and killed, or to leave him outside, where she feared it would certainly die of cold. She went to U.G. for advice. His response: 'Why don't you knit a sweater for him?'

U.G. is drawing a detailed map of an area in London. This is to help me find the book shops I would like to visit while I'm there. I'm quite amazed by this seventy-seven-year-old man's memory. It has not faded with time. Not a trace of senility here. 'No images for me. When I draw the H.M.V. shop on the map, I don't have an image of it inside of me. All I have is just a word. You can't understand what I am saying. If you did, it would put an end to you.'

Marisa, who is also listening to what U.G. is saying, turns to me and unhesitantly says, 'We don't have to use all that U.G. says, Mahesh. If we did, that would put an end to our art. No painting for me, buddy, and no movies for you. Can you imagine living a life without being able to recreate images? Who the hell wants this? It would be a terrible life.' And to this U.G. adds, 'Not only would you not be able to paint. You would not be able to have any relationship with anything or anybody.'

The Last Supper

Lisa is going away tomorrow to the United States. U.G. for a change is cooking for a lot more people tonight than he usually does. He's in a foul mood right now. 'I don't like to cook and feed all these people. I don't even like to cook and feed myself. I am like a dog. I detest your civilized manners of sitting around a table and having food orgies. I'm going to get rid of that table. This is not an ashram. Food is at the bottom of all my needs,' he roars. Everyone sits around and quietly listens to him. Then, when the food is ready to be served, each person happily gets up and eats. The angel hair pasta U.G. has cooked is delicious. U.G. is a great cook. And perhaps the fastest. He cooks a meal, consisting of a single dish, in just five minutes. I love his food.

Tonight's movie is *Blown Away*, starring Tommy Lee Jones and Jeff Bridges. The film has all the visual dazzle and action, but it just doesn't work. There is no internal progression in the screenplay. The sub-text just does not work. Gosh, even to make a bad film one has to work hard.

August 6 ... DAY TWENTY-EIGHT

'They talk very lightly of money as if it has no importance for them, when in fact it is one of the most important things in their lives. These holy men are greedy, jealous and vindictive bastards, just like everybody else. You want to live through your work, and through your children. These people want to live through their religious institutions,' says U.G. early in the morning when I mention to him that Swamiji had called for him from Bangalore while U.G. was having his bath. Bramachari Sivarama Sarma, whom everyone fondly calls 'Swamiji', is a holy man. He was once contending to be the pontiff of a well-known and fabulously rich religious order in South India. 'I have for the past five days been translating your biography on U.G. into Kannada,' he says boastfully, knowing very well that this news would make me immensely happy. It does. Never could I imagine that this biography of U.G. that I wrote would one day be translated into Telugu, Hindi, Kannada, and also Chinese. Later, Swamiji calls again. He is seeking some financial advice from U.G. He wants to invest his money safely so that he has no problems in the future. Swamiji is getting old, and like all normal people, wants to make sure that he has enough to live on in his old age.

U.G. suggests that he should invest all his money in The Valentine Model School, and gives him a personal assurance that he will see that he gets 1,000 rupees every month from that as long as he lives. 'But we will throw your body on the garbage heap when you die. No religious rites will be performed. We will not take care of your corpse. We will just leave it there in the dump for the insects to feast on. They will have a field day on your fat body,' warns U.G. jokingly.

Ellen Chrystal sits inches away from me, reliving her memories spent in the 'Divine Presence' of Da Free John, the self-announced American Avatar. Bizarre tales of food and sex orgies climax with a dull account of her sleeping with her Bhagwan. The charismatic Avatar used to condescend to have Tantric Sex only with a handful of female devotees whom he found highly evolved. This act, said the Avatar, forged an eternal bond between him and the devotee, she said. Scenes from her life serve as a potent magnifying lens through which we get an extreme and close view of the debauchery that goes on in the name of 'divine love' in the holy business.

'The world has not seen, nor will ever see, a pimp of the magnitude of Rajneesh. Pimps at least take the money from the boys and give it to the girls. They make a living out of the cut they get from such a deal. But Rajneesh took money both from the boys and the girls, and kept everything for himself,' says U.G., savaging the Rajneeshis who have assembled to see him today.

'I will destroy Mahesh. Ask him to come to me personally and return my mala. This is a breach of trust. He cannot do this. I worked so hard...,' said Rajneesh to my actor friend, Vinod Khanna, way back in 1978. I was a Rajneeshi sannyasi then. The Bhagwan was unable to cope with the news of me dumping his mala into a toilet, and walking out on him. Why did he keep giving discourses on 'unconditional love', I still wonder. He behaved just like any jilted lover. 'Rajneesh's empty threats to destroy you obviously did not work. You're still here and he's dead and gone,' says U.G. summing up the topic of holy men.

We are lost in Lausanne and looking for a restaurant that sells pizza. It's Sunday and the town is empty. 'Burn all maps. So what if you get lost? You can always turn back. Your anxiety to know whether you are heading in the right direction is making you take all the wrong turns. Look! Don't think!' says U.G., knowing very well that he was failing to get his point across to Paul. This has been an ongoing dialogue between Paul Sempé and U.G. for years. Finally, using U.G.'s dog sense, we get to our destination.

People always seem to have felt an urge to record, to make marks that jog memory. Historians believe that the bison drawn on cave walls was humanity's first diary entry. Just think. We make a few abstract marks on a piece of paper in a certain order and someone a world away and a thousand years from now can know our deepest thoughts. Writing transcends boundaries of time and space and even the limitation of death.

August 7 ... DAY TWENTY-NINE

Ending: time to move. I have packed my bags and I will be leaving for London tomorrow. I toss and turn trying to sleep. I cannot. I step out into the dark night and look at the moonlit sky. A strange question begins to formulate itself inside of me. Who am I now? Am I in any way different from that guy who came here thirty days ago? As I sit here attempting to answer the question, I begin to discover that I am, and will always be, a stranger in the story of my own life. Going back to Bombay, and picking up the threads of my life, feels as if one is returning to a novel one had left off reading many summers ago. It is so easy to lose the thread of our own story. As I scan through the collage of a thousand images of my time spent here in Switzerland with U.G., I feel as if I have taken them apart and put them back together again in a new way. A writer comes to his craft only after he has been shattered by life in some way. Having lived through these thirty days and thirty nights in Gstaad, I know nothing for me will be the same again. People pay good money for a taste of death. Sky diving, bungee jumping, and terrifying amusement-park rides give people a jolt that awakens a fuller appreciation of life. That is why adventure films and stories are always popular, because they offer a less risky way to experience death and rebirth through heroes we can identify with.

U.G. is my hero. My coming to meet U.G. is perhaps my way of having a taste of death, and then springing back into life. Having survived all the ordeals of this summer, and having lived through a kind of 'death,' I return home. I have stood on the shoulders of this giant called U.G. and had a glimpse of a world which is awesome. I have known this phenomenon called U.G. for eighteen years now. But never have I felt in his presence what I have felt this summer. U.G. is now effecting people physically. 'Don't mystify it...,' said U.G. one quiet evening, when I spoke to him alone about my experiences. I promise myself not to. But story-telling probably began with people like me who struggle to relate their experiences and adventures to the world outside.

Kids like to bring back souvenirs from summer vacations, partly to remind them of the trip, but also to prove to the other kids that they really visited those exotic locales. A common fairy-tale motif is that proof brought back from the magic world tends to evaporate. A sack full of gold coins won from the fairies will be opened in the 'ordinary world' and found to contain nothing but dead leaves, leading other people to believe that the traveller was just dreaming. Yet the traveller knows the experience was real. All deeply felt emotional experiences are hard to explain to others and often even to oneself.

August 8 ... DAY THIRTY

'India has no future. You people got your freedom on a platter. Indians did not shed any blood. You think that you got your freedom because of the speeches that your leaders had made? No, you must thank Hitler and the Germans for that. Britain was in a shambles after the Second World War. Holding on to its colonies became a hassle for the battle-weary English. So they let go of India. Even the U.S.A. should thank Hitler for what it is today. The Second World War gave a major boost to its war industry. But enough is enough. The United States and the industrial nations have ganged up and bullied the rest of the world too long. They have to be stopped in their tracks and this, I'm afraid, will be done only by the Islamic fundamentalists or China,' says U.G.

'I don't know about India but what he is saying about America and the Western nations is true. But I keep my mouth shut. It is too subversive. I would lose my job. If I said all this in my country they would lock me up in a prison...,' says Jim, an American Jew who has lived in Europe for years, at the end of an intense discussion which is triggered by my query to U.G. about the future of India. As the evening deepens, U.G. goes on to spotlight the harsh economic realities which confront the world. It sends me hurtling down into a quagmire of depression.

Robert Towne, the screenplay writer of *Chinatown* said the process of writing is also a way of discarding. As soon as you get an experience out from inside, it's gone. Once you objectify it, in a sense you have exercised it. It doesn't belong to you anymore. You have purged it. When the sand gets into the oyster's craw, the oyster's response to protect himself is to spin this thing around. The sand then becomes a beautiful pearl. The oyster's object is not to admire it, but to get rid of something that hurts.

'Are you ready for the parting message?' asks U.G., sinking into the front seat of the car and fastening the seat-belt. 'Yes,' I whisper, and pulling out a small diary get ready to jot down what he is about to say. 'Unless humankind comes to terms with the blunt truth that it is no more important than the mosquito or the field rat, it is doomed. This individual called U.G. is just an animal, nothing more.

'Whatever happened to me cannot be used to promote myself or promote any cause for the welfare of mankind. What I say undermines the very foundation of human thought. How can society be interested in what I say? Nature does not use anything else as a model. I cannot make any definitive statement, but even physically this cannot reproduce another one like itself. It is anybody's guess as to whether the sperm of this individual can impregnate a female or not. I have no interest in becoming a guinea pig for the medical technologists who will, in any case, use all the insights they gain during the course of their experiments to ultimately destroy life. All that they have discovered about the body so far has not been helpful to understand the innate intelligence the body is born with. The natural immunity of the body is destroyed by everything they are doing. When this body drops dead, it will be recycled by nature just like a garden slug to enrich the soil. In short, it will just rot.'

So total and complete is his self-demolition that it makes me shudder. As I look away, I see the full moon is just beginning its climb into a dark, cold sky.

A sparkling, new dawn is here. We are just fifty kilometres away from Geneva. Suddenly U.G. turns towards us. The golden glow of the morning light makes him look divine. As we drive through a field of sunflowers, U.G. says 'I invited Bob and Paul to come here to Gstaad. I want them to sort out the course of their lives while they are here. There is a conflict going on there inside of them. I want them to resolve it. I can only extend my help to you guys in the area of your practical lives.' U.G.'s concern for people manifests itself through his actions, not words. Don't believe him when he says 'I won't lift my little finger to help anyone. You can all rot in hell....' That's a lie. He is the most concerned guy I have ever met in my life.

As I pass through the Immigration, savouring the aftertaste of my experiences with U.G. in Gstaad, U.G.'s voice suddenly erupts within me: 'All experiences, no matter how extraordinary they are, separate you from life. You will never know what life is, never.... ' As my aircraft takes off from the Geneva Airport, and heads for London, I find myself once again asking the same ageless, childlike questions. 'Who am I? Where did I come from? What happens when I die? What does it mean? Where do I fit in? Where am I going? —Home, stupid! Home.'

Index